Internet of Things with Python

Interact with the world and rapidly prototype IoT applications using Python

Gastón C. Hillar

BIRMINGHAM - MUMBAI

Internet of Things with Python

First published: May 2016

Production reference: 1170516

Published by Packt Publishing Ltd.
Livery Place
35 Livery Street
Birmingham B3 2PB, UK.

ISBN 978-1-78588-138-1

www.packtpub.com

Credits

Author
Gastón C. Hillar

Reviewer
Navin Bhaskar

Commissioning Editor
Kartikey Pandey

Acquisition Editor
Reshma Raman

Content Development Editor
Divij Kotian

Technical Editor
Nirant Carvalho

Copy Editor
Sneha Singh

Project Coordinator
Nikhil Nair

Proofreader
Safis Editing

Indexer
Hemangini Bari

Graphics
Gastón C. Hillar

Jason Monteiro

Production Coordinator
Shantanu N. Zagade

Cover Work
Shantanu N. Zagade

About the Author

Gastón C. Hillar is Italian and has been working with computers since he was eight. He began programming with the legendary Texas TI-99/4A and Commodore 64 home computers in the early 80s. He has a bachelor's degree in computer science, in which he graduated with honors, and an MBA, in which he graduated with an outstanding thesis. At present, Gastón is an independent IT consultant and freelance author who is always looking for new adventures around the world.

He has been a senior contributing editor at Dr. Dobb's and has written more than a hundred articles on software development topics. Gaston was also a Microsoft MVP in technical computing. He has received the prestigious Intel® Black Belt Software Developer award seven times.

He is a guest blogger at Intel® Software Network (`http://software.intel.com`). You can reach him at `gastonhillar@hotmail.com` and follow him on Twitter at `http://twitter.com/gastonhillar`.

His blog is `http://csharpmulticore.blogspot.com`.

He lives with his wife, Vanesa, and his two sons, Kevin and Brandon.

Acknowledgments

At the time of writing this book, I was fortunate to work with an excellent team at Packt Publishing Ltd, whose contributions vastly improved the presentation of this book. Reshma Raman allowed me to provide her with ideas to develop this book and I jumped into the exciting project of teaching how to combine electronic components, sensors, actuators, the Intel Galileo Gen 2 board, and Python to create exciting Internet of Things projects. Divij Kotian helped me realize my vision for this book and provided many sensible suggestions regarding the text, the format, and the flow. The reader will notice his great work. It was great working with Divij in another book. I would like to thank my technical reviewers and proofreaders for their thorough reviews and insightful comments. I was able to incorporate some of the knowledge and wisdom they have gained in their many years in the software development industry. This book was possible because they gave valuable feedback.

Special thanks go to my father, José C. Hillar, who introduced me to electronics before I started speaking. I grew up among transistors, resistors, and soldering irons. His clear vision of the evolution of electronic components, microcontrollers, and microprocessors made it possible for me to learn everything that was necessary to build Internet of Things projects. He worked with me while testing all the sample projects included in the book.

The interaction with a huge number of experts at Intel Developer Zone made it possible for me to become extremely familiar with the Intel Galileo and Intel Edison platforms, and start running Python code on them. My visits to Intel Developer Forum 2013, 2014 and 2015 made me understand all the things that developers must know in order to successfully create modern IoT projects. Special thanks go to Kathy Farrel and Aaron Tersteeg. Many conversations with them in San Francisco, California, kicked off my idea of writing this book.

The entire process of writing a book requires a huge number of lonely hours. I wouldn't have been able to write an entire book without dedicating some time to playing soccer with my sons, Kevin and Brandon, and my nephew, Nicolas. Of course, I never won a match. However, I did score a few goals.

About the Reviewer

Navin Bhaskar has over 4 years of experience in embedded systems, having written code ranging from device drivers to firmware for smart cards. He won the Distinctive Excellence award in the mbed design challenge for his *Reconfigurable Computing for Embedded System* project and the third prize for his EvoMouse in the OpenWorld contest. You can find his blog at `https://navinbhaskar.wordpress.com/`, where you can find tutorials on IoT and related topics.

www.PacktPub.com

eBooks, discount offers, and more

Did you know that Packt offers eBook versions of every book published, with PDF and ePub files available? You can upgrade to the eBook version at www.PacktPub.com and as a print book customer, you are entitled to a discount on the eBook copy. Get in touch with us at customercare@packtpub.com for more details.

At www.PacktPub.com, you can also read a collection of free technical articles, sign up for a range of free newsletters and receive exclusive discounts and offers on Packt books and eBooks.

https://www2.packtpub.com/books/subscription/packtlib

Do you need instant solutions to your IT questions? PacktLib is Packt's online digital book library. Here, you can search, access, and read Packt's entire library of books.

Why subscribe?

- Fully searchable across every book published by Packt
- Copy and paste, print, and bookmark content
- On demand and accessible via a web browser

To my sons, Kevin and Brandon, and my wife, Vanesa

Table of Contents

Preface

Internet of Things, also known as IoT, is changing the way we live and represents one of the biggest challenges in the IT industry. Developers are creating low-cost devices that collect huge amounts of data, interact with each other, and take advantage of cloud services and cloud-based storage. Makers all over the world are working on fascinating projects that transform everyday objects into smart devices with sensors and actuators.

A coffee cup is not a simple object anymore—it can send a message to your smartwatch indicating that the liquid inside has the right temperature so that you can drink it without worrying about checking whether it is too hot. In case you move the coffee cup before you receive the message, your wearable vibrates to indicate that you don't have to drink it yet.

You can check the coffee level of the coffee dispenser in your smartphone, and you won't have to worry about ordering more coffee: the coffee dispenser will automatically place an online order to request coffee when the coffee level is not enough to cover the rest of the day. You just need to approve the online order that the coffee dispenser suggests from your smartwatch. Based on certain statistical algorithms, the coffee dispenser will know the appropriate time to make the order.

What happens when more usual visitors arrive at the office? Their smartwatches or smartphones will communicate with the coffee dispensers and they will place orders in case the probable consumption of decaffeinated coffee increases too much. We have smart coffee cups, smart coffee dispensers, smartwatches, smartphones, and wearables. All of them take advantage of the cloud to create a smart ecosystem capable of providing us with all the different types of coffees we need for our day.

The Intel Galileo Gen 2 board is an extremely powerful and versatile minicomputer board for IoT projects. We can boot a Linux version and easily execute Python scripts that can interact with the different components included on the board. This book will teach you to develop IoT prototypes, from selecting the hardware to all the necessary stacks with Python 2.7.3, its libraries, and tools. In case you need a smaller board or an alternative, all the examples included in the book are compatible with Intel Edison boards, and therefore, you can switch to this board in case you need to.

Python is one of the most popular programming languages. It is open source, multiplatform, and you can use it to develop any kind of application, from websites to extremely complex scientific computing applications. There is always a Python package that makes things easier for us in order to avoid reinventing the wheel and solve problems faster. Python is an ideal choice for developing a complete IoT stack. This book covers all the things you need to know to transform everyday objects into IoT projects.

This book will allow you to prototype and develop IoT solutions from scratch with Python as the programming language. You will leverage your existing Python knowledge to capture data from the real world, interact with physical objects, develop APIs, and use different IoT protocols. You will use specific libraries to easily work with low-level hardware, sensors, actuators, buses, and displays. You will learn how to take advantage of all the Python packages with the Intel Galileo Gen 2 board. You will be ready to become a maker and to be a part of the exciting IoT world.

What this book covers

Chapter 1, *Understanding and Setting up the Base IoT Hardware*, start us off on our journey towards Internet of Things (IoT) with Python and the Intel Galileo Gen 2 board. We will learn the different features offered by this board and visualize its different components. We will understand the meaning of the different pins, LEDs, and connectors. We will learn to check the board's firmware version and to update if necessary.

Chapter 2, *Working with Python on Intel Galileo Gen 2*, leads us through many procedures that make it possible to work with Python as the main programming language to create IoT projects with our Intel Galileo Gen 2 board. We will write a Linux Yocto image to a microSD card, configure the board to make it boot this image, update many libraries to use their latest versions, and launch the Python interpreter.

Chapter 3, Interacting with Digital Outputs with Python, teaches us how to work with two different libraries to control digital outputs in Python: mraa and wiring-x86. We will connect LEDs and resistors to a breadboard and write code to turn on between 0 to 9 LEDs. Then, we will improve our Python code to take advantage of Python's object-oriented features, and we will prepare the code to make it easy to build an API that will allow us to print numbers with LEDs with a REST API.

Chapter 4, Working with a RESTful API and Pulse Width Modulation, has us working with Tornado Web Server, Python, the HTTPie command-line HTTP client, and the mraa and wiring-x86 libraries. We will generate many versions of RESTful APIs that will allow us to interact with the board in computers and devices connected to the LAN. We will be able to compose and send HTTP requests that print numbers in LEDs, change the brightness levels for three LEDs, and generate millions of colors with an RGB LED.

Chapter 5, Working with Digital Inputs, Polling and Interrupts, explains the difference between reading pushbutton statuses with polling and working with interrupts and interrupt handlers. We will write code that will allow the user to perform the same actions with either pushbuttons in the breadboard or HTTP requests. We will combine code that reacts to changes in the statuses of the pushbuttons with a RESTful API built with Tornado Web Server. We will create classes to encapsulate pushbuttons and the necessary configurations with the mraa and wiring-x86 libraries.

Chapter 6, Working with Analog Inputs and Local Storage, explains how to work with analog inputs to measure voltage values. We will measure voltages with an analog pin and both the mraa and the wiring-x86 libraries. We will be able to transform a variable resistor into a voltage source and make it possible to measure the darkness level with an analog input, a photoresistor, and a voltage divider. We will fire actions when the environment light changes, and we will work with both analog inputs and outputs. We will register events by taking advantage of the logging features included in the Python standard library and the USB 2.0 connector included in the Intel Galileo Gen 2 board.

Chapter 7, Retrieving Data From the Real World with Sensors, has us working with a variety of sensors to retrieve data from the real world. We will take advantage of the modules and classes included in the upm library that will make it easy for us to start working with analog and digital sensors. We will learn the importance of considering units of measurement because sensors always provide values measured in a specific unit, which we must consider. We will measure the magnitude and direction of proper acceleration or g-force, ambient temperature, and humidity.

Chapter 8, Displaying Information and Performing Actions, teaches us about different displays the we can connect to our board through the I²C bus. We will work with an LCD display with an RGB backlight, and we will then replace it with an OLED dot matrix. We will write code that takes advantage of the modules and classes included in the upm library to work with LCD and OLED displays and show text on them. We will also write code that interacts with an analog servo. We will control the shaft to allow us to create a gauge chart to display the temperature value retrieved with a sensor. Our Python code will make things move.

Chapter 9, Working with the Cloud, teaches you how to combine many cloud-based services that will allow us to easily publish data collected from sensors and visualize it in a web-based dashboard. We will work with the MQTT protocol and its publish/subscribe model to process commands in our board and indicate when the commands are successfully processed through messages. First, we will work with the PubNub cloud that works with the MQTT protocol under the hood. Then, we will develop the same example with Mosquitto and Eclipse Paho. We will be able to write applications that can establish bidirectional communications with our IoT devices.

Chapter 10, Analyzing Huge Amounts of Data with Cloud-based IoT Analytics, explains the close relationship between IoT and Big Data. We will work with Intel IoT Analytics, a cloud-based service that allows us to organize huge amounts of data collected by multiple IoT devices and their sensors. We will use the requests package to write a few lines of Python code to interact with the Intel IoT Analytics REST API. We will learn about the different options that Intel IoT Analytics offers us to analyze huge amounts of data, and we will define rules to trigger alerts.

What you need for this book

In order to work with the different tools required to connect to the Intel Galileo Gen 2 board and launch the Python samples, you will need any computer with an Intel Core i3 or higher CPU and at least 4 GB of RAM. You can work with any of the following operating systems:

- Windows 7 or higher (Windows 8, Windows 8.1, or Windows 10)
- Mac OS X Mountain Lion or higher
- Any Linux version capable of running Python 2.7.x
- Any modern browser with JavaScript support.

You will also need an Intel Galileo Gen 2 board and a breadboard with 830 tie points (holes for connections) and 2 power lanes.

In addition, you will need different electronic components and breakout boards to build the examples included in many chapters.

Who this book is for

This book is ideal for Python programmers who want to explore the tools available in the Python ecosystem in order to build their own IoT web stack and IoT-related projects. People from creative and designing backgrounds will also find this book equally useful.

Conventions

In this book, you will find a number of text styles that distinguish between different kinds of information. Here are some examples of these styles and an explanation of their meaning.

Code words in text, database table names, folder names, filenames, file extensions, pathnames, dummy URLs, user input, and Twitter handles are shown as follows: " By default, the pip package management system that makes it easy to install and manage software packages written in Python isn't installed."

A block of code is set as follows:

```
if __name__ == "__main__":
    print ("Mraa library version: {0}".format(mraa.getVersion()))
    print ("Mraa detected platform name: {0}".format(mraa.
getPlatformName()))

    number_in_leds = NumberInLeds()
    # Count from 0 to 9
    for i in range(0, 10):
        number_in_leds.print_number(i)
        time.sleep(3)
```

When we wish to draw your attention to a particular part of a code block, the relevant lines or items are set in bold:

```
class NumberInLeds:
    def __init__(self):
        self.leds = []
        for i in range(9, 0, -1):
            led = Led(i, 10 - i)
            self.leds.append(led)
```

```
def print_number(self, number):
    print("==== Turning on {0} LEDs ====".format(number))
    for j in range(0, number):
        self.leds[j].turn_on()
    for k in range(number, 9):
        self.leds[k].turn_off()
```

New terms and **important words** are shown in bold. Words that you see on the screen, for example, in menus or dialog boxes, appear in the text like this: " The next time you have to upload a file to the board, you don't need to set up a new site in the **Site Manager** dialog box in order to establish an SFTP connection."

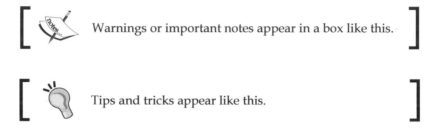

Warnings or important notes appear in a box like this.

Tips and tricks appear like this.

Reader feedback

Feedback from our readers is always welcome. Let us know what you think about this book—what you liked or disliked. Reader feedback is important for us as it helps us develop titles that you will really get the most out of.

To send us general feedback, simply e-mail feedback@packtpub.com, and mention the book's title in the subject of your message.

If there is a topic that you have expertise in and you are interested in either writing or contributing to a book, see our author guide at www.packtpub.com/authors.

Customer support

Now that you are the proud owner of a Packt book, we have a number of things to help you to get the most from your purchase.

Downloading the example code

You can download the example code files for this book from your account at
`http://www.packtpub.com`. If you purchased this book elsewhere, you can visit
`http://www.packtpub.com/support` and register to have the files e-mailed directly
to you.

You can download the code files by following these steps:

1. Log in or register to our website using your e-mail address and password.
2. Hover the mouse pointer on the **SUPPORT** tab at the top.
3. Click on **Code Downloads & Errata**.
4. Enter the name of the book in the **Search** box.
5. Select the book for which you're looking to download the code files.
6. Choose from the drop-down menu where you purchased this book from.
7. Click on **Code Download**.

You can also download the code files by clicking on the **Code Files** button on the
book's webpage at the Packt Publishing website. This page can be accessed by
entering the book's name in the **Search** box. Please note that you need to be
logged in to your Packt account.

Once the file is downloaded, please make sure that you unzip or extract the folder
using the latest version of:

*   WinRAR / 7-Zip for Windows
*   Zipeg / iZip / UnRarX for Mac
*   7-Zip / PeaZip for Linux

The code bundle for the book is also hosted on GitHub at `https://github.com/
PacktPublishing/Internet-of-Things-with-Python`. We also have other code
bundles from our rich catalog of books and videos available at `https://github.
com/PacktPublishing/`. Check them out!

Downloading the color images of this book

We also provide you with a PDF file that has color images of the screenshots/
diagrams used in this book. The color images will help you better understand the
changes in the output. You can download this file from `https://www.packtpub.
com/sites/default/files/downloads/InternetofThingswithPython_
ColorImages.pdf`.

Errata

Although we have taken every care to ensure the accuracy of our content, mistakes do happen. If you find a mistake in one of our books—maybe a mistake in the text or the code—we would be grateful if you could report this to us. By doing so, you can save other readers from frustration and help us improve subsequent versions of this book. If you find any errata, please report them by visiting http://www.packtpub.com/submit-errata, selecting your book, clicking on the **Errata Submission Form** link, and entering the details of your errata. Once your errata are verified, your submission will be accepted and the errata will be uploaded to our website or added to any list of existing errata under the Errata section of that title.

To view the previously submitted errata, go to https://www.packtpub.com/books/content/support and enter the name of the book in the search field. The required information will appear under the **Errata** section.

Piracy

Piracy of copyrighted material on the Internet is an ongoing problem across all media. At Packt, we take the protection of our copyright and licenses very seriously. If you come across any illegal copies of our works in any form on the Internet, please provide us with the location address or website name immediately so that we can pursue a remedy.

Please contact us at copyright@packtpub.com with a link to the suspected pirated material.

We appreciate your help in protecting our authors and our ability to bring you valuable content.

Questions

If you have a problem with any aspect of this book, you can contact us at questions@packtpub.com, and we will do our best to address the problem.

1
Understanding and Setting up the Base IoT Hardware

In this chapter, we will start our journey towards **Internet of Things (IoT)** with Python and the Intel Galileo Gen 2 board. Python is one of the most popular and versatile programming languages. You can use Python to create multiplatform desktops and Web, mobile, and scientific applications. You can work with huge amounts of data and develop the complex algorithms that are popular in Big Data scenarios with Python. There are thousands of Python packages, which allow you to extend Python capabilities to any kind of domain you can imagine.

We can leverage our existing knowledge of Python and all of its packages to code the different pieces of our IoT ecosystem. We can use the object-oriented features, which we love from Python. in code that interacts with the Intel Galileo Gen 2 board and the electronic components connected to it. We can use the different packages that make it possible for us to easily run a Web server and provide a RESTful API. We can use all the packages that we already know to interact with databases, Web services, and different APIs. Python makes it easy for us to jump into the IoT world. We don't need to learn another programming language, we can use the one we already know and love.

First, we will learn about the features included in the Intel Galileo Gen 2 board. We will:

- Understand the Intel Galileo Gen 2 board and its components
- Recognize the Input/Output and the Arduino 1.0 pinout
- Learn about the additional expansion and connectivity capabilities
- Understand the buttons and the LEDs found in the board
- Check and upgrade the board's firmware

Understanding the Intel Galileo Gen 2 board and its components

We want to bring our ideas to life, easily. We want to be able to display a happy birthday message on a screen when we clap our hands. We want to collect huge amounts of data from the real world. We want to create wearables that keep track of all our activities during an entire day. We want to use the data to perform actions and interact with real-world elements. We want to use our mobile devices to control robots. We want to be able to determine whether the weather is hot or cold based on the data retrieved from a temperature sensor. We want to make decisions based on the values collected from a humidity sensor.

We want to measure how much of our favorite beverage is there in the cup and display the information on an LCD dot matrix display. We want to analyze all the data collected by things that are connected to the Internet. We want to become makers in the Internet of Things era by leveraging our existing Python programming skills.

We will use Python as the main programming language to control the different components connected to an Intel Galileo Gen 2 board, specifically Python 2.7.3. However, before we can become makers, it is necessary to understand some of this board's features.

After we unbox an Intel Galileo Gen 2, we will find the following elements:

- The Intel Galileo Gen 2 board
- A 12 VDC (Volts direct current), 1.5 A (Amperes) power supply

The following image shows the front view for an unboxed Intel Galileo Gen 2 board:

Let's have a look at the front view of the board for a few minutes. We will notice many familiar elements, such as an Ethernet jack, host USB port, and many labeled pins. In case we have previous experience with an Arduino UNO R3 board, we will easily realize that many elements are in the same locations as in that board. In case we have previous experience with embedded systems and electronics, we will easily realize that the board provides the necessary pins (SCL and SDA) to talk with the devices that support the I²C bus. In case we don't have any previous experience, we will learn what we can do with all these pins in the examples included in the forthcoming chapters.

The next image shows the graphical representation of the Intel Galileo Gen 2 board in the Fritzing open source and free software. As you might notice, the graphical representation includes only the important pieces of the board and all the things we can wire and connect, with the necessary labels to help recognize them easily. We will use the Fritzing diagrams to illustrate all the wirings that we must do in order to complete each sample project through the book.

 You can download the latest version of Fritzing from `http://fritzing.org/download/`. Fritzing runs on Windows, Mac OS X and Linux. You will find the Fritzing sketches for all the examples included throughout the book in files with an FZZ extension (`*.fzz`) as a part of the code files that you can download for this book. The files are saved with Fritzing 0.92. Thus, you can open the sketches in Fritzing, check the breadboard view, and make any changes to it based on your needs.

The next image shows the electronic schematic representation of the Intel Galileo Gen 2 board, that is, the symbolic representation of the board to make it easy to understand the interconnections of the electronic circuits related to the board. The electronic schematic is also known as circuit diagram or electrical diagram. The symbol includes all the pins provided by the board shown as connectors. We can easily recognize the many labels that appear on the board as labels for each connector in the symbol. Fritzing allows us to work with both the breadboard and the electronic schematic representation.

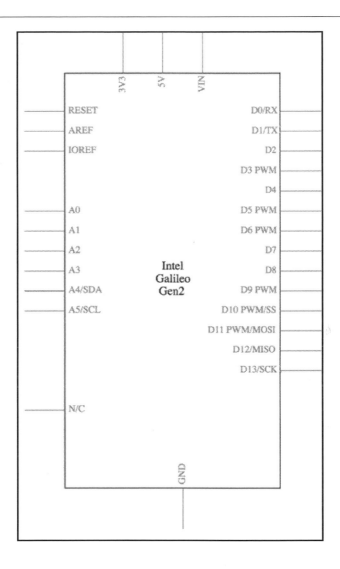

 When you open the Fritzing file for each sample included in the book, you will be able to easily switch from the breadboard view to the schematic view by clicking on either the Breadboard or the Schematic buttons located at the top of the main Fritzing window.

The next image shows the system block diagram for the Intel Galileo Gen 2 board. The diagram is a part of the content included in the Intel Galileo Gen 2 design document: http://www.intel.com/content/dam/www/public/us/en/documents/guides/galileo-g2-schematic.pdf.

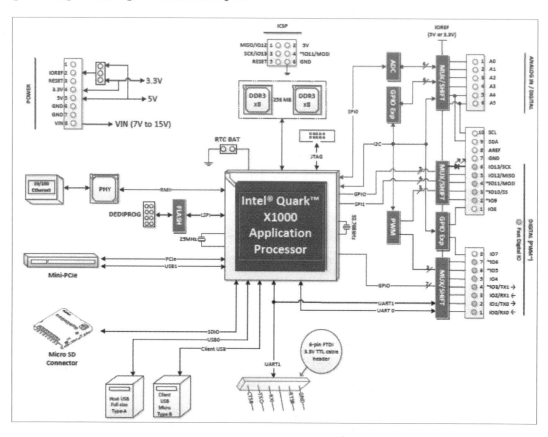

The Intel Galileo Gen 2 board is an Arduino certified embedded computer that we will use to develop and prototype our IoT projects. The board is based on Intel architecture and uses an Intel Quark SoC X1000 system on a chip, known as SoC or application processor. The SoC is a single-core and single-threaded application processor that is compatible with the Intel Pentium 32-bit **instruction set architecture (ISA)**. Its operating speed is up to 400 MHz. The following image shows the SoC, located approximately at the center of the board. The following page provides detailed information about the Intel Quark SoC X1000: http://ark.intel.com/products/79084/Intel-Quark-SoC-X1000-16K-Cache-400-MHz

On the right-hand side of the CPU, the board has two integrated circuits that provide 256 MB of DDR3 **RAM** (short for **Random Access Memory**) memory. The operating system and Python will be able to work with this RAM memory. As it happens in any computer, RAM memory loses its information after we turn off the board. Thus, we say that RAM is volatile, as the data stored in it is lost when the memory isn't powered. The following image shows the DDR3 memory chips.

In addition, the board provides access to the following onboard memories:

- 512 KB embedded **SRAM** (short for **Static Random Access Memory**).
- 8 MB Legacy SPI NOR Flash, non-volatile memory. Its goal is to store the board's firmware and sketches.
- 11 KB **EEPROM** (short for **Electrically Erasable Programmable Read-Only Memory**). It is non-volatile and we can store data in it for our own purposes.

Recognizing the Input/Output and the Arduino 1.0 pinout

The board provides the following I/O pins:

- 14 digital I/O pins
- Six **PWM** (short for **Pulse Width Modulation**) output pins
- Six analog input pins

The board is hardware and software pin-compatible with Arduino shields designed for the Arduino Uno R3. The 14 digital I/O pins numbered from 0 to 13 are located in the upper-right corner of the board and they also include the adjacent **AREF** and **GND** pins, as in the Arduino Uno R3. The pins configuration is also known as Arduino 1.0 pinout.

 Shields are boards that we can plug on top of the Intel Galileo Gen 2 board to extend its capabilities. For example, you can plug a shield that provides two high current motor controllers or a shield that adds an LED matrix.

As it happens in the Arduino Uno R3, we can use six of these digital I/O pins as PWM (Pulse Width Modulation) output pins. Specifically, the pins labeled with a tilde symbol (~) as a prefix to the number have this capability: pins ~**11**, ~**10**, ~**9**, ~**6**, ~**5** and ~**3**. The following are the pins that compose the header from left to right:

- SCL
- SDA
- AREF
- GND
- 13
- 12

- ~11
- ~10
- ~9
- 8
- 7
- ~6
- ~5
- 4
- ~3
- 2
- TX->1
- RX<-0

The next image shows the 14 digital I/O pins and the six PWM output pins labeled with a tilde symbol (~) as a prefix for the number. The first two pins, starting from the left are for the two I²C bus lines: **SCL** (**Serial CLock**) and **SDA** (**Serial DAta**). The last two pins, starting from the left, labeled **TX->1** and **RX<-0** are the UART 0 port pins. A **UART** port stands for **Universal Asynchronous Receiver/Transmitter**.

The six analogous input pins numbered from **A0** to **A5** are located in the lower-right corner of the board, as in the Arduino Uno R3. On the left-hand side of the analog input pins, we can see the following power pins that compose the power header:

- POWER
- IOREF
- RESET
- 3.3V
- 5V
- GND
- GND
- VIN

The **VIN** pin in the power header provides the input voltage that is supplied to the board through its power jack. The power supply included in the box provides 12V. However, the board can operate with an input voltage ranging from 7V to 15V. The board also provides support to Power over Ethernet, also known as PoE, this passes the electrical power to the board along with data on the Ethernet cable.

The following screenshot shows the power pins, also known as power headers, and the six analog input pins:

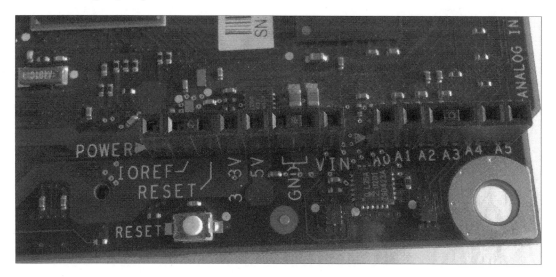

The board includes a jumper labeled **IOREF** that allows us to select between a 3.3V or 5V shield operation and provides voltage-level translation to all the I/O pins. Based on the jumper position, the board can work with either a 3.3V or 5V Arduino shield. By default, the **IOREF** jumper is set to the 5V position, and therefore, the initial setting allows us to work with 5V shields. The following screenshot shows the **IOREF** jumper set to the 5V position.

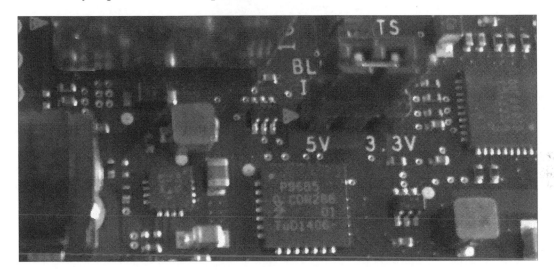

 The **IOREF** pin in the power header provides the operational voltage reference based on the **IOREF** jumper position. Thus, based on the **IOREF** jumper position, the voltage reference in the **IOREF** pin can be either 5V or 3.3V.

On the right-hand side of the board, there is a 6 pin, specifically 2x3 pin, ICSP (In-Circuit Serial Programming) header, labeled **ICSP**. The location of this header is also compatible with the Arduino 1.0 pinout. The following screenshot shows the ICSP header:

Recognizing additional expansion and connectivity capabilities

The power jack is located on the left-hand side of the board and it is labeled **PWR**. Below the power jack, there is a microSD card connector, labeled **SDIO**. The microSD card connector supports microSD cards with a maximum support capacity of 32 GB. We will use the microSD card as our main storage to store the operating system, Python, and the necessary libraries. The board can boot from the microSD card. Thus, we can think of the microSD card as our main hard drive to work with IoT projects. The following screenshot shows the power jack with the power supply connected to it and the microSD card connector with an 8 GB microSD card being connected to it.

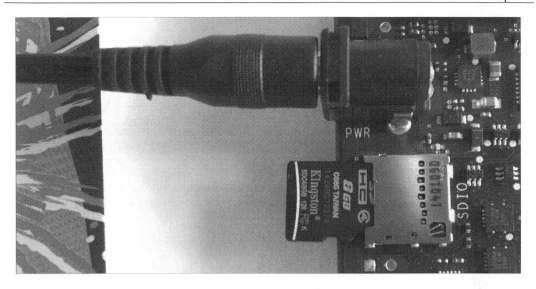

The Ethernet jack is located in the upper-left corner of the board, labeled **10/100 LAN**, above the power jack. The Ethernet port supports both the Ethernet and Fast Ethernet standards, and therefore, it can work with either 10 Mbps or 100 Mbps nominal throughput rates. The Ethernet port is extremely useful to connect the board to our LAN and access it through an IP address. There is an adhesive label with the MAC (Media Access Control) address for the Ethernet onboard network interface card. The MAC address is also known as physical address.

The following screenshot shows this adhesive label on the Ethernet jacket and a cable plugged in it. The MAC address for the board shown in the image is A1B2C3D4E5F6. If we use the convention that expresses a MAC address as six groups of two hexadecimal digits separated by colons (:), the MAC address will be expressed as A1:B2:C3:D4:E5:F6. The MAC address is extremely useful to identify the board in our LAN DHCP client list. For security reasons, the original MAC address has been erased and we use a fake MAC address for our example.

A six pin, 3.3V USB TTL UART header is located next to the Ethernet jack, specifically UART 1, the second UART port in the board. The six pin, 3.3V USB TTL UART header has the following labels on the right-hand side:

- CTS
- TXO
- RXI
- No label (empty)
- RTS
- GND

Next to the Ethernet jack and the UART header, there is a micro USB Type B connection, labeled **USB CLIENT**. We can use this connection to connect the computer to the board, in order to perform firmware updates or transfer sketches.

> However, it is important to know that you cannot power the board off USB. In addition to it, never connect a cable to the micro USB Type B connection before you connect the power supply to the board.

Next to the micro USB connection, there is a USB 2.0 host connector, labeled **USB HOST**. The connector supports a maximum of 128 USB endpoint devices. We can use this connector to plug a USB thumb drive for additional storage, USB keyboard, USB mouse, or any other USB device that we might need. However, we must consider the necessary drivers and their compatibility with the Linux distribution that we will be using with the board, before we plug any device.

The following image shows the UART header, micro USB connector, and the USB 2.0 port, from left to right, next to the Ethernet jack.

The following image shows the side view with all the connectors and jacks. From left to right, the USB 2.0 port, the micro USB connector, the UART header, and the Ethernet jack with the green (SPEED) and yellow (LINK) LEDs.

The back of the board provides a mini PCI Express slot, also known as the mPICe slot, compliant with PCIe 2.0 features, labeled **PCIE**. The slot is compatible with both full size and half size mPCIe modules that we can connect to the board to expand its capabilities. The half size mPCIe module requires an adapter to be connected to the slot on the board.

 It is possible to add another USB host port via the mPCIe slot. The mPCIe slot is extremely useful to provide WiFi, Bluetooth, and other types of connectivity that aren't included as onboard features.

Next to the mPCIe slot, there is a 10-pin JTAG (Joint Test Action Group) header, labeled **JTAG**. It is possible to use the JTAG interface for debugging purposes in combination with debugging software that supports the Intel Quark SoC X1000 application processor, such as the free and open source on-chip debugging software OpenOCD.

The next image shows the back-view for the board with mPCIe slot and the JTAG header.

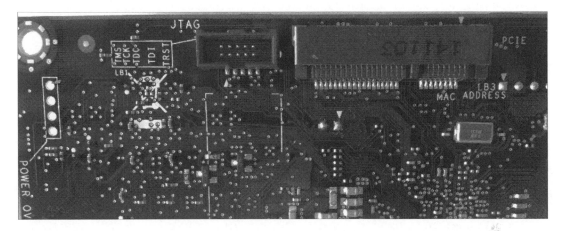

Understanding the buttons and the LEDs

The front of the board provides two buttons located at the bottom labeled **REBOOT** and **RESET**. The following image shows these two buttons:

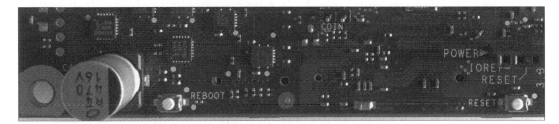

The button labeled **REBOOT** resets the Intel Quark SoC X1000 application processor. The button labeled **RESET** resets the sketch and any shield attached to the board. In this book, we won't be working with the Arduino sketches but we might need to reset a shield.

There are five rectangular LEDs located next to the USB 2.0 host connector: two LEDs on the left-hand side of the connector and three LEDs on the right-hand side. The following are the labels and the meaning of the LEDs:

- **OC**: The LED signals over-current when the board is powered through the micro USB connector. However, this feature is not enabled on Intel Galileo Gen 2 boards, and therefore, we just have the LED turned off. If the LED turns on, it means that the board is not working OK or the power supply is failing. This LED usually turns on when the board is bricked. We say a board is bricked when it doesn't work anymore and is technologically as useful as a brick.

- **USB**: It is the micro USB ready LED. The LED turns on after the board has finished the boot process and allows us to connect the micro USB cable to the micro USB connection labeled **USB CLIENT**. We should never connect a cable to the micro USB connection before this LED turns on because we can damage the board.

- **L**: The LED is connected to pin 13 of the digital I/O pins, and therefore, a high level sent to pin 13 will turn on this LED and a low level will turn it off.

- **ON**: It is a power LED and indicates that the board is connected to the power supply.

- **SD**: The LED indicates I/O activity with the microSD card connector, labeled **SDIO**, and therefore, this LED will blink whenever the board is reading or writing on the microSD card.

The following image shows the **OC** and **USB** LEDs on the left-hand side of the USB 2.0 host connector and the **L**, **ON** and **SD** LEDs on its right-hand side.

The board includes an integrated real-time clock, known as RTC. It is possible to connect a 3V coin-cell battery to keep the RTC operation between turn-on cycles. Unluckily, the battery is not included in the box. The two RTC coin-cell connector pins are located in the lower-left corner of the Intel Quark SoC X1000 application processor, labeled **COIN** and with a battery icon. The next image shows the two RTC coin-cell connector pins.

Checking and upgrading the board's firmware

Sometimes, the original firmware included in the board is the latest one available for Intel Galileo Gen 2. However, in some cases, we might need a firmware update, and therefore it is always convenient to make sure that we are working with the latest available version for the onboard firmware.

> Firmware updates solve bugs and compatibility issues. Thus, it is always convenient to work with the latest firmware. However, in case you don't feel sure about following the procedure to update the firmware, it is convenient to keep the version that came with the board. A wrong procedure while updating the firmware or a power loss during the process might damage the board, that is, it might transform the board into a bricked one. You definitely don't want this to happen to your board.

If you want to check the current firmware version and check whether it is necessary to upgrade the board's firmware, you must follow the following steps:

Go to the Intel Galileo Firmware and Drivers download page at `http://downloadcenter.intel.com/download/24748/Intel-Galileo-Firmware-and-Drivers-1-0-4`. The URL is for the latest firmware version at the time this book has been written: 1.0.4. However, always make sure that you are downloading the latest available version from Intel Drivers & Software Download Center. In case the version is higher than 1.0.4, the procedure will be the same but you just need to replace 1.0.4 with the new version numbers.

The Web browser will display the available downloads for the supported operating systems. The Web page doesn't detect the operating system you are using, and therefore, it offers the downloads for all the supported operating systems: Windows, Mac OS X, and Linux. The following image shows the contents for the Web page:

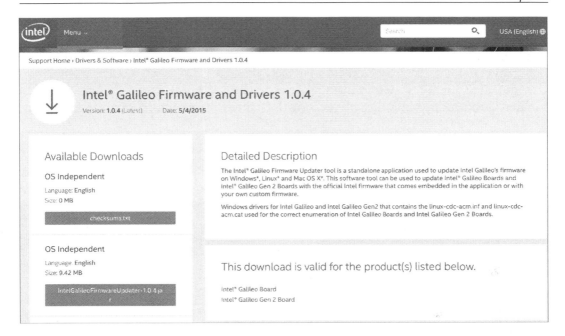

You will find a PDF user guide under **OS Independent: IntelGalileoFirmwa reUpdaterUserGuide-1.0.4.pdf**. Click on the button, read and accept the Intel Software License Agreement, and read the Intel Galileo Firmware Updater Tool documentation. The documentation includes all the necessary steps to install the drivers in Windows and Linux. The Mac OS X doesn't require any driver installation.

Before you install the drivers or start the process to check the firmware version in your board, remove all the connections from the board, such as the microUSB cable and any USB device plugged into the USB 2.0 host connector. Remove any sketches and also the microSD card. Your Intel Galileo Gen 2 board should be empty just as when you unboxed it.

Connect the power supply to the board and wait a few seconds until the rectangular LED labeled **USB** turns on. Once this LED is turned on, the boot process has already finished and it is safe to connect a USB Type A to Micro-B USB cable from your computer to the micro USB connector labeled **USB CLIENT** in the board. Unluckily, the cable isn't included within the board's box. The following image shows an Intel Galileo Gen 2 board with the connections done and the firmware updater tool running on Mac OS X.

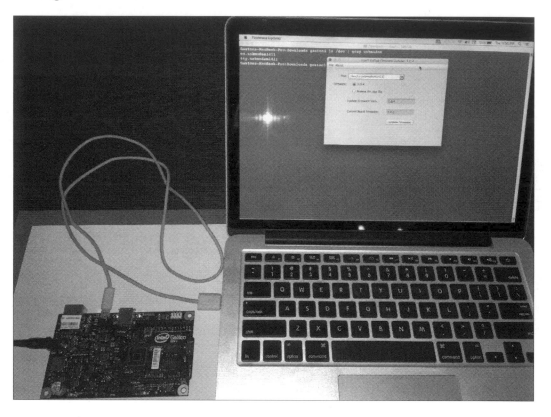

In case you are working with either Windows or Linux, follow the procedure to install the necessary drivers as explained in the **IntelGalileoFirmwareUpdaterUserG uide-1.0.4.pdf** document.

You already have the board connected to your computer, and therefore, you can skip this step in the document. In fact, many versions of this document didn't explain that you had to wait for the USB LED to turn on before you can connect the board to a computer through the micro USB connector and that caused many boards to have unexpected problems.

Once you have the drivers installed in your computer and your board is connected to it, you can download and execute the ZIP file of the Intel Galileo Firmware Updater for your operating system. For Windows, the file is **IntelGalileoFirmwareUpdater-1.0.4-Windows.zip**. For Mac OS X, the file is **IntelGalileoFirmwareUpdater-1.0.4-OSX.zip**. You usually have to scroll down the Web page to find the appropriate file for your operating system. Once you click on the desired file button, it is necessary to read and accept the Intel Software License Agreement before you can download the zip file.

In Windows, download the **IntelGalileoFirmwareUpdater-1.0.4-Windows.zip** file, open it, and execute the **firmware-updater-1.0.4.exe** application included in the zip file. The **Intel Galileo Firmware Updater Tool** window will appear and it will automatically select the virtual COM port number, such as **COM3**, generated by the previously installed driver in the **Port** dropdown. The application will communicate with the board and then display the firmware version included with the tool in **Update Firmware Version** and the current board's firmware version in **Current Board Firmware**.

The following image shows the Intel Galileo Firmware Updater Tool running on Windows 10. In this case, the tool has the newest version for the firmware because it offers version **1.0.4** and the current board's firmware is **1.0.2**.

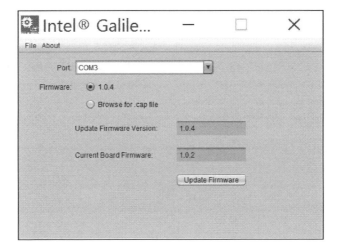

In Mac OS X, download the **IntelGalileoFirmwareUpdater-1.0.4- OSX.zip** file and then execute the downloaded **Firmware Updater** application. Take into account that you might need to authorize the operating system to run the application based on your security settings and your OS X version. The **Intel Galileo Firmware Updater Tool** window will appear and it will automatically select the generated USB modem device for the connected board, such as **/dev/cu.usbmodem1411**, in the **Port** dropdown. The application will communicate with the board and then it will display the firmware version included with the tool in **Update Firmware Version** and the current board's firmware version in **Current Board Firmware**.

The following image shows the Intel Galileo Firmware Updater Tool running on OS X El Capitan. In this case, the tool has the newest version for the firmware because it offers version **1.0.4** and the current board's firmware is **1.0.2**, as it happened with the Windows version.

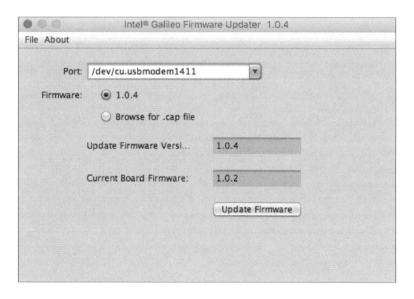

In case you decide that you need and want to update the firmware, considering the previously explained risks, you just need to click on the **Update Firmware** button and wait for the tool to indicate that the process has finished. The procedure is the same for either Windows or Mac OS X.

Don't unplug the USB cable from your computer connected to the board, don't disconnect the power supply from the board, and don't close the application until the tool indicates that the firmware update has finished. The safest way to perform a firmware update is to plug the power supply to a UPS (Uninterruptible Power Supply) to protect it from a power failure during the firmware update process.

Once the firmware update process has finished and the tool displays that you have the same firmware version on the board that the firmware version that the tool offers, you can close the application and disconnect the USB cable from your computer and the board. Make sure that you don't leave the USB cable connected to your board and then unplug the power supply.

Test your knowledge

1. The Intel Galileo Gen 2 board includes:

    1. WiFi connectivity onboard with three antennas.

    2. Ethernet connectivity onboard.

    3. Bluetooth connectivity onboard.

2. The Intel Galileo Gen 2 board is hardware and pin compatible with a wide range of:

    1. Arduino Uno R3 shields.

    2. Arduino Pi shields.

    3. Raspberry Pi shields.

3. The jumper labeled IOREF allows us to:

    1. Select between 3.5V or 7V shield operation and provide voltage-level translation to all the I/O pins.

    2. Select between 3.3V or 5V shield operation and provide voltage-level translation to all the I/O pins.

    3. Reset the board.

4. The LED labeled L is connected to the following pins of the digital I/O pins:

    1. 11.

    2. 12.

    3. 13.

5. The back of the board provides the following slot:

    1. Mini PCI Express.

    2. PCMCIA.

    3. Thunderbolt.

Summary

In this chapter, we learnt the different features offered by the Intel Galileo Gen 2 board. We visualized the different components of the board and we understood the meaning of the different pins, LEDs, and connectors. We also learned to check the board's firmware version and to update it in case it is necessary to do so.

Now that we recognize the different components of the board, we have to prepare it to work with Python as our main programming language, which is what we are going to discuss in the next chapter.

2
Working with Python on Intel Galileo Gen 2

In this chapter, we will start our journey towards Internet of Things (IoT) with Python and the Intel Galileo Gen 2 board. We shall:

- Set up the environment to start working with Python as the main programming language
- Retrieve the board's assigned IP address after it boots a Yocto Linux distribution
- Connect to the board's operating system and run commands on it
- Install and upgrade the necessary libraries to interact with the board's component with Python
- Run our first lines of Python code in the board

Setting up the board to work with Python as the programming language

There is some work to be done in order to start working with Python as the main programming language to control this board. We need the following additional elements that aren't included in the board's box:

- A microSD card of at least 4 GB with a maximum supported capacity of 32 GB. It is convenient to use a speed class 4 or a faster microSD card. Note that you will lose all the contents of the microSD card.
- A microSD to SD memory card adapter. The adapter is usually included within a microSD card's package.

- A computer with an SD memory card reader. Most modern laptops and desktop computers include SD mermory card readers. However, in case you don't have one, you can buy a USB SD memory card reader and plug it to a free USB port in your computer. SD memory card readers are in fact read/write devices, and therefore, we can use them to write to a microSD card via the microSD to SD memory card adapter.

- An Ethernet cable.

- An Ethernet switch or a WiFi router with a free Ethernet port. You will connect the Intel Galileo Gen 2 board to your LAN.

> In case you do not have access to your LAN's switch, you will have to ask your network administrator for advice.

The next picture shows an 8 GB speed class 4 microSD card labeled **SDC4/8GB** (left) and a microSD to SD memory card adapter (right).

We have to download the latest version of the Yocto Linux meta distribution boot image from the Intel IoT Development Kit Images Repository website. Open `http://iotdk.intel.com/images/` in your Web browser and download the `iot-devkit-latest-mmcblkp0.direct.bz2` compressed file with the boot image listed on the Web page. You can also download it by entering the full URL in your Web browser: `http://iotdk.intel.com/images/iot-devkit-latest-mmcblkp0.direct.bz2`.

We will use the `devkit-latest-mmcblkp0.direct.bz2` file, last modified on July 2, 2015. Make sure that you don't download any version releases sooner than this date because there are many differences in the package names used in previous releases that aren't compatible with the instructions provided later on in this chapter.

Once you have downloaded the file, it is necessary to decompress the downloaded image file and write the extracted image to the microSD card. The procedure is different in Windows and Mac OS X.

In Windows, you can use 7-Zip to extract the contents from the downloaded `.bz2` file. 7-Zip is a free and open source software that you can download from `http://www.7-zip.org`.

Once you extract the Yocto Linux meta distribution boot image `iot-devkit-latest-mmcblkp0.direct` from the `.bz2` file, you have to write this image to the microSD card. Insert the microSD card into the microSD to SD memory card adapter and insert the adapter into the computer's SD memory card reader.

The Win32 Disk Imager tool is an image writer for Windows that allows us to write images to USB sticks or SD/CF cards. You can use this free software to write the image to the microSD card. You can download it from `http://sourceforge.net/projects/win32diskimager/files/Archive`. The installer for the latest version is the `Win32DiskImager-0.9.5-install.exe` file. Once you install the software, take into account that you must execute the application as an administrator in Windows. You can right-click on the application's icon and select **Run as administrator**.

Click on the icon on the right-hand side of the **Image File** textbox and change the files filter from **Disk Images (*.img *.IMG)** to ***.*** so that you can select the Yocto Linux boot image with a **direct** extension.

Select the drive letter that Windows assigned to the microSD card in the **Device** dropdown.

Make sure that you select the right drive letter because all the contents for the drive will be erased and overwritten with the boot image. If you select the incorrect drive letter, you will lose the contents of the entire drive.

Click on **Write** and then click on **Yes** in the confirm overwrite dialog box. Now, wait until the tool finishes writing the contents to the microSD card. The following screenshot shows the **Win32 Disk Imager** tool displaying the progress while it writes the image to the microSD card in Windows 10.

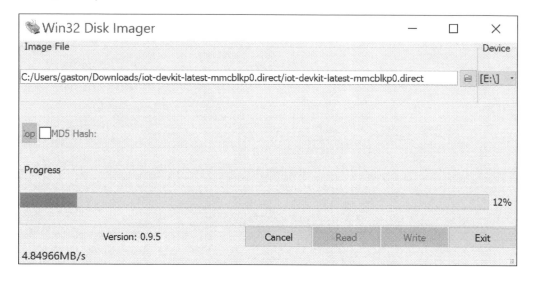

It will take a few minutes until the tool finishes writing the image to the microSD card. Once the writing process has finished, the tool will display a **Complete** dialog box with a **Write successful** message. Click on **OK** to close the dialog box and close the Win32 Disk Imager window.

Eject the microSD card in Windows and then remove the SD memory card adapter from the SD card reader.

In Mac OS X and Linux, you can use `bunzip2` to extract the contents from the downloaded **bz2** file, `diskutil` to unmount the microSD card, and `dd` to write the image to the microSD card. It is also possible to open a **Terminal** and unzip the downloadeded bz2 file by running the following command in the folder in which you downloaded the file:

```
bunzip -c iot-devkit-latest-mmcblkp0.direct
```

 You need to be very careful with the commands to avoid erasing a wrong device such as a partition of your hard drive.

It is also possible to unzip the downloaded bz2 file by double-clicking on it on Finder. However, we will be running more commands in the **Terminal** window, and therefore, it is easier to start unzipping the file with a command.

Once you extract the Yocto Linux boot image `iot-devkit-latest-mmcblkp0.`
`direct` from the bz2 file, you have to write this image to the microSD card. Insert
the microSD card into the microSD to SD memory card adapter and then insert
the adapter into the computer's SD memory card reader. Launch the **Disk Utility**
application and check the details for the media connected to the card reader. For
example, in any MacBook laptop, you will find the info by clicking on **APPLE SD**
Card Reader Media and then on the **Info** button. Check the name listed in **Device**
name or **BSD device node**. We will use this name in a command that will write
the boot image to the microSD card. The following picture shows the **Disk Utility**
application and the information for a microSD card whose device name is **disk2**. We
just need to add `/dev/` as a prefix to the gathered device name, and therefore, in this
sample case, the complete name is `/dev/disk2`.

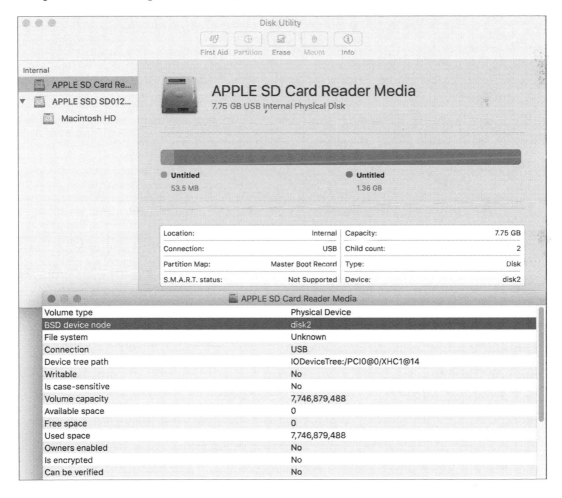

It is also possible to gather the information by running the `diskutil` command to list all the devices and find out the device name assigned to the microSD card. However, the information provided by this command is a bit difficult to read and the **Disk Utility** application makes it easy to understand which is the device name for the memory card reader. The following command lists all the devices:

```
diskutil list
```

The following is the sample output generated by this command. The highlighted lines show the device name for the microSD card: `/dev/disk2`.

```
/dev/disk0 (internal, physical):
   #:                       TYPE NAME                    SIZE
IDENTIFIER
   0:      GUID_partition_scheme                    *121.3 GB
disk0
   1:                       EFI EFI                  209.7 MB
disk0s1
   2:      Apple_CoreStorage Macintosh HD           120.5 GB
disk0s2
   3:             Apple_Boot Recovery HD            650.0 MB
disk0s3
/dev/disk1 (internal, virtual):
   #:                       TYPE NAME                    SIZE
IDENTIFIER
   0:             Apple_HFS Macintosh HD           +120.1 GB
disk1
                            Logical Volume on disk0s2
                            4BADDDC3-442C-4E75-B8DC-82E38D8909AD
                            Unencrypted
/dev/disk2 (internal, physical):
   #:                       TYPE NAME                    SIZE
IDENTIFIER
   0:      FDisk_partition_scheme                    *7.7 GB
disk2
   1:                      Linux                      53.5 MB
disk2s1
   2:                      Linux                       1.4 GB
disk2s2
```

 Make sure that you take note of the right device name because all the contents for the drive will be erased and overwritten with the boot image. If you specify a wrong device name, you will lose the contents of the entire drive.

Unmount the microSD card with the following command. You need to replace `/dev/devicename` with `/dev/disk2` in case the device name you gathered was `disk2`. If not, replace it with the appropriate device name.

```
sudo diskutil unmountDisk /dev/devicename
```

The **Terminal** will ask for your password and will unmount the microSD card. Run the following `dd` command to write the image in the input file named `iot-devkit-latest-mmcblkp0.direct` to the microSD card in the device name you gathered in the previous step. You need to replace `of=/dev/devicename` with `of=/dev/disk2` in case the device name you gathered was `disk2`. If not, replace it with the appropriate device name. The command doesn't include a device name so that you don't overwrite any of your disks by accident.

```
sudo dd if=iot-devkit-latest-mmcblkp0.direct of=/dev/devicename bs=8m
```

Then, it will take some time to write the image to the microSD card. Wait until the command finishes and the `Terminal` displays the prompt again. Notice that it usually takes a few minutes and there is no output with any progress indication until the write process finishes. You will see the following output after the command finishes:

```
169+1 records in
169+1 records out
1417675776 bytes transferred in 1175.097452 secs (1206433 bytes/sec)
```

Now, unmount the microSD card with the following command. You need to replace `/dev/devicename` with `/dev/disk2` in case the device name you gathered was `disk2`. If not, replace it with the appropriate device name.

```
sudo diskutil unmountDisk /dev/devicename
```

Close the terminal window and then remove the SD memory card adapter from the SD card reader.

Now, we have a microSD card with a Yocto Linux distribution that includes Python 2.7.3 and many useful libraries and utilities. It is time to make the Intel Galileo Gen 2 board boot from the Yocto image written to the microSD card.

Make sure that the board is unplugged and place the microSD card with the Yocto image in the microSD card slot on the board, labeled **SDIO**. The following picture shows a microSD card inserted in the slot on the board.

Then, connect the board to your LAN with the Ethernet cable and plug the board's power supply to turn on the board and start it up. You will notice that the rectangular onboard LED labeled **SD** indicates that there is activity with the microSD card. Wait for approximately 30 seconds to make sure that the board finishes the boot process. You will notice that the LED labeled **SD** stops blinking after the boot process finishes.

Retrieving the board's assigned IP address

The board has finished the boot process with the Yocto Linux microSD card and is connected to our LAN throught the Ethernet port. The DHCP server has assigned the board an IP address and we need to know it in order to run commands on a Yocto Linux console. There are many ways for us to retrieve the board's assigned IP address. We will explore the different options and you can choose the most convenient one based on your LAN configuration.

If the board is connected to one of the Ethernet ports of a Wireless router and we have access to the router's Web interface, we can easily know the IP address assigned to the board. Some router's Web interfaces display the wired clients list. As our board is connected through an Ethernet wire, it will be listed as one of the wired clients and the device MAC address will match the MAC address printer in the adhesive label on the board's Ethernet jacket. The following picture shows the Wired-clients list in a router's Web interface and the list includes a device named **galileo** with **A1-B2-C3-D4-E5-F6** as the MAC address that matches the MAC address printed without hyphens (-) in the board: **A1B2C3D4E5F6**. The IP address assigned to the board is **192.168.1.104**. For security reasons, the original MAC address has been erased and we are using a fake MAC address for our example.

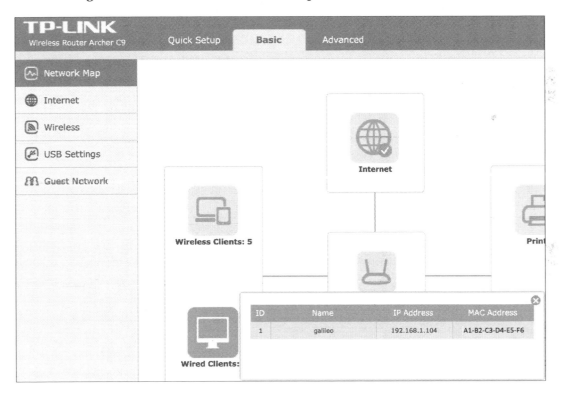

Sometimes, the router's Web interface doesn't provide an option that displays the wired clients list. If this is the case for our router, we will always be able to retrieve the DHCP client list that provides all the IP addresses assigned to either the wireless or wired devices connected to the LAN. We just need to find the device that has the MAC address for the board. The following picture shows the DHCP Client List in a router's Web interface and the list includes a device named **galileo** with **A1-B2-C3-D4-E5-F6** as the MAC address that matches the MAC address printed without hyphens (-) in the board: **A1B2C3D4E5F6**. The IP address assigned to the board is **192.168.1.104**.

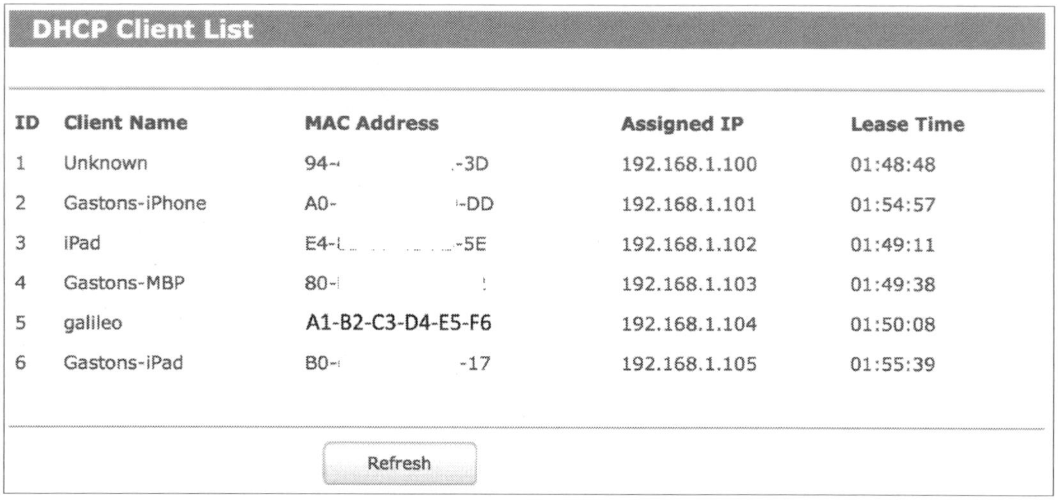

DHCP Client List

ID	Client Name	MAC Address		Assigned IP	Lease Time
1	Unknown	94-⸱	.-3D	192.168.1.100	01:48:48
2	Gastons-iPhone	A0-	⸱-DD	192.168.1.101	01:54:57
3	iPad	E4-Ⴑ ⸱ ⸱ ⸱⸱-5E		192.168.1.102	01:49:11
4	Gastons-MBP	80-ⵏ	ⵏ	192.168.1.103	01:49:38
5	galileo	A1-B2-C3-D4-E5-F6		192.168.1.104	01:50:08
6	Gastons-iPad	B0-ⵏ	-17	192.168.1.105	01:55:39

Refresh

Another option is to install a Bonjour Browser to discover the board and its services on the LAN automatically through this zero-configuration networking implementation, without knowing the IP assigned to the board.

In Windows, download, install, and launch the free Bonjour Browser for Windows from `http://hobbyistsoftware.com/bonjourbrowser`. The application will display many available Bonjour services with **galileo** as their name. The following screenshot shows the **_ssh._tcp** service type with **galileo** as its name selected with the details. The **IP Adresses** section shows the IP address and the port number for the SSH service: **192.168.1.105:22**. We can use the IP address with any SSH client to connect to the board. In addition, the Bonjour browser lets us know that the board has an SFTP service that will make it easy for us to transfer files from and to the Yocto Linux running on the board.

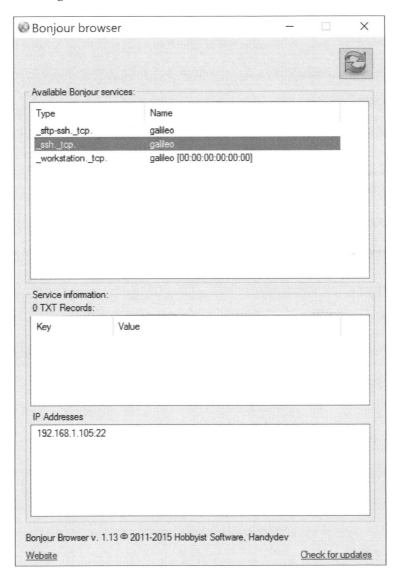

In OS X, download and run the free Bonjour Browser from http://www.tildesoft. com. You can click on **Reload Services** to refresh the discovered devices and their services. The following picture shows a board and its services listed in the Bonjour Browser. You have to click on each right-arrow to expand the details for each listed service. In this case, all the services are provided by the same device named **galileo**. Once you expand the device, the application displays the IPv4 and IPv6 addresses. The **SSH (_ssh._tcp.)** service type lists a device with **galileo** as its name and with **192.168.1.105:22** as the IPv4 address and the port number. We can use the IP address with any SSH client to connect to the board. The Bonjour Browser also displays the details for the SFTP service.

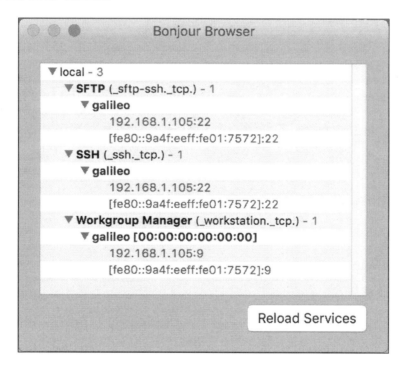

SSH stands for Secure Shell Protocol and its default port is 22. Yocto Linux runs the SSH server in the default port, and therefore, there is no need to specify the port in SSH clients, we can just specify the discovered IP address.

Connecting to the board's operating system

Now, we need to use an SSH client to connect to the Yocto Linux running on the board and update some libraries that we will use to interact with the board's components and features. Both OS X and Linux include the ssh command in the Terminal. However, Windows doesn't include an ssh command and we have to install an SSH client.

In Windows, we can use the free and open source PuTTY SSH and telnet client. However, if you have any other preference for an SSH client in Windows, you can use any other software. The commands we execute in the terminal will be the same no matter what SSH client we use.

We can download and install PuTTY in Windows from http://www.putty.org or http://www.chiark.greenend.org.uk/~sgtatham/putty/download.html. Once you install it, launch it and make sure you allow Windows firewall or any other installed firewall to open the necessary ports to make the connections. You will see warnings popping up depending on the firewall software that is running on Windows.

After you launch PuTTY, the application will display the **PuTTY Configuration** dialog box. Enter the IP address assigned to your board in the **Host Name (or IP address)** textbox and leave the **Port** value to its default **22** value. The following picture shows the dialog box with the settings to connect to the board whose assigned IP is **192.168.1.105**. You can leave the default settings. However, you should definitely change the **Window | Appearance** settings to change the default font.

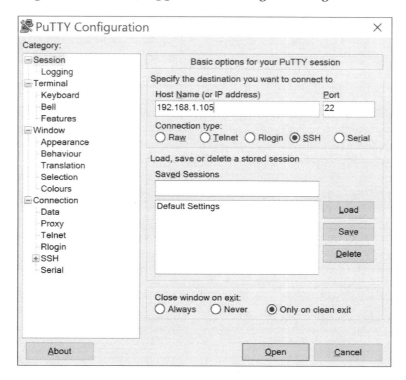

Click on **Open** and the first time you want to establish a connection; PuTTY will display a security alert because the server's host key is not cached in the registry. You trust your board and the Yocto Linux that is running on it, and therefore, just click on **Yes**. The following picture shows the security alert.

PuTTY will display a new window, specifically a terminal window, with the IP address included in the title. You will see the following message asking you to enter the login user.

```
login as:
```

Enter **root** and press *Enter*. You will login as the `root` user that doesn't require a password in the Yocto Linux default configuration. Now, you can run any shell commands. For example, you can enter the following command to check the installed python version:

```
python --version
```

The following picture shows a PuTTY terminal window with the results of logging in as root and running a few commands:

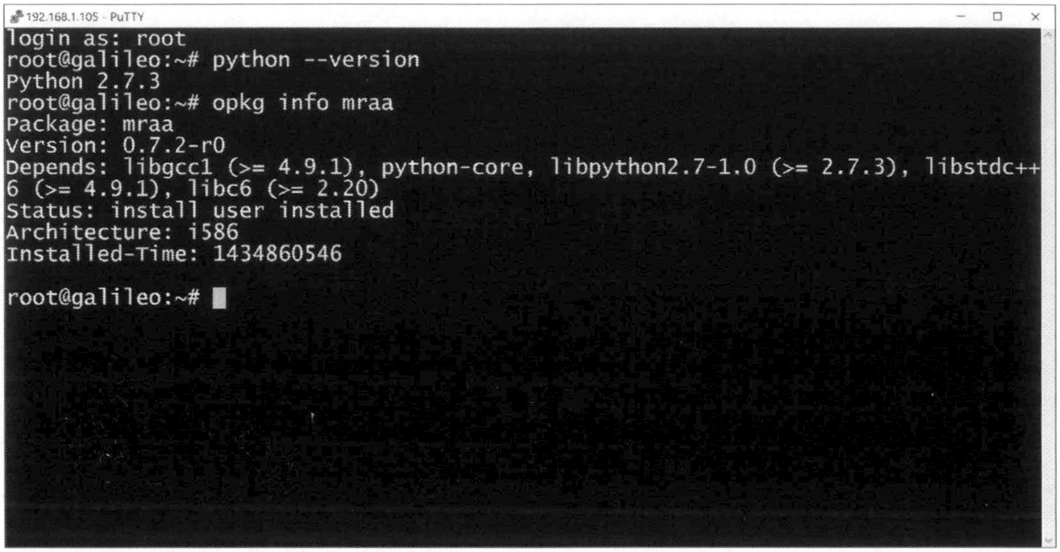

```
192.168.1.105 - PuTTY                                                    —   □   ×
login as: root
root@galileo:~# python --version
Python 2.7.3
root@galileo:~# opkg info mraa
Package: mraa
Version: 0.7.2-r0
Depends: libgcc1 (>= 4.9.1), python-core, libpython2.7-1.0 (>= 2.7.3), libstdc++
6 (>= 4.9.1), libc6 (>= 2.20)
Status: install user installed
Architecture: i586
Installed-Time: 1434860546

root@galileo:~#
```

In OS X and Linux, you can open a **Terminal** and run the ssh command to connect to the Yocto Linux running on the board. You have to enter ssh followed by a space, the user name, an arrow (@), and the IP. In this case, we want to connect with root as the user name, and therefore, we will enter ssh followed by a space, root@, and then the IP address. The following command works with the board that is running the SSH server in the 192.168.1.105 IP address and port number 22. You have to replace 192.168.1.105 with the IP address you retrieved.

```
ssh root@192.168.1.105
```

The first time you want to establish a connection, the ssh command will display a security alert because the authenticity of the host can't be established. You trust your board and the Yocto Linux that is running on it, and therefore, answer **yes** to a question that will be similar to the following one and press *Enter*.

```
The authenticity of host '192.168.1.105 (192.168.1.105)' can't be
established.
ECDSA key fingerprint is SHA256:Ln7j/g1Np4igsgaUP0ujFC2PPcb1pnkLD8Pk0
AK+Vow.
Are you sure you want to continue connecting (yes/no)?
```

The `ssh` command will display a message similar to the following line after you answer **yes** and press *Enter*:

```
Warning: Permanently added '192.168.1.105' (ECDSA) to the list of
known hosts.
```

You will log in as the `root` user that does not require a password in the Yocto Linux default configuration. Now, you can run any shell command. For example, you can enter the following command to check the installed Python version.

```
python --version
```

Notice that while you see the following prompt **root@galileo:~#**, it means that all your commands are running on the Yocto Linux on the board and not on your OS X Terminal or your Linux Terminal. The following picture shows an OS X **Terminal** window with the results of logging in as `root` and running a few commands:

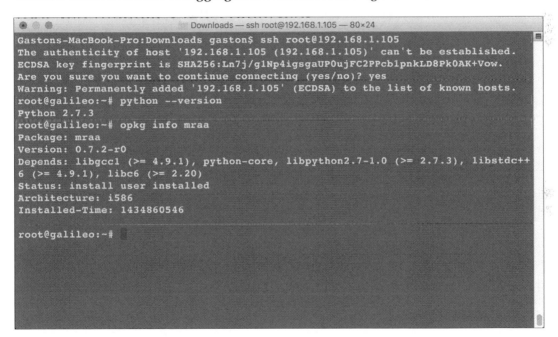

 The Yocto Linux that the board has booted includes Python 2.7.3 pre-installed.

We can also run any SSH client in a mobile device such as a tablet or smartphone. There are many SSH clients developed for iOS and Android. It is possible to work with a tablet and a Bluetooth keyboard linked to it and easily run the commands in the SSH client.

Installing and upgrading the necessary libraries to interact with the board

Now, we will run many commands in the SSH client. Make sure that your SSH client is connected to the Yocto Linux SSH server running on the board as explained in the preceding section before running the commands. Specially, if you are working with either OS X or Linux, you have to make sure that you don't run the commands on your computer instead of doing this on the remote shell. Its simple, just make sure you always see the prompt **root@galileo:~#** before running any command.

 Your board should be connected to a LAN with Internet access because we will download content from the Internet.

We will use the opkg utility to download and install the updated version of both the mraa and upm libraries. The mraa library, also known as libmraa, is a low level C/C++ library with bindings to Python that allows us to interface with the I/O features on the Intel Galileo Gen 2 board and other supported platforms. The upm library provides high-level interfaces for sensors and actuators that we can plug to the platforms supported by the mraa library. The upm library simplifies working with sensors and actuators and includes bindings to Python. We will be working with both libraries in the forthcoming chapters, and therefore, we want to have their latest versions installed.

The opkg utility is a lightweight package manager that allows us to easily download and install OpenWrt packages. OpenWrt is a Linux distribution for embedded devices. First, we will check both the mraa and upm installed versions by using the opkg utility.

Run the following command to check the installed mraa version:

```
opkg info mraa
```

The following lines show the output with the version and dependencies for the mraa package. In this case, the output shows that the installed version for mraa is **0.7.2-r0**.

```
Package: mraa
Version: 0.7.2-r0
Depends: libgcc1 (>= 4.9.1), python-core, libpython2.7-1.0 (>= 2.7.3),
libstdc++6 (>= 4.9.1), libc6 (>= 2.20)
Status: install user installed
Architecture: i586
Installed-Time: 1434860546
```

Run the following command to check the installed upm version:

```
opkg info upm
```

The following lines show the output with the version and dependencies for the upm package. In this case, the output shows that the installed version for upm is **0.3.1-r0**.

```
Package: upm
Version: 0.3.1-r0
Depends: libgcc1 (>= 4.9.1), libpython2.7-1.0 (>= 2.7.3), libc6 (>=
2.20), python-core, libstdc++6 (>= 4.9.1), mraa (>= 0.7.2)
Status: install user installed
Architecture: i586
Installed-Time: 1434860596
```

Run the following command to check the repository configuration for both the `mraa` and upm libraries.

```
cat /etc/opkg/mraa-upm.conf
```

If you see the following line as a response, it means that the repository is configured to work with the 1.5 version and we need to change its configuration to make it possible to update both the mraa and upm libraries to their latest versions.

```
src mraa-upm http://iotdk.intel.com/repos/1.5/intelgalactic
```

Run the following command to configure the repository for both the mraa and upm libraries to work with version 2.0 instead of 1.5:

```
echo "src mraa-upm http://iotdk.intel.com/repos/2.0/intelgalactic" > /
etc/opkg/mraa-upm.conf
```

Now, run the following command to check the repository configuration for both the mraa and upm libraries and you will notice that 1.5 has been replaced by 2.0 in the output.

```
cat /etc/opkg/mraa-upm.conf
```

You should see the results shown in the next line:

```
src mraa-upm http://iotdk.intel.com/repos/2.0/intelgalactic
```

We will use the opkg utility to update packages from the previously configured repository located on the Internet. Run the following command to make the opkg utility update the list of available packages after we changed the configuration of the repositories for both the mraa and upm libraries.

```
opkg update
```

The previous command will generate the following output that indicates the list of available packages that have been updated. Notice that the last lines of the output indicate that the command has been downloaded from http://iotdk.intel.com/repos/2.0/intelgalactic/Packages and saved the available packages in /var/lib/opkg/mraa-upm.

```
Downloading http://iotdk.intel.com/repos/1.5/iotdk/all/Packages.
Updated list of available packages in /var/lib/opkg/iotdk-all.
Downloading http://iotdk.intel.com/repos/1.5/iotdk/i586/Packages.
Updated list of available packages in /var/lib/opkg/iotdk-i586.
Downloading http://iotdk.intel.com/repos/1.5/iotdk/quark/Packages.
Updated list of available packages in /var/lib/opkg/iotdk-quark.
Downloading http://iotdk.intel.com/repos/1.5/iotdk/x86/Packages.
Updated list of available packages in /var/lib/opkg/iotdk-x86.
Downloading http://iotdk.intel.com/repos/2.0/intelgalactic/Packages.
Updated list of available packages in /var/lib/opkg/mraa-upm.
```

Run the following command to check the versions for both the mraa and upm libraries stored in /var/lib/opkg/mraa-upm.

```
cat /var/lib/opkg/mraa-upm
```

The following lines show the results. Notice that the version numbers might vary because both the mraa and upm libraries are very active projects and they are frequently updated. Thus, the version numbers might be higher when you run the previous command.

```
Package: mraa
Version: 0.9.0
Provides: mraa-dev, mraa-dbg, mraa-doc
```

```
Replaces: mraa-dev, mraa-dbg, mraa-doc, libmraa, libmraa-dev, libmraa-
doc
Conflicts: mraa-dev, mraa-dbg, mraa-doc
Section: libs
Architecture: i586
Maintainer: Intel IoT-Devkit
MD5Sum: b92167f26a0dc0dba4d485b7bedcfb47
Size: 442236
Filename: mraa_0.9.0_i586.ipk
Source: https://github.com/intel-iot-devkit/mraa
Description: mraa built using CMake
Priority: optional


Package: upm
Version: 0.4.1
Depends: mraa (>= 0.8.0)
Provides: upm-dev, upm-dbg, upm-doc
Replaces: upm-dev, upm-dbg, upm-doc
Conflicts: upm-dev, upm-dbg, upm-doc
Section: libs
Architecture: i586
Maintainer. Intel IoT-Devkit
MD5Sum: 13a0782e478f2ed1e65b33249be41424
Size: 16487850
Filename: upm_0.4.1_i586.ipk
Source: https://github.com/intel-iot-devkit/upm
Description: upm built using CMake
Priority: optional
```

In this case, we have mraa version **0.9.0** and upm version **0.4.1**. The version numbers are higher than the initially installed ones. We definitely want to upgrade mraa **0.7.2-r0** to **0.9.0** and upm **0.3.1-r0** to 0.4.1. As shown in the preceding lines, upm depends on mraa version 0.8.0 or greater, and therefore, we will upgrade mraa first.

Run the following command to install the latest available version of the mraa library:

```
opkg install mraa
```

The following lines show the results:

```
Upgrading mraa from 0.7.2-r0 to 0.9.0 on root.
Downloading http://iotdk.intel.com/repos/2.0/intelgalactic/mraa_0.9.0_
i586.ipk.
Removing package mraa-dev from root...
```

```
Removing package mraa-doc from root...
Removing obsolete file /usr/lib/libmraa.so.0.7.2.
Removing obsolete file /usr/bin/mraa-gpio.
Configuring mraa.
```

Run the following command to install the latest available version of the upm library:

```
opkg install upm
```

The following lines show some lines with the results and the final line. Note that the package installation removes an important number of obsolete files:

```
Upgrading upm from 0.3.1-r0 to 0.4.1 on root.
Downloading http://iotdk.intel.com/repos/2.0/intelgalactic/upm_0.4.1_
i586.ipk.
Removing package upm-dev from root...
Removing obsolete file /usr/lib/libupm-wt5001.so.0.3.1.
Removing obsolete file /usr/lib/libupm-adc121c021.so.0.3.1.
Removing obsolete file /usr/lib/libupm-joystick12.so.0.3.1.
Removing obsolete file /usr/lib/libupm-grove.so.0.3.1.
Removing obsolete file /usr/lib/libupm-tm1637.so.0.3.1.
...
Removing obsolete file /usr/lib/libupm-groveloudness.so.0.3.1.
Configuring upm.
```

Now, run the following command to check the installed mraa version:

```
opkg info mraa
```

The following lines show the output with the version and dependencies for the mraa package. The first lines show that mraa version **0.7.2-r0** is not installed anymore and the highlighted lines show that mraa version **0.9.0** is installed.

```
Package: mraa
Version: 0.7.2-r0
Depends: libgcc1 (>= 4.9.1), python-core, libpython2.7-1.0 (>= 2.7.3),
libstdc++6 (>= 4.9.1), libc6 (>= 2.20)
Status: unknown ok not-installed
Section: libs
Architecture: i586
Maintainer: Intel IoT Devkit team <meta-intel@yoctoproject.org>
MD5Sum: b877585652e4bc34c5d8b0497de04c4f
Size: 462242
Filename: mraa_0.7.2-r0_i586.ipk
Source: git://github.com/intel-iot-devkit/mraa.git;protocol=git;rev=29
9bf5ab27191e60ea0280627da2161525fc8990
```

```
Description: Low Level Skeleton Library for Communication on Intel
platforms  Low
 Level Skeleton Library for Communication on Intel platforms.
```

```
Package: mraa
Version: 0.9.0
Provides: mraa-dev, mraa-dbg, mraa-doc
Replaces: mraa-dev, mraa-dbg, mraa-doc, libmraa, libmraa-dev, libmraa-
doc
Conflicts: mraa-dev, mraa-dbg, mraa-doc
Status: install user installed
Section: libs
Architecture: i586
Maintainer: Intel IoT-Devkit
MD5Sum: b92167f26a0dc0dba4d485b7bedcfb47
Size: 442236
Filename: mraa_0.9.0_i586.ipk
Source: https://github.com/intel-iot-devkit/mraa
Description: mraa built using CMake
Installed-Time: 1452800349
```

Run the following command to check the installed upm version:

```
opkg info upm
```

The following lines give the output with the version and dependencies for the upm package. The first lines display that upm version **0.3.1-r0** is not installed anymore and the highlighted lines show that upm version **0.4.1** is installed.

```
Package: upm
Version: 0.3.1-r0
Depends: libgcc1 (>= 4.9.1), libpython2.7-1.0 (>= 2.7.3), libc6 (>=
2.20), python-core, libstdc++6 (>= 4.9.1), mraa (>= 0.7.2)
Status: unknown ok not-installed
Section: libs
Architecture: i586
Maintainer: Intel IoT Devkit team <meta-intel@yoctoproject.org>
MD5Sum: 9c38c6a23db13fbeb8c687336d473200
Size: 10344826
Filename: upm_0.3.1-r0_i586.ipk
Source: git://github.com/intel-iot-devkit/upm.git;protocol=git;rev=3
d453811fb7760e14da1a3461e05bfba1893c2bd file://0001-adafruitms1438-
CMakeLists.txt-stop-RPATH-being-added.patch
Description: Sensor/Actuator repository for Mraa  Sensor/Actuator
repository for Mraa.
```

```
Package: upm
Version: 0.4.1
Depends: mraa (>= 0.8.0)
Provides: upm-dev, upm-dbg, upm-doc
Replaces: upm-dev, upm-dbg, upm-doc
Conflicts: upm-dev, upm-dbg, upm-doc
Status: install user installed
Section: libs
Architecture: i586
Maintainer: Intel IoT-Devkit
MD5Sum: 13a0782e478f2ed1e65b33249be41424
Size: 16487850
Filename: upm_0.4.1_i586.ipk
Source: https://github.com/intel-iot-devkit/upm
Description: upm built using CMake
Installed-Time: 1452800568
```

Now, we have the latest versions of both the mraa and upm libraries installed and we will be able to use them from any Python program.

Installing pip and additional libraries

By default, the `pip` package management system that makes it easy to install and manage software packages written in Python isn't installed. We are going to use Python as our main programming language, and therefore, we will definitely benefit from installing `pip`.

Enter the following `curl` command to download the `get-pip.py` file from `https://bootstrap.pypa.io`, into the current folder.

```
curl -L "https://bootstrap.pypa.io/get-pip.py" > get-pip.py
```

You will see an output similar to the following lines that will indicate the download progress:

```
  % Total    % Received % Xferd  Average Speed   Time    Time     Time
Current
                                 Dload  Upload   Total   Spent    Left
Speed
100 1379k  100 1379k    0     0   243k      0  0:00:05  0:00:05 --:--
:--  411k
```

Once the download has finished, run `python` with `get-pip.py` as an argument.

```
python get-pip.py
```

You will see an ouput similar to the following lines that will indicate the installation progress and a few warnings related to the SSLContext. Don't worry about the warnings.

```
Collecting pip
/tmp/tmpe2ukgP/pip.zip/pip/_vendor/requests/packages/urllib3/util/
ssl_.py:90: InsecurePlatformWarning: A true SSLContext object
is not available. This prevents urllib3 from configuring SSL
appropriately and may cause certain SSL connections to fail. For more
information, see https://urllib3.readthedocs.org/en/latest/security.
html#insecureplatformwarning.
  Downloading pip-7.1.2-py2.py3-none-any.whl (1.1MB)
    100% |################################| 1.1MB 11kB/s
Collecting wheel
  Downloading wheel-0.26.0-py2.py3-none-any.whl (63kB)
    100% |################################| 65kB 124kB/s
Installing collected packages: pip, wheel
Successfully installed pip-7.1.2 wheel-0.26.0
/tmp/tmpe2ukgP/pip.zip/pip/_vendor/requests/packages/urllib3/util/
ssl_.py:90: InsecurePlatformWarning: A true SSLContext object
is not available. This prevents urllib3 from configuring SSL
appropriately and may cause certain SSL connections to fail. For more
information, see https://urllib3.readthedocs.org/en/latest/security.
html#insecureplatformwarning.
```

Now, we can use the `pip` installer to easily install additional Python 2.7.3 packages. We will use the `pip` installer to get the `wiring-x86` package from PyPI, the Python Package Index, and install it. The `wiring-x86` package is a Python module that provides a simple API similar to the WiringPi module to use the general purpose I/O pins on the Intel Galileo Gen 2 board and other supported platforms. We just need to run the following command to install the package:

```
pip install wiring-x86
```

The last lines for the ouput will indicate that the `wiring-x86` package has been successfully installed. Don't worry about the error messages related to building a wheel for `wiring-x86`.

```
Installing collected packages: wiring-x86
  Running setup.py install for wiring-x86
Successfully installed wiring-x86-1.0.0
```

Invoking the Python interpreter

We have installed the most updated versions of the most important libraries we required to interact with the features included in the Intel Galileo Gen 2 board. Now, we can invoke the Python interpreter by typing the classic command:

```
python
```

Now, enter the following two lines of Python code:

```
import mraa
mraa.getVersion()
```

The Python interpreter will display the following output:

```
'v0.9.0'
```

We imported the `mraa` library and called the `mraa.getVersion` method to check whether Python is able to retrieve the installed version of the `mraa` library. The result of calling the method displays the version we installed for the `mraa` library, and therefore, we know that Python is going to work with the version we expect. Note that the Python code is running on the Yocto Linux on the Intel Galileo Gen 2 board.

Now, enter the following line to check whether the `mraa` library has successfully detected the board type:

```
mraa.getPlatformName()
```

The Python interpreter will display the following output:

```
'Intel Galileo Gen 2'
```

We called the `mraa.getPlatformName` method and the result of calling the method displays our board's name: Intel Galileo Gen 2. The following screenshot shows the results of calling the previous methods:

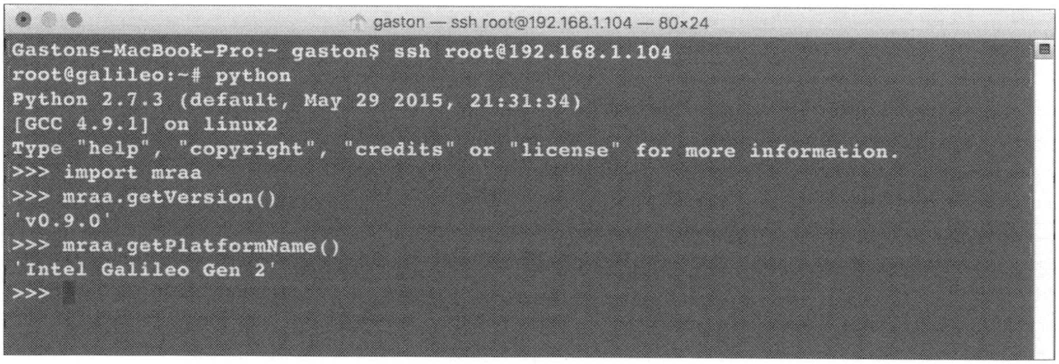

Now, open a Web browser in any computer or device connected to your LAN and enter the board's assigned IP address. For example, in case the IP address is **192.168.1.104**, enter it as the URL to browse. The following screenshot shows the content you will see on your Web browser: **It works!**

The board is working as a Web server and it returns the contents of the /www/pages/ index.html file to the Web browser request.

Test your knowledge

1. We can access Python 2.7.x on the Intel Galileo Gen 2 board:

    1. After booting the pre-installed SPI image from the flash memory.

    2. After booting a Yocto Linux from the microSD card, specifically, the IoT Devkit image.

    3. After booting the pre-installed SPI image and pressing the reboot button three times.

2. Once an Intel Galileo Gen 2 board is connected to our LAN, we can access its shell with any utility that allows us to use the following interface and protocol:

    1. SSH.

    2. Telnet.

    3. X.25.

3. Which of the following libraries has bindings to Python and allows us to work with the I/O on Intel Galileo Gen 2:

    1. IotGalileoGen2.

    2. Mraa.

    3. Mupm.

4. Which of the following packages is a Python module that provides an API similar to the WiringPi module to use general purpose I/O pins on the Intel Galieo Gen 2:

    1. wiring-py-galileo.

    2. galileo-gen2-x86.

    3. wiring-x86.

5. Which of the following methods return the board that the mraa library automatically detects:

    1. mraa.getPlatformName().

    2. mraa.getBoardName().

    3. mraa.getGalileoBoardName().

Summary

In this chapter, we followed many procedures to make is possible to work with Python as the main programming language to create IoT projects with our Intel Galileo Gen 2 board. We wrote a Linux Yocto image to a microSD card and we configured the board to make it boot this image, so that we can access Python and other useful libraries to interact with the board. We updated many libraries to use their latest versions and we launched the Python interpreter.

Now that our board is ready to be coded with Python, we can start wiring electronic components to the board and work with Python and the libraries to write digital values, which is the topic of the next chapter.

3
Interacting with Digital Outputs with Python

In this chapter, we will work with digital inputs with Python and two libraries: `mraa` and `wiring-x86`. We shall:

- Wire our first connections between an Intel Galileo Gen 2 and a breadboard with electronic components
- Write a first version of a Python script that turns on and off electronic components connected to the board
- Transfer Python code to the Yocto Linux running on the board
- Execute Python scripts that interact with the board
- Learn to take advantage of Python's object-oriented features to improve the code and make it easier to understand
- Prepare the code to make it easy to build an API that will allow us to interact with the IoT device

Turning on and off an onboard component

First, we will take advantage of an onboard LED (Light Emitting Diode) to write our first Python lines that interact with the digital output capabilities included in the Intel Galileo Gen 2 board. The simple example will allow us to understand how the `mraa` library allows us to easily turn on and off one of the onboard components with Python code.

In the previous chapter, we recognized the different elements included in the Intel Galileo Gen 2 board. We know that there are three rectangular LEDs located at the right hand side of the USB 2.0 host connector. The first LED, labeled **L** is connected to pin 13 of the digital I/O pins, and therefore, a high level sent to pin 13 will turn on this LED and a low level will turn it off.

We will write a few lines of Python code that will use the mraa library to make the onboard LED labeled **L** to repeat the following loop until the Python program is interrupted:

- Turn on
- Stay turned on for 3 seconds
- Turn off
- Stay turned off for 2 seconds.

The following lines show the Python code that performs the previously explained actions. The code file for the sample is iot_python_chapter_03_01.py.

```python
import mraa
import time


if __name__ == "__main__":
    print ("Mraa library version: {0}".format(mraa.getVersion()))
    print ("Mraa detected platform name: {0}".format(mraa.
getPlatformName()))

    # Configure GPIO pin #13 to be an output pin
    onboard_led = mraa.Gpio(13)
    onboard_led.dir(mraa.DIR_OUT)

    while True:
        # Turn on the onboard LED
        onboard_led.write(1)
        print("I've turned on the onboard LED.")
        # Sleep 3 seconds
        time.sleep(3)
        # Turn off the onboard LED
        onboard_led.write(0)
        print("I've turned off the onboard LED.")
        time.sleep(2)
```

Detailed steps to download the code bundle are mentioned in the Preface of this book. Please have a look.

The code bundle for the book is also hosted on GitHub at `https://github.com/PacktPublishing/Internet-of-Things-with-Python`. We also have other code bundles from our rich catalog of books and videos available at `https://github.com/PacktPublishing/`. Check them out!

In the previous chapter, we learned that the Yocto Linux running on the board provided both **SSH** and **SFTP** (short for **SSH File Transfer Protocol** or **Secure File Transfer Protocol**) services by running a Bonjour browser. We can use any SFTP client to connect to the board and transfer the file that we created in any computer or mobile device. Of course, we can also use any Linux editor, such as vi, in the SSH terminal, or just enter the code in the Python interpreter. However, it is usually more convenient to use our favorite editor or IDE in our computer or mobile device and then transfer the file to the board with any SFTP client.

Some Python IDEs have remote development capabilities and allow us to easily transfer the necessary files and launch their execution on the board. An example is the paid Professional Edition of JetBrains PyCharm. Unluckily, the Community Edition doesn't include this feature.

We don't want the process to be linked to a specific IDE, and therefore, we will transfer the file with an SFTP client. FileZilla Client is a free, open source and multiplatform FTP client that supports SFTP. You can download and install it here: `http://filezilla-project.org`.

Once you have installed and executed FileZilla Client, you must follow the next steps to add the SFTP server running on the board in with the application's Site Manager:

1. Select **File | Site Manager**.
2. Click **New Site** on the **Site Manager** dialog box. Enter the desired name, such as **IntelGalileo2** to easily identify the board's SFTP service.
3. Enter the board's IP address in **Host**. You don't need to enter any value in **Port** because the SFTP server uses the default SFTP port, that is, the same port in which the SSH daemon listens: port 22.
4. Select **SFTP - SSH File Transfer Protocol** in the Protocol dropdown.
5. Select **Normal** in the **Logon Type** dropdown.

6. Enter **root** in **User**. The next screenshots shows the configuration values for a board that has **192.168.1.107** as its assigned IP address.

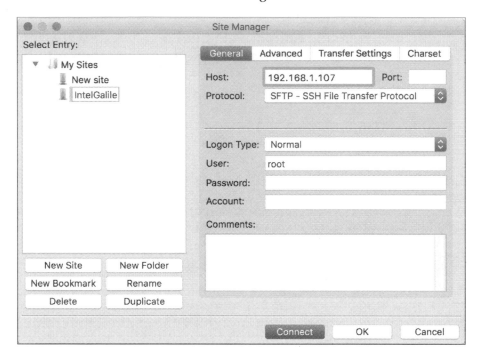

7. Click **Connect**. FileZilla will display an Unknown host key dialog box, indicating that the server's host key is unknown. It is similar to the information provided when you established the first connection to the board with an SSH client. The details include the host and the fingerprint. Activate the **Always trust this host, add this key to the cache** checkbox and click **OK**.

8. FileZilla will display the /home/root folder for the Yocto Linux running on the board at the right-hand side of the window, under **Remote Site**.

9. Navigate to the folder in which you saved the Python files you want to transfer in your local computer under **Local site**.

10. Select the file you want to transfer and press *Enter* to transfer the file to the /home/root folder on the board. Another way is to right-click on the desired file and select **Upload**. FileZilla will display the uploaded file in the /home/root folder under **Remote Site**. This way, you will be able to access the Python file in the default location that Yocto Linux uses when you login with an SSH terminal, that is, in your home folder for your root user. The following picture shows many Python files uploaded to the /home/root folder with FileZilla and listed in the contents of the /home/root folder.

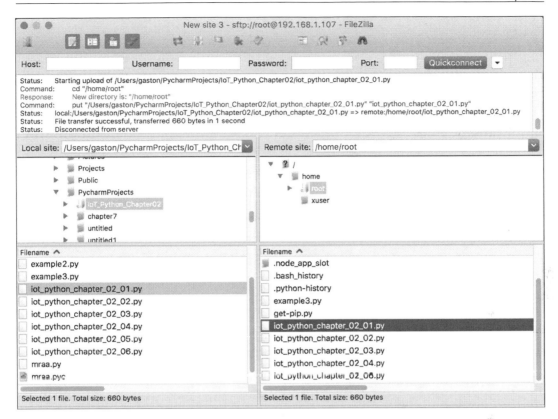

Status: Starting upload of /Users/gaston/PycharmProjects/IoT_Python_Chapter02/iot_python_chapter_02_01.py
Command: cd "/home/root"
Response: New directory is: "/home/root"
Command: put "/Users/gaston/PycharmProjects/IoT_Python_Chapter02/iot_python_chapter_02_01.py" "iot_python_chapter_02_01.py"
Status: local:/Users/gaston/PycharmProjects/IoT_Python_Chapter02/iot_python_chapter_02_01.py => remote:/home/root/iot_python_chapter_02_01.py
Status: File transfer successful, transferred 660 bytes in 1 second
Status: Disconnected from server

As you work with additional projects, you will want to create new folders under /home/root to provide a better organization for your Python code in the Yocto Linux filesystem.

The next time you have to upload a file to the board, you don't need to setup a new site in the **Site Manager** dialog box in order to establish an SFTP connection. You just need to select **File | Site Manager**, select the site name under **Select Entry** and click **Connect**.

If you run the following command in the SSH terminal after you login, Linux will print your current folder or directory:

```
pwd
```

The result of the previous command will be the same folder in which we uploaded the Python code file.

```
/home/root
```

Once we transfer the file to the board, we can run the previous code with the following command on the board's SSH terminal:

```
python iot_python_chapter_03_01.py
```

The previous code is extremely simple. We have used many print statements to make it easy for us to understand what is going on with messages on the console. The following lines show the generated output after we run the code for a few seconds:

```
Mraa library version: v0.9.0
Mraa detected platform name: Intel Galileo Gen 2
Setting GPIO Pin #13 to dir DIR_OUT
I've turned on the onboard LED.
I've turned off the onboard LED.
I've turned on the onboard LED.
I've turned off the onboard LED.
```

The first lines print the `mraa` library version and the detected platform name. This way, we have information about the `mraa` library version that Python is using and we make sure that the `mraa` library has been able to initialize itself and detect the right platform: Intel Galileo Gen 2. In case we have a specific issue, we can use this information to check about specific problems related to the `mraa` library and the detected platform.

The next line creates an instance of the `mraa.Gpio` class. **GPIO** stands for **General Purpose Input/Output** and an instance of the `mraa.Gpio` class represents a general purpose Input/Output pin on the board. In this case, we pass `13` as an argument for the `pin` parameter, and therefore, we are creating an instance of the `mraa.Gpio` class that represents the pin number 13 of the GPIO pins in the board. We named the instance `onboard_led` to make it easy to understand that the instance allows us to control the status of the onboard LED.

```
onboard_led = mraa.Gpio(13)
```

> We just need to specify the value for the pin parameter to initialize an instance of the `mraa.Gpio` class. There are two additional optional parameters (`owner` and `raw`), but we should leave them with the default values. By default, whenever we create an instance of the `mraa.Gpio` class, we own the pin and the `mraa` library will close it on destruct.

As we might guess from its name, an instance of the `mraa.Gpio` class allows us to work with pins as either Input or Output. Thus, it is necessary to specify the desired direction for our `mraa.Gpio` instance. In this case, we want to use pin 13 as an output pin. The following line calls the `dir` method to configure the pin to be an output pin, that is, to set is direction to the `mraa.DIR_OUT` value.

```
onboard_led.dir(mraa.DIR_OUT)
```

Then, the code runs a loop forever, that is, until you interrupt the execution by pressing *Ctrl* + *C* or the button to stop the process in case you are using a Python IDE with remote development features to run the code in your board.

The first line within the `while` loop calls the `write` method for the `mraa.Gpio` instance, `onboard_led`, with 1 as an argument for the `value` required parameter. This way, we send a high value (1) to the pin 13 configured for digital output. Because the pin 13 has the onboard LED connected to it, the result of a high value in pin 13 is that the onboard LED turns on.

```
onboard_led.write(1)
```

After we turn on the LED, a line of code uses the `print` statement to print a message to the console output, so that we know the LED should be turned on. A call to `time.sleep` with 3 as the value for the `seconds` argument delays the execution for three seconds. Because we didn't change the status of pin 13, the LED will stay turned on during this delay.

```
time.sleep(3)
```

The next line calls the `write` method for the `mraa.Gpio` instance, `onboard_led`, but this time with 0 as an argument for the `value` required parameter. This way, we send a low value (0) to the pin 13 configured for digital output. Because the pin 13 has the onboard LED connected to it, the result of a low value in pin 13 is that the onboard LED turns off.

```
onboard_led.write(0)
```

After we turn off the LED, a line of code uses the `print` statement to print a message to the console output, so that we know the LED should be turned off. A call to `time.sleep` with 2 as the value for the seconds argument delays the execution for 2 seconds. Because we didn't change the status of pin 13, the LED will stay turned off during this delay. Then, the loop starts over again.

[

As we can use any `ssh` client to run the Python code, we can see the results of the `print` statements in the console output and they are extremely useful for us to understand what should be happening with the digital outputs. We will take advantage of more advanced logging features included in Python for more complex scenarios later.
]

As we could learn from the previous example, the `mraa` library encapsulates all the necessary methods to work with the GPIO pins in the `mraa.Gpio` class. The previous code didn't take advantage of Python's object-oriented features, it just interacted with one of the classes included in the `mraa` library. We will take advatange of many Python features in the forthcoming examples. In addition, once we start working with more complex examples, we will make the board interact through the network.

Prototyping with breadboards

In the previous example, we interacted with the onboard LED, and therefore, we didn't wire any additional electronic component to the board. Now, it is time to move to more complex samples in which we will have to start working with additional components and tools.

We don't want to create a new printed circuit board (PCB) and solder electronic components to the board each time we want to wire some electronic components to the board. We will be prototyping many electronics projects throught the book and we will also continue prototyping after we learn each lesson towards our IoT adventure. Thus, we will use a solderless breadboard as our construction base for our electronic prototypes.

[

Solderless breadboards are also known as breadboards, solderless plug-in breadboards or prototype boards. We will call them with their shortests name: breadboards.
]

We will use an 830 tie points (holes for connections) with 2 power lanes breadboard for all our prototypes that require electronic components wired to the board. The following picture shows this kind of breadboard that consists of a chunk of plastic of approximately 6.5" x 2.1" with a bunch number of holes.

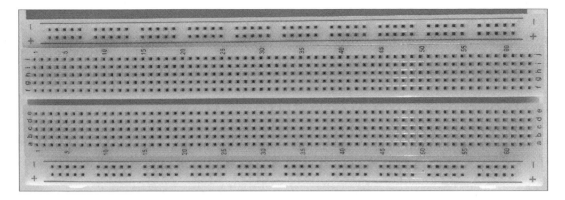

The next picture shows the internal connections for an 830 tie points with 2 power lanes breadboard. There are metal strips inside the breadboard that connect the holes as shown in this picture.

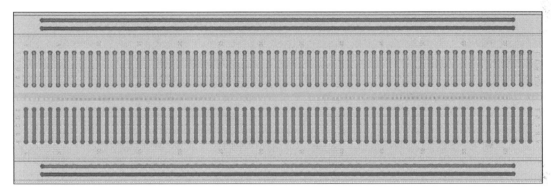

The breadboard provides two power lanes, bus strips or horizontal buses at the top and at the bottom of the board. These power lanes connect all the holes within the row. Each column has five row holes connected.

However, we must be careful because there are similar breadboards that break the power lanes or horizontal buses in the middle, and therefore, the power lanes don't connect all the holes within the row. The following picture shows the connections for these kinds of breadboards.

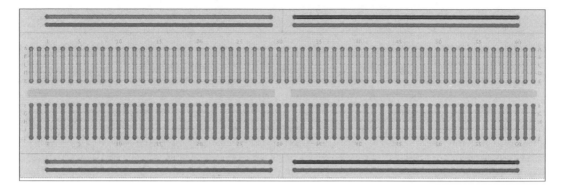

In case you decide to work with this kind of breadboard, you have to make the following connections to the buses. This way, you will mimic the wires shown for the first breadboard.

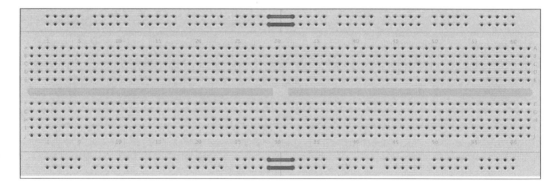

We can stick wire ends without insulation into the breadboard holes in order to wire elements. It is convenient to prepare jumper wires with different lengths and using cables with diverse colors. The following picture shows many cables of different lengths without their insulation that will work as jumper wires.

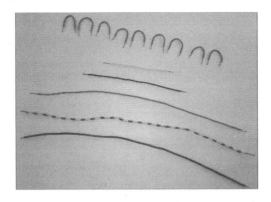

In case we don't want to spend time building our own jumper wires, we can buy prebuilt male to male solderless flexible breadboard jumper wires with tiny plugs attached to the wire ends.

You can use any of the previously explained options to make the necessary connections for each of the examples in which we will be working throught this book. In case you decide to use male to male breadboard jumper wires, make sure they are high quality ones.

Working with schematics to wire digital outputs

Now, it is time to take advantage of the prototyping capabilities of the breadboard and start working on a more complex example. We will turn on and off 9 LEDs by using 9 digital outputs of the Intel Galileo Gen 2 board. Each digital output is going to control whether an LED is turned on or turned off.

After we finish the necessary wirings, we will write Python code that counts from 1 to 9 by controlling the digital output to turn on the necessary number of LEDs. In this case, our first approach won't be the best one. However, after we learn many things, we will create new versions and we will improve both the initial prototype and the Python code.

We need the following parts to work with this example:

- Three red ultrabright 5mm LEDs
- Three white ultrabright 5mm LEDs
- Three green ultrabright 5mm LEDs
- Nine 270Ω resistors with 5% tolerance (red violet brown gold)

The following diagram shows the components connected to the breadboard, the necessary wirings and the wirings from the Intel Galileo Gen 2 board to the breadboard. The Fritzing file for the sample is `iot_fritzing_chapter_03_02.fzz` and the following picture is the breadboard view.

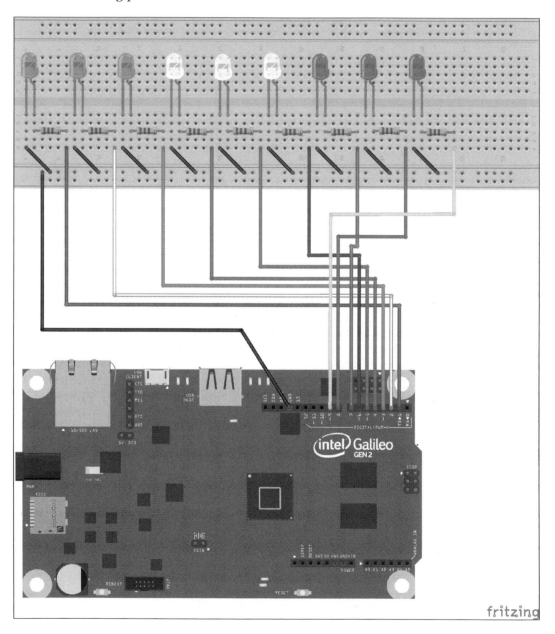

In this case, we decided to match the GPIO pin number with the LED number. This way, whenever we want to turn on LED 1, we write a high (1) value to GPIO pin number 1, whenever we want to turn on LED 2, we write a high (1) value to GPIO pin number 2, and so on. Later, we will realize it is not the best decision because the wiring becomes a bit more complex than expected due to the positions of the pins in the board. However, we will analyze this situation later and we will create a new version of this example with improvements based on everything we learned from the first version.

The following picture shows the schematic with the electronic components represented as symbols. The schematic makes it easier to understand the connections between the Intel Galileo Gen 2 board GPIO pins and the electronic components. Clearly, the schematic benefits from the fact that the GPIO pin number matches the LED number and it will be easy to write our first version of the code.

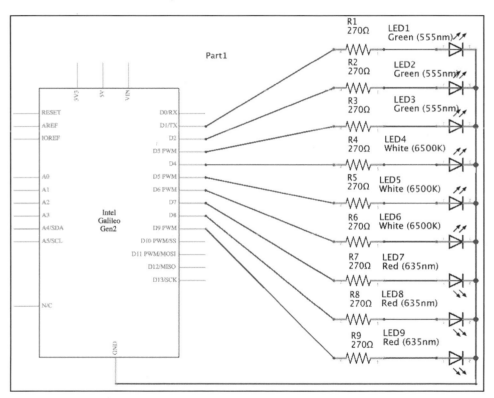

As seen in the previous schematic, each GPIO pin labeled from **D1** to **D9** in the board's symbol is connected to a **270Ω** resistor, wired to an LED's anode, and each LED's cathode is connected to ground. This way, whenever we write a high (1) value to any of the GPIO pins, the board will put 5V on the pin and the LED will turn on. Whenever we write a low (0) value to any of the GPIO pins, the board will put 0V on the pin and the LED will turn off.

As we left the jumper labeled **IOREF** in its default 5V position, the board will be operating with 5V for its GPIO pins. Thus, a GPIO pin will have 5V when we write a high value to it. If we change the position of this jumper to 3.3V, a GPIO pin will have 3.3V when we write a high value to it. Unless specified otherwise, we are using the default position for this jumper in all the examples.

Now, it is time to insert the components in the breadboard and make all the necessary wirings.

Always shutdown the Yocto Linux, wait for all the onboard LEDs to turn off, and unplug the power supply from the Intel Galileo Gen 2 board before adding or removing any wire from the board's pins. Do the same before plugging or unplugging any shield.

In order to shutdown the Yocto Linux, enter the following command in your ssh terminal. Make sure you have exited the Python interpreter when you enter the command.

```
shutdown
```

As a result of the previous command, you will see the time at which the shutdown process is going to begin. The message will be similar to the following output but with different dates and times.

```
Shutdown scheduled for Mon 2016-01-25 23:50:04 UTC, use 'shutdown -c'
to cancel.
root@galileo:~#
Broadcast message from root@galileo (Mon 2016-01-25 23:49:04 UTC):

The system is going down for power-off at Mon 2016-01-25 23:50:04 UTC!
```

Then, wait around 1 minute until the operating system closes down and all the onboard LEDs turn off. At this time, you can safely remove the power supply from the board.

We have to pay special attention when inserting the LEDs in the breadboard. As we can notice in the schematic, the resistor is wired to an LED's anode, and each LED's cathode is connected to ground.

We can easily identify the LED's anode, that is, its positive lead, because its lead is slightly longer than the other lead. The LED's cathode, that is, its negative lead is shorter than the other lead. In the following picture, the LED's cathode, that is, its negative lead is the lead located at the left-hand side (the shorter lead). The LED's anode, that is, its positive lead, is the lead located at the right-hand side (the slightly longer lead). You can also notice that the metal piece inside the LED connected to the LED's anode, that is, its positive lead, is smaller than the metal piece inside the LED connected to the LED's cathode, that is, its negative lead.

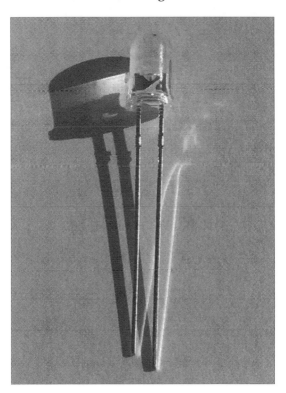

The LED in the picture is located in the same position than the LEDs are connected in the previously shown breadboard picture. Thus, we have to connect the shorter lead at the left and the larger lead at the right in the breadboard. The next picture shows the LED representation in the breadboard picture with its cathode and anode.

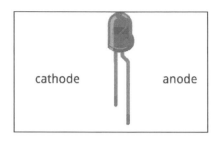

The following picture shows the schematic electronic symbol for the LED with the same positions for the cathode and anode than in the previous picture that showed the breadboard picture.

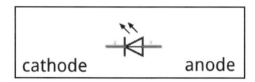

The following picture shows all the LEDs connected to the breadboard. You can check the cathode and the anode based on the metal parts that you can see through the LED's plastic.

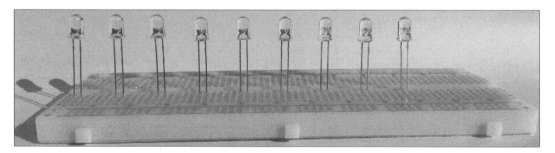

The following picture shows all the LEDs connected to the breadboard where you can check that the LEDs are connected as we have seen in the breadboard view for the Fritzing diagram.

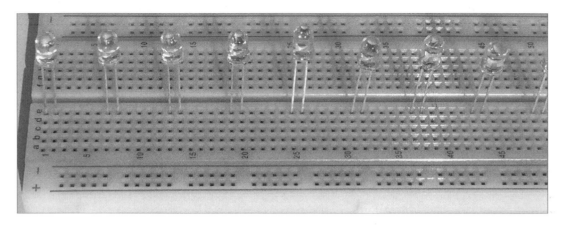

Resistors are the same forward and backwards, and therefore, it doesn't matter which way you use them in the breadboard. The following picture shows a 270Ω axial-lead resistor with 5% tolerance. Notice that the color bands from left to right are red, violet, brown and gold. The color bands allow us to know the resistance in ohms and their tolerance value without having to measure the resistor.

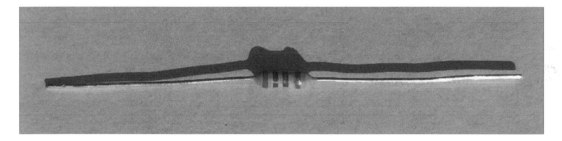

The following picture shows the components connected to the breadboard, the necessary wirings and the wirings from the Intel Galileo Gen 2 board to the breadboard.

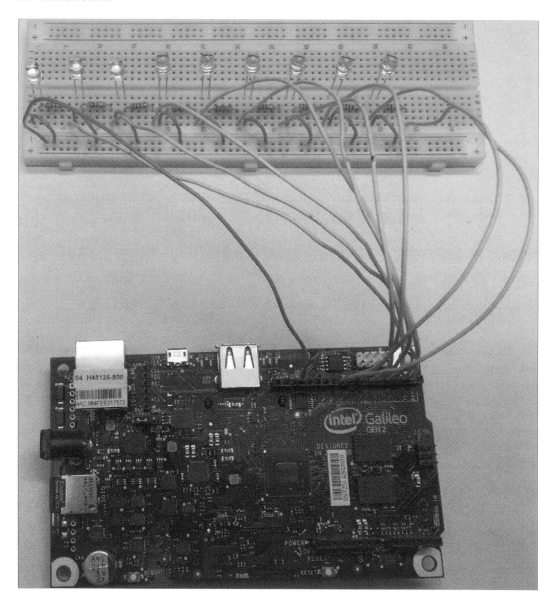

Counting from 1 to 9 with LEDs, Python code and the mraa library

Once we finish the wirings and we make sure that all the components and the wires are in the right place, we can write our first version of the Python code to count from 1 to 9 with the LEDs, transfer it to the board via SFTP and execute it.

We will write a few lines of Python code that will use the mraa library to run the following steps to count from 1 to 9, with a 3 seconds pause between each step:

- Turn on LED1
- Turn on LED1 and LED2
- Turn on LED1, LED2 and LED3
- Turn on LED1, LED2, LED3 and LED4
- Turn on LED1, LED2, LED3, LED4 and LED5
- Turn on LED1, LED2, LED3, LED4, LED5 and LED6
- Turn on LED1, LED2, LED3, LED4, LED5, LED6 and LED7
- Turn on LED1, LED2, LED3, LED4, LED5, LED6, LED7 and LED8
- Turn on LED1, LED2, LED3, LED4, LED5, LED6, LED7, LED8 and LED9

The following lines show the Python code that performs the previously explained actions. The code file for the sample is iot_python_chapter_03_02.py.

```python
import mraa
import time


if __name__ == "__main__":
    print ("Mraa library version: {0}".format(mraa.getVersion()))
    print ("Mraa detected platform name: {0}".format(mraa.
getPlatformName()))

    # Configure GPIO pins #1 to 9 to be output pins
    output = []
    for i in range(1, 10):
        gpio = mraa.Gpio(i)
        gpio.dir(mraa.DIR_OUT)
        output.append(gpio)
```

```
    # Count from 1 to 9
    for i in range(1, 10):
        print("==== Turning on {0} LEDs ====".format(i))
        for j in range(0, i):
            output[j].write(1)
            print("I've turned on the LED connected to GPIO Pin
#{0}.".format(j + 1))
        time.sleep(3)
```

Once we transfer the file to the board, we can run the previous code with the following command on the board's SSH terminal:

```
python iot_python_chapter_03_02.py
```

We have used many `print` statements to make it easy for us to understand what is going on with messages on the console. The following lines show the generated output after we run the code:

```
Mraa library version: v0.9.0
Mraa detected platform name: Intel Galileo Gen 2
Setting GPIO Pin #1 to dir DIR_OUT
Setting GPIO Pin #2 to dir DIR_OUT
Setting GPIO Pin #3 to dir DIR_OUT
Setting GPIO Pin #4 to dir DIR_OUT
Setting GPIO Pin #5 to dir DIR_OUT
Setting GPIO Pin #6 to dir DIR_OUT
Setting GPIO Pin #7 to dir DIR_OUT
Setting GPIO Pin #8 to dir DIR_OUT
Setting GPIO Pin #9 to dir DIR_OUT
==== Turning on 1 LEDs ====
I've turned on the LED connected to GPIO Pin #1.
==== Turning on 2 LEDs ====
I've turned on the LED connected to GPIO Pin #1.
I've turned on the LED connected to GPIO Pin #2.
==== Turning on 3 LEDs ====
I've turned on the LED connected to GPIO Pin #1.
I've turned on the LED connected to GPIO Pin #2.
I've turned on the LED connected to GPIO Pin #3.
==== Turning on 4 LEDs ====
I've turned on the LED connected to GPIO Pin #1.
I've turned on the LED connected to GPIO Pin #2.
I've turned on the LED connected to GPIO Pin #3.
I've turned on the LED connected to GPIO Pin #4.
==== Turning on 5 LEDs ====
```

```
I've turned on the LED connected to GPIO Pin #1.
I've turned on the LED connected to GPIO Pin #2.
I've turned on the LED connected to GPIO Pin #3.
I've turned on the LED connected to GPIO Pin #4.
I've turned on the LED connected to GPIO Pin #5.
==== Turning on 6 LEDs ====
I've turned on the LED connected to GPIO Pin #1.
I've turned on the LED connected to GPIO Pin #2.
I've turned on the LED connected to GPIO Pin #3.
I've turned on the LED connected to GPIO Pin #4.
I've turned on the LED connected to GPIO Pin #5.
I've turned on the LED connected to GPIO Pin #6.
==== Turning on 7 LEDs ====
I've turned on the LED connected to GPIO Pin #1.
I've turned on the LED connected to GPIO Pin #2.
I've turned on the LED connected to GPIO Pin #3.
I've turned on the LED connected to GPIO Pin #4.
I've turned on the LED connected to GPIO Pin #5.
I've turned on the LED connected to GPIO Pin #6.
I've turned on the LED connected to GPIO Pin #7.
==== Turning on 8 LEDs ====
I've turned on the LED connected to GPIO Pin #1.
I've turned on the LED connected to GPIO Pin #2.
I've turned on the LED connected to GPIO Pin #3.
I've turned on the LED connected to GPIO Pin #4.
I've turned on the LED connected to GPIO Pin #5.
I've turned on the LED connected to GPIO Pin #6.
I've turned on the LED connected to GPIO Pin #7.
I've turned on the LED connected to GPIO Pin #8.
==== Turning on 9 LEDs ====
I've turned on the LED connected to GPIO Pin #1.
I've turned on the LED connected to GPIO Pin #2.
I've turned on the LED connected to GPIO Pin #3.
I've turned on the LED connected to GPIO Pin #4.
I've turned on the LED connected to GPIO Pin #5.
I've turned on the LED connected to GPIO Pin #6.
I've turned on the LED connected to GPIO Pin #7.
I've turned on the LED connected to GPIO Pin #8.
I've turned on the LED connected to GPIO Pin #9.
```

The following nine pictures show the sequence of LEDs that are turned on in the breadboard by executing the Python code.

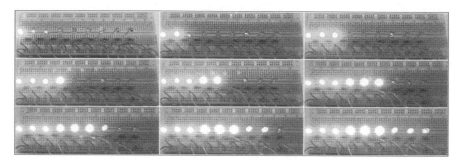

First, the code declares an empty list named output. Then, a for loop creates nine instances of the mraa.Gpio class and each of them represent a general purpose Input/Output pin on the board. We pass i as an argument for the pin parameter, and therefore, each instance represents the pin number equal to i of the GPIO pins in the board. After we create the instance, we call the dir method to configure the pin to be an output pin, that is, to set is direction to the mraa.DIR_OUT value. Then we call the append method for the output list to add the mraa.Gpio instance (gpio) to the output list. It is important to understand that range(1, 10) generates the following list: [1, 2, 3, 4, 5, 6, 7, 8, 9]. Thus, our for loop will start with i equal to 1 and its last iteration will be with i equal to 9.

```
output = []
for i in range(1, 10):
    gpio = mraa.Gpio(i)
    gpio.dir(mraa.DIR_OUT)
    output.append(gpio)
```

Another for loop determines the number of LEDs to be turned on. We use range(1, 10) to generate the same list than in the previous loop. The first line within the for loop calls a print method to display the number of LEDs that we are going to turn on in the iteration. A loop within the loop uses range(0, i) to generate the list of indexes of the elements in the output list that we have to turn on for the iteration of the main for loop (i).

The inner loop uses j as its variable and the code within this inner loop just calls the write method for each mraa.Gpio instance, output[j], with 1 as an argument for the value required parameter. This way, we send a high value (1) to the pin that is equal to j + 1, configured for digital output. If j is equal to 0, the first element of the output list is the mraa.Gpio instance that is configured for pin 1 (j + 1). Because each pin from 1 to 9 has an LED connected to it, the result of a high value in one or more pins are LEDs turned on. Then, the code prints a message indicating the LED number that has been turned on.

Once the inner loop finishes, a call to `time.sleep` with 3 as the value for the `seconds` argument delays the execution for three seconds. This way, the LED or LEDs stay turned on during this delay before the outer loop performs another iteration.

```
for i in range(1, 10):
    print("==== Turning on {0} LEDs ====".format(i))
    for j in range(0, i):
        output[j].write(1)
        print("I've turned on the LED connected to GPIO Pin
#{0}.".format(j + 1))
    time.sleep(3)
```

The following picture shows the console output printed on an SSH terminal in a laptop, the 9 LEDs turned on in the protoboard connected to the board that is running Python code.

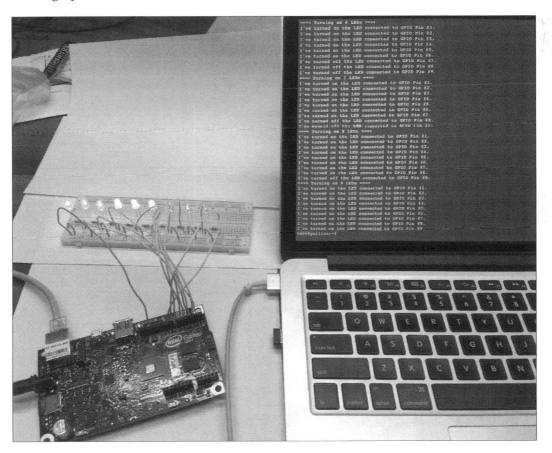

Taking advantage of object-oriented code to control digital outputs

The previous example just turns on the LEDs. Thus, in case we want to count in a reverse order, that is, from 9 to 1, the results are not going to be as expected. After the code turns on 9 LEDs, the code will turn on 8 LEDs but there are still going to be 9 LEDs turned. The problem is that we never turn off the LEDs that we don't need to be turned on, and therefore the 9 LEDs will stay on until the edited loop finishes its execution.

We are always talking about LEDs turning on and turning off LEDs. However, we have been using just instanced of the `mraa.Gpio` class and called the `write` method. Python is an object-oriented programming language, and therefore, we can definitely take advantage of its object-oriented features to write reusable, easier to understand and simpler to maintain code. For example, in this case, it makes a lot of sense to create an `Led` class to represent an LED connected to our board.

The following lines show the code for the new `Led` class. The code file for the sample is `iot_python_chapter_03_03.py`.

```
import mraa
import time


class Led:
    def __init__(self, pin):
        self.gpio = mraa.Gpio(pin)
        self.gpio.dir(mraa.DIR_OUT)

    def turn_on(self):
        self.gpio.write(1)
        print("I've turned on the LED connected to GPIO Pin
#{0}.".format(self.gpio.getPin()))

    def turn_off(self):
        self.gpio.write(0)
        print("I've turned off the LED connected to GPIO Pin
#{0}.".format(self.gpio.getPin()))
```

We have to specify the pin number to which the LED is connected when we create an instance of the `Led` class in the `pin` required argument. The constructor, that is, the `__init__` method, creates a new `mraa.Gpio` instance with the received `pin` as its `pin` argument, saves its reference in the `gpio` attribute and calls its `dir` method to configure the pin to be an output pin.

The class defines the following two methods:

- `turn_on`: Calls the `write` method for the related `mraa.Gpio` instance to send a high value (1) to the pin and turn on the LED connected to this pin. Then, it prints a message with details about the performed action.
- `turn_off`: Calls the `write` method for the related `mraa.Gpio` instance to send a low value (0) to the pin and turn off the LED connected to this pin. Then, it prints a message with details about the performed action.

Now, we can write code that uses the new `Led` class to create the necessary instances based on the number of LEDs we want to control and the pins to which they are connected. The following lines show an improved version of the code that uses the new `Led` class to count from 1 to 9 with the LEDs. The code file for the sample is `iot_python_chapter_03_03.py`.

```python
if __name__ == "__main__":
    print ("Mraa library version: {0}".format(mraa.getVersion()))
    print ("Mraa detected platform name: {0}".format(mraa.
getPlatformName()))

    # Configure GPIO pins #1 to 9 to be output pins
    leds = []
    for i in range(1, 10):
        led = Led(i)
        leds.append(led)

    # Count from 1 to 9
    for i in range(1, 10):
        print("==== Turning on {0} LEDs ====".format(i))
        for j in range(0, i):
            leds[j].turn_on()
        for k in range(i, 9):
            leds[k].turn_off()
        time.sleep(3)
```

First, the code declares an empty list named `leds`. Then, a `for` loop creates nine instances of the `Led` class and each of them represent an LED connected to a GPIO pin on the board. We pass `i` as an argument for the `pin` parameter. Then, we call the `append` method for the `leds` list to add the `Led` instance (`led`) to the `leds` list. Our `for` loop will start with `i` equal to 1 and its last iteration will be with `i` equal to 9.

Another `for` loop determines the number of LEDs to be turned on. We use `range(1, 10)` to generate the same list than in the previous loop. The first line within the `for` loop calls a `print` method to display the number of LEDs that we are going to be turned on in the iteration.

An inner loop within the loop uses `range(0, i)` to generate the list of indexes of the elements in the `leds` list that we have to turn on for the iteration of the main `for` loop (i). The inner loop uses `j` as its variable and the code within this inner loop just calls the `turn_on` method for each `Led` instance.

Another inner loop wihin the loop uses `range(i, 9)` to generate the list of indexes of the elements in the `leds` list that we have to turn off for the iteration of the main `for` loop (i). The inner loop uses `k` as its variable and the code within this inner loop just calls the `turn_off` method for each `Led` instance.

 The code is easier to understand than the previous version and the `Led` class handles everything related to an LED. We can easily understand that the line that calls the `turn_on` method for `leds[j]` is turning on an LED. We definitely know that an LED is being turned off in the line that calls the `turn_off` method for `leds[k]`.

As the new code turns off the LEDs that don't have be turned on, we can easily create a new version that counts from 9 to 1 by changing one line. The following lines show the new version of the code that works with the `Led` class to count from 9 to 1 with the LEDs. The only line that had to be edited is the highlighted one. The code file for the sample is `iot_python_chapter_03_04.py`.

```python
if __name__ == "__main__":
    print ("Mraa library version: {0}".format(mraa.getVersion()))
    print ("Mraa detected platform name: {0}".format(mraa.
getPlatformName()))

    # Configure GPIO pins #1 to 9 to be output pins
    leds = []
    for i in range(1, 10):
        led = Led(i)
        leds.append(led)

    # Count from 9 to 1
    for i in range(9, 0, -1):
        print("==== Turning on {0} LEDs ====".format(i))
        for j in range(0, i):
            leds[j].turn_on()
        for k in range(i, 9):
            leds[k].turn_off()
        time.sleep(3)
```

Improving our object-oriented code to provide new features

Now that we have our counter working with the LEDs connected to the board, we want to add new features. We want to be able to easily transform a number between 1 and 9 into its representation in LEDs connected to the board.

The following lines show the code for the new NumberInLeds class. The code file for the sample is iot_python_chapter_03_05.py.

```
class NumberInLeds:
    def __init__(self):
        self.leds = []
        for i in range(1, 10):
            led = Led(i)
            self.leds.append(led)

    def print_number(self, number):
        print("==== Turning on {0} LEDs ====".format(number))
        for j in range(0, number):
            self.leds[j].turn_on()
        for k in range(number, 9):
            self.leds[k].turn_off()
```

The constructor, that is, the __init__ method, declares an empty list attribute named leds (self.leds). Then, a for loop creates nine instances of the Led class and each of them represent an LED connected to a GPIO pin on the board. We pass i as an argument for the pin parameter. Then, we call the append method for the self.leds list to add the Led instance (led) to the self.leds list. Our for loop will start with i equal to 1 and its last iteration will be with i equal to 9.

The class defines a print_number method that requires the number that we want to represent with LEDs turned on in the number argument. The method uses a for loop with j as its variable to turn on the necessary LEDs by accesing the appropriate members of the self.leds list and calling the turn_on method. Then, the method uses another for loop with k as its variable to turn off the remaining LEDs by accesing the appropriate members of the self.leds list and calling the turn_off method. This way, the method makes sure that only the LEDs that have to be turned on are really turned on and the rest of them are turned off.

Now, we can write code that uses the new `NumberInLeds` class to count from 0 to 9 with the LEDs. In this case, we start with 0 because the new class is able to turn off all the LEDs that shouldn't be turned on to represent a specific number. The code file for the sample is `iot_python_chapter_03_05.py`.

```
if __name__ == "__main__":
    print ("Mraa library version: {0}".format(mraa.getVersion()))
    print ("Mraa detected platform name: {0}".format(mraa.
getPlatformName()))

    number_in_leds = NumberInLeds()
    # Count from 0 to 9
    for i in range(0, 10):
        number_in_leds.print_number(i)
        time.sleep(3)
```

The code is very easy to understand, we just create an instance of the `NumberInLeds` class, named `number_in_leds`, and then we call its `print_number` method with i as its argument within the `for` loop.

We took advantage of Python's object-oriented features to create classes that represent the LEDs and the generation of numbers with LEDs. This way, we wrote higher level code that is easier to understand because we don't just read code that writes 0s and 1s to specific pin numbers, we can read code that prints numbers in LEDs, turns on and turns off LEDs.

Isolating the pin numbers to improve wirings

Obviously, it is easy to turn on the LED that represents number 1 when it is connected to GPIO pin number 1. In our previous wiring, the LED that represented each number was connected to the same GPIO pin number. The schema was also very easy to understand with the connections where the LED number matched the pin number.

However, the wirings between the board and the breadboard were a bit complicated because the GPIO pins in the board go from 13 down to 1, from left to right. The breadboard has the LEDs in the opposite direction, that is, from 1 to 9, left to right. Thus, the wire that connect the GPIO pin number 1 with LED number 1 has to go from right to left and crosses the other jumper wires. We will change the jumper wires to improve our wiring and then we will make the necessary changes to our object-oriented Python code to isolate the pin numbers and make it possible to have a nicer wiring. Don't forget to shutdown the operating system and unplug the power supply from the board before you make changes to the wirings.

The following diagram shows the components connected to the breadboard and the new wirings from the Intel Galileo Gen 2 board to the breadboard. The Fritzing file for the sample is `iot_fritzing_chapter_03_06.fzz` and the following picture is the breadboard view.

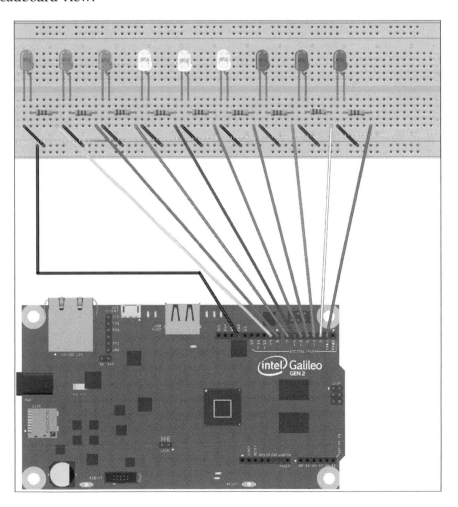

Now, whenever we want to turn on LED 1, we must write a high (1) value to GPIO pin number 9, whenever we want to turn on LED 2, we write a high (1) value to GPIO pin number 8, and so on. Because we changed the wirings, the schematic with the electronic components represented as symbols also changed. The following picture shows the new version of the schematic.

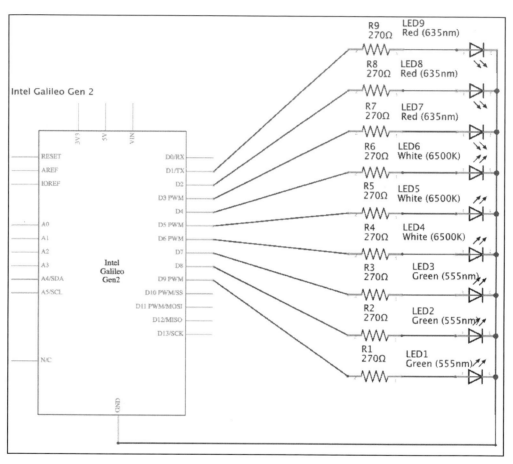

The following lines show the new code for the Led class. The code file for the sample is iot_python_chapter_03_06.py.

```python
import mraa
import time


class Led:
    def __init__(self, pin, position):
        self.position = position
```

```
        self.gpio = mraa.Gpio(pin)
        self.gpio.dir(mraa.DIR_OUT)


    def turn_on(self):
        self.gpio.write(1)
        print("I've turned on the LED connected to GPIO Pin #{0}, in
position {1}.".format(self.gpio.getPin(), self.position))



    def turn_off(self):
        self.gpio.write(0)
        print("I've turned off the LED connected to GPIO Pin #{0}, in
position {1}.".format(self.gpio.getPin(), self.position))
```

Now, we have to specify an additional parameter when we create an instance of the Led class: the position in the breadboard, that is the LED number in the breadboard. The constructor, that is, the __init__ method, saves the position value in an attribute with the same name. Both the turn_on and turn_off methods use the self.position attribute value to print a message indicating the position of the LED that has been turned on or off. As the position doesn't match the pin anymore, the message had to be improved to specify the position.

The following lines show the code for the new version of the NumberInLeds class. The code file for the sample is iot_python_chapter_03_06.py.

```
class NumberInLeds:
    def __init__(self):
        self.leds = []
        for i in range(9, 0, -1):
            led = Led(i, 10 - i)
            self.leds.append(led)

    def print_number(self, number):
        print("==== Turning on {0} LEDs ====".format(number))
        for j in range(0, number):
            self.leds[j].turn_on()
        for k in range(number, 9):
            self.leds[k].turn_off()
```

It was necessary to make changes to the highlighted lines in the constructor, that is, the __init__ method. The for loop that creates the nine instances of the Led class now starts with i equal to 9 and its last itearation will be with i equal to 1. We pass i as an argument for the pin parameter and 10 - i as an argument for the position parameter. This way, the first Led instance in the self.leds list will be the one with pin equal to 9 and position equal to 1.

The code that uses the new version of the `NumberInLeds` class to count from 0 to 9 with the LEDs is the same than the previous code. The code file for the sample is `iot_python_chapter_03_06.py`.

```python
if __name__ == "__main__":
    print ("Mraa library version: {0}".format(mraa.getVersion()))
    print ("Mraa detected platform name: {0}".format(mraa.
getPlatformName()))

    number_in_leds = NumberInLeds()
    # Count from 0 to 9
    for i in range(0, 10):
        number_in_leds.print_number(i)
        time.sleep(3)
```

We just needed to make a few changes in the class that encapsulates a LED (`Led`) and in the class that encapsulates a number represented with LEDs (`NumberInLeds`). The following picture shows the 9 LEDs turned on in the breadboard with the new wirings connected between the breadboard and the board that is running the new Python code running.

We can easily build an API and provide a REST API to allow any client that has connection to the board to be able to print numbers through HTTP. Our REST API just needs to create an instance of the `NumberInLeds` class and call the `print_number` method with the specified number to be printed with LEDs. We will build this REST API in the next chapter.

Controlling digital outputs with the wiring-x86 library

One of the great advantages of working with Python as our programming language to interact with the board is that we have plenty of packages available for Python. We have been using the `mraa` library to interact with the digital outputs. However, in the previous chapter, we also installed the `wiring-x86` library. We can change just a few lines of our object-oriented code to replace the `mraa` library with the `wiring-x86` one to turn on and off the LEDs.

The following lines shows the code for a `Board` class followed by the new version of the `Led` class that works with the `wiring-x86` library instead of using `mraa`. The code file for the sample is iot_python_chapter_03_07.py.

```python
from wiringx86 import GPIOGalileoGen2 as GPIO
import time


class Board:
    gpio = GPIO(debug=False)


class Led:
    def __init__(self, pin, position):
        self.pin = pin
        self.position = position
        self.gpio = Board.gpio
        self.gpio.pinMode(pin, self.gpio.OUTPUT)

    def turn_on(self):
        self.gpio.digitalWrite(self.pin, self.gpio.HIGH)
        print("I've turned on the LED connected to GPIO Pin #{0}, in
position {1}.".format(self.pin, self.position))

    def turn_off(self):
        self.gpio.digitalWrite(self.pin, self.gpio.LOW)
        print("I've turned off the LED connected to GPIO Pin #{0}, in
position {1}.".format(self.pin, self.position))
```

The `wiring-x86` library doesn't include automatic detection of the board, and therefore, it is necessary to use the class that represents our board. The GPIOGalileoGen2 represents the Intel Galileo Gen 2 board, and therefore, the first line of code uses an `import` statement to import it as `GPIO` from `wiringx86`. This way, whenever we reference `GPIO`, we will be really using `wiringx86`. `GPIOGalileoGen2`. Notice that the library name is `wiring-x86` but the module name is `wiringx86`.

When we create an instance of the `Led` class, we have to specify the GPIO digital `pin` to which the LED is connected and the `position` in the breadboard, that is the LED number in the breadboard. The constructor, that is, the `__init__` method, saves a reference to the `Board.gpio` class attribute in `self.gpio` and calls its `pinMode` method with the received pin as its `pin` argument and `self.gpio.OUTPUT` as its `mode` argument. This way, we configure the pin to be an output pin. All the `Led` instances will save a reference to the same `Board.gpio` class attribute that created an instance of the `GPIO` class, specifically, the `wiringx86.GPIOGalileoGen2` class with its `debug` argument set to `False` to avoid unnecessary debug information for the low-level communications.

The `turn_on` method calls the `digitalWrite` method for the GPIO instance to send a high value (`self.GPIO.HIGH`) to the pin specified by the `self.pin` attribute value and prints a message about the performed action.

The `turn_off` method calls the `digitalWrite` method for the GPIO instance to send a low value (`self.GPIO.LOW`) to the pin specified by the `self.pin` attribute value and prints a message about the performed action.

The code for the `NumberInLeds` class remains the same one that we have used for the previous example. There is no need to make changes to this class because it will automatically work with the new `Led` class and there were no changes in the arguments for its constructor or its two methods. We just need to replace the lines that printed information about the `mraa` library in the `__main__` method because we aren't using the `mraa` library anymore.

The following lines shows the code for the `NumberInLeds` class and the `__main__` method. The code file for the sample is `iot_python_chapter_03_07.py`.

```
class NumberInLeds:
    def __init__(self):
        self.leds = []
        for i in range(9, 0, -1):
            led = Led(i, 10 - i)
            self.leds.append(led)
```

```
def print_number(self, number):
    print("==== Turning on {0} LEDs ====".format(number))
    for j in range(0, number):
        self.leds[j].turn_on()
    for k in range(number, 9):
        self.leds[k].turn_off()


if __name__ == "__main__":
    print ("Working with wiring-x86 on Intel Galileo Gen 2")

    number_in_leds = NumberInLeds()
    # Count from 0 to 9
    for i in range(0, 10):
        number_in_leds.print_number(i)
        time.sleep(3)
```

We just needed to change a few lines of code and we can see how the Python code makes LEDs in the breadboard count from 0 to 9 using the `wiring-x86` library. The way in which we work with the GPIO pins for digital output with this library is a bit different from the mechanism used in the `mraa` library. However, we could easily encapsulate the changes by taking advantage of Python's object-oriented features. We can decide which library is more convenient for our projects based on our preferences and needs. It is always a nice idea to have more than just one option.

Test your knowledge

1. When we send a high value (1) to a GPIO pin configured as output, the GPIO pin will have:

    1. 0 V.

    2. 6 V.

    3. The voltage specified in the position in which the IOREF jumper is located.

2. An instance of the `mraa.Gpio` class represents:

    1. A single GPIO pin in the board.

    2. All the I/O pins in the board.

    3. Two GPIO pins in the board.

3. When we create an instance of the `mraa.Gpio` class, we must specify:

    1. The pin number as an argument.

    2. The specific board and a pin number as arguments.

    3. The pin number and the desired direction: `mraa.DIR_OUT` or `mraa.DIR_IN`.

4. Which of the following lines write a high value to the GPIO pin configured as output with the instance of `mraa.Gpio` named `gpio10`:

    1. `gpio10.write(0)`

    2. `gpio10.write(1)`

    3. `gpio10.write(mraa.HIGH_VALUE)`

5. Which of the following lines configure the instance of `mraa.Gpio` named `gpio10` for digital output:

    1. `gpio10.dir(mraa.DIR_DIGITAL).out()`

    2. `gpio10.dir(mraa.DIR_OUT)`

    3. `gpio10.dir(mraa.DIR_OUT, mraa.DIGITAL)`

Summary

In this chapter, we worked with Python with two different libraries: `mraa` and `wiring-x86`. We connected LEDs and resistors to a breadboard and we wrote code to turn on from 0 to 9 LEDs. We improved our Python code to take advantage of Python's object-oriented features and we prepared the code to make it easy to build an API that will allow us to print numbers with LEDs with a REST API.

Now that we finished our first wirings and we started controlling the board with Python, we can start working with additional outputs and combine them with a REST API, which is the topic of the next chapter.

4
Working with a RESTful API and Pulse Width Modulation

In this chapter, we will interact with the board with HTTP requests and we will use pulse width modulation to generate different output voltages. We shall:

- Work with the Tornado web server to build a RESTful API in Python
- Compose and send HTTP requests to print numbers in LEDs
- Work with pulse width modulation to control the output voltage in pins
- Fade in and fade out LEDs connected to the board
- Use different tools to compose and send HTTP requests that interact with the board
- Build a RESTful API to mix red, green and blue and generate millions of colors with an RGB LED
- Use the `mraa` and `wiring-x86` libraries to control pulse width modulation

Printing numbers in LEDs with a RESTful API

Tornado is a Python web framework and asynchronous networking library. It is well known for providing great scalability due to its non-blocking network I/O. We will take advantage of the fact that Tornado makes it really easy to build a RESTful API and make it possible for any client to consume this API and print numbers in LEDs connected to the board. The following is the web page for the Tornado web server: http://www.tornadoweb.org.

In *Chapter 1, Understanding and Setting up the Base IoT Hardware,* we installed the `pip` installer to easily install additional Python 2.7.3 packages in the Yocto Linux that we are running on the board. Now, we will use a `pip` installer to install Tornado 4.3. We just need to run the following command in the SSH terminal to install the package.

```
pip install tornado
```

The last lines for the output will indicate that the `tornado` package has been successfully installed. Don't worry about the error messages related to building wheel and the insecure platform warning.

```
Collecting tornado
/usr/lib/python2.7/site-packages/pip/_vendor/requests/packages/
urllib3/util/ssl_.py:90: InsecurePlatformWarning: A true SSLContext
object is not available. This prevents urllib3 from configuring SSL
appropriately and may cause certain SSL connections to fail. For more
information, see https://urllib3.readthedocs.org/en/latest/security.
html#insecureplatformwarning.
  InsecurePlatformWarning
  Downloading tornado-4.3.tar.gz (450kB)
    100% |################################| 454kB 25kB/s
Collecting backports.ssl-match-hostname (from tornado)
  Downloading backports.ssl_match_hostname-3.5.0.1.tar.gz
Collecting singledispatch (from tornado)
  Downloading singledispatch-3.4.0.3-py2.py3-none-any.whl
Collecting certifi (from tornado)
  Downloading certifi-2015.11.20.1-py2.py3-none-any.whl (368kB)
    100% |################################| 372kB 31kB/s
Collecting backports-abc>=0.4 (from tornado)
  Downloading backports_abc-0.4-py2.py3-none-any.whl
Collecting six (from singledispatch->tornado)
  Downloading six-1.10.0-py2.py3-none-any.whl
...
Installing collected packages: backports.ssl-match-hostname, six,
singledispatch, certifi, backports-abc, tornado
  Running setup.py install for backports.ssl-match-hostname
  Running setup.py install for tornado
Successfully installed backports-abc-0.4 backports.ssl-match-
hostname-3.5.0.1 certifi-2015.11.20.1 singledispatch-3.4.0.3 six-
1.10.0 tornado-4.3
```

Now, we will install HTTPie, a command-line HTTP client written in Python that makes it easy to send HTTP requests and uses a syntax that is easier than curl (also known as cURL). HTTPie displays colorized output and will make it easy for us to send HTTP requests to test our RESTful API. We just need to run the following command in the SSH terminal to install the package.

```
pip install --upgrade httpie
```

The last lines for the output will indicate that the `httpie` package has been successfully installed. Don't worry about the insecure platform warning.

```
Collecting httpie
/usr/lib/python2.7/site-packages/pip/_vendor/requests/packages/
urllib3/util/ssl_.py:90: InsecurePlatformWarning: A true SSLContext
object is not available. This prevents urllib3 from configuring SSL
appropriately and may cause certain SSL connections to fail. For more
information, see https://urllib3.readthedocs.org/en/latest/security.
html#insecureplatformwarning.
  InsecurePlatformWarning
  Downloading httpie-0.9.3-py2.py3-none-any.whl (66kB)
    100% |############################| 69kB 117kB/s
Collecting Pygments>=1.5 (from httpie)
  Downloading Pygments-2.0.2-py2-none-any.whl (672kB)
    100% |############################| 675kB 17kB/s
Collecting requests>=2.3.0 (from httpie)
  Downloading requests-2.9.1-py2.py3-none-any.whl (501kB)
    100% |############################| 503kB 23kB/s
Installing collected packages: Pygments, requests, httpie
Successfully installed Pygments-2.0.2 httpie-0.9.3 requests-2.9.1
```

Now, we can use an `http` command to easily send HTTP requests to `localhost` and test the RESTful API built with Tornado. Obviously, after we test that the RESTful API is working OK locally, we want to send HTTP requests from a computer or device connected to our LAN. You can install HTTPie in your computer or use any other application that allows you to compose and send HTTP requests, such as the previously mentioned curl utility (`http://curl.haxx.se`) or Telerik Fiddler (`http://www.telerik.com/fiddler`) in case you are working on Windows. Telerik Fiddler is a free web debugging proxy with a GUI but it only runs on Windows. You can even use apps that can compose and send HTTP requests from mobile devices and test the RESTful API by using them.

If you are working on either OS X or Linux, you can open a Terminal and start using curl from the command line. If you are working on Windows, you can easily install curl from the Cygwin package installation option, and execute it from the Cygwin terminal.

In order to build a RESTful API with Tornado, first we have to create subclasses of the `tornado.web.RequestHandler` class and override the necessary methods to handle the HTTP requests to the URL. For example, if we want to handle an HTTP GET request with a synchronous operation, we must create a new subclass of the `tornado.web.RequestHandler` class and define the `get` method with the required arguments, if any. If we want to handle an HTTP PUT request, we just need to define the `put` method with the required arguments. Then, we have to map the URL pattern in an instance of the `tornado.web.Application` class.

The following lines show the new classes that we must add to our existing code with either the `mraa` or the `wiring-x86` libraries that made it possible to print numbers in LEDs in the previous chapter. We already had the Led and NumberInLeds classes and the code adds the following classes: BoardInteraction, VersionHandler, PutNumberInLedsHandler, GetCurrentNumberHandler. The code file for the sample is iot_python_chapter_04_01.py.

```python
import mraa
from datetime import date
import tornado.escape
import tornado.ioloop
import tornado.web


class BoardInteraction:
    number_in_leds = NumberInLeds()
    current_number = 0



class VersionHandler(tornado.web.RequestHandler):
    def get(self):
        response = {'version': '1.0',
                    'last_build': date.today().isoformat()}
        self.write(response)


class PutNumberInLedsHandler(tornado.web.RequestHandler):
    def put(self, number):
        int_number = int(number)
```

```
        BoardInteraction.number_in_leds.print_number(int_number)
        BoardInteraction.current_number = int_number
        response = {'number': int_number}
        self.write(response)


class GetCurrentNumberHandler(tornado.web.RequestHandler):
    def get(self):
        response = {'number': BoardInteraction.current_number}
        self.write(response)
```

The `BoardInteraction` class declares two class attributes: `number_in_leds`
and `current_number`. The other classes define methods that work with these
class attributes, to access a common `NumberInLeds` instance, saved in `number_in_leds`, and the current number that is being displayed with LEDs, saved in
`current_number`.

The code declares the following three subclasses of `tornado.web.RequestHandler`:

- `VersionHandler`: Defines the parameter less `get` method that returns a
  response with the version number and the last build date.

- `PutNumberInLedsHandler`: Defines the `put` method that requires a number
  argument that specifies the number that has to be printed with LEDs. The
  method calls the `print_number` method for the `NumberInLeds` instance
  stored in the `BoardInteraction.number_in_leds` class attribute with the
  desired number of LEDs to be turned on specified in the `number` attribute.
  Then, the code saves the number that is being printed with LEDs in the
  `BoardInteraction.current_number` class attribute and returns a response
  with the printed number.

- `GetCurrentNumberHandler`: Defines the parameter less `get` method that
  returns a response with the value of the `BoardInteraction.current_number` class attribute, that is, the number that is being printed with LEDs.

The following lines use the previously declared subclasses of `tornado.web.RequestHandler` to make up the web application with Tornado that represents
the RESTful API and the new `__main__` method. The code file for the sample is
`iot_python_chapter_04_01.py`.

```
application = tornado.web.Application([
    (r"/putnumberinleds/([0-9])", PutNumberInLedsHandler),
    (r"/getcurrentnumber", GetCurrentNumberHandler),
    (r"/version", VersionHandler)])
```

```
if __name__ == "__main__":
        print("Listening at port 8888")
    BoardInteraction.number_in_leds.print_number(0)
    application.listen(8888)
    tornado.ioloop.IOLoop.instance().start()
```

First, the code creates an instance of the `tornado.web.Application` class named `application` with the list of request handlers that make up the web application. The code passes a list of tuples to the `Application` constructor. The list is composed of a regular expression (`regexp`) and a subclass of `tornado.web.RequestHandler` (`request_class`).

The `__main__` method prints a message indicating the port number in which the HTTP server is listening and uses the `NumberInLeds` instance saved in `BoardInteraction.number_in_leds` to print number 0, that is, to turn off the nine LEDs. The next line calls the `application.listen` method to build an HTTP server for the application with the defined rules on the specified port. The code passes `8888` for the `port` argument, that is, the default port value for the Tornado HTTP server.

Then, the call to `tornado.ioloop.IOLoop.instance().start()` starts the server created with `application.listen`. This way, whenever the web application receives a request, Tornado iterates over the list of request handlers that make up the web application and creates an instance of the first `tornado.web.RequestHandler` subclass whose associated regular expression matches the request path. Then, Tornado calls one of the following methods the corresponding parameters for the new instance based on the HTTP request:

- head
- get
- post
- delete
- patch
- put
- options

The following table shows some HTTP requests that match the regular expressions defined in the preceding code. In this case, the HTTP requests use localhost because they are executed locally on the Yocto Linux running on the board. If we replace localhost with the board's assigned IP address, we can make the HTTP requests from any computer or device connected to our LAN.

HTTP verb and request URL	Tuple (regexp, request_class) that matches the request path	RequestHandler **subclass and method that is called**
GET http://localhost:8888/version	(r"/version", VersionHandler)])	VersionHandler.get()
PUT http://localhost:8888/ putnumberinleds/5	(r"/putnumberinleds/ ([0-9])", PutNumberInLedsHandler)	PutNumberInLedsHandler.put(5)
PUT http://localhost:8888/ putnumberinleds/8	(r"/putnumberinleds/ ([0-9])", PutNumberInLedsHandler)	PutNumberInLedsHandler.put(8)
GET http://localhost:8888/ getcurrentnumber	(r"/getcurrentnumber", GetCurrentNumberHandler)	GetCurrentNumberHandler.get()

The RequestHandler class declares a SUPPORTED_METHODS class attribute with the following code. In this case, we haven't overridden the class attribute, and therefore, we inherit superclass declaration:

```
SUPPORTED_METHODS = ("GET", "HEAD", "POST", "DELETE", "PATCH", "PUT",
"OPTIONS")
```

The default code declared in the superclass for the get, head, post, delete, patch, put, and options methods is a single line that raises an HTTPError. For example, the following line shows the code for the get method defined in the RequestHandler class.

```
def get(self, *args, **kwargs):
    raise HTTPError(405)
```

Whenever the web application receives a request and matches the URL pattern, Tornado performs the following actions:

1. Create a new instance of the RequestHandler subclass that has been mapped to the URL pattern.

2. Call the initialize method with the keyword arguments specified in the application configuration. We can override the initialize method to save the arguments into member variables.

3. No matter which is the HTTP request, call the prepare method. If we call either finish or send_error, Tornado won't call any additional methods. We can override the prepare method to execute code that is necessary for any HTTP request and then write the specific code in the get, head, post, delete, patch, put or options methods.

4. Call the method according to the HTTP request with the arguments based on the URL regular expression that captured the different groups. As previously explained, we must override the methods we want our `RequestHandler` subclass to be able to process. For example, if there was an HTTP GET request, Tornado will call the `get` method with the different arguments.

5. In this case, we are working with synchronous handlers, and therefore, Tornado calls `on_finish` after the previous method called according to the HTTP request returned. We can override the `on_finish` method to perform cleanup or logging. It is very important to understand that Tornado calls `on_finish` after it sent the response to the client.

The following line will start the HTTP server and our RESTful API in the Yocto Linux running on the board. Don't forget that you need to transfer the Python source code file to the Yocto Linux with an SFTP client, as explained in the previous chapter.

```
python iot_python_chapter_04_01.py
```

After we start the HTTP server, we will see the following output and all the LEDs on the board are going to be turned off.

```
Listening at port 8888
==== Turning on 0 LEDs ====
I've turned off the LED connected to GPIO Pin #9, in position 1.
I've turned off the LED connected to GPIO Pin #8, in position 2.
I've turned off the LED connected to GPIO Pin #7, in position 3.
I've turned off the LED connected to GPIO Pin #6, in position 4.
I've turned off the LED connected to GPIO Pin #5, in position 5.
I've turned off the LED connected to GPIO Pin #4, in position 6.
I've turned off the LED connected to GPIO Pin #3, in position 7.
I've turned off the LED connected to GPIO Pin #2, in position 8.
I've turned off the LED connected to GPIO Pin #1, in position 9.
```

Composing and sending HTTP requests

The HTTP server is running in Yocto Linux and waiting for our HTTP requests to control the LEDs on connected to the Intel Galileo Gen 2 board. Now, we will compose and send HTTP requests locally in Yocto Linux and then from other computer or devices connected to our LAN.

HTTPie supports curl-like shorthands for localhost. For example, `:8888` is a shorthand that expands to `http://localhost:8888`. We already have an SSH terminal running the HTTP server, and therefore, we can run the following command in another SSH terminal.

```
http GET :8888/version
```

The previous command will compose and send the following HTTP request:
GET http://localhost:8888/version. The request is the simplest case in our
RESTful API because it will match and run the VersionHandler.get method that
just receives self as a parameter because the URL pattern doesn't include any
parameters. The method creates a response dictionary and then calls the self.write
method with response as a parameter. The self.write method writes the received
chunk to the output buffer. Because the chunk (response) is a dictionary, self.
write writes it as JSON and sets the Content-Type of the response to application/
json. The following lines show an example response for the HTTP request, including
the response headers:

```
HTTP/1.1 200 OK
Content-Length: 46
Content-Type: application/json; charset=UTF-8
Date: Thu, 28 Jan 2016 03:15:21 GMT
Etag: "fb066668a345b0637fdc112ac0ddc37c318d8709"
Server: TornadoServer/4.3

{
    "last_build": "2016-01-28",
    "version": "1.0"
}
```

We can execute HTTPie with the -b option in case we don't want to include the
header in the response. For example, the following line performs the same HTTP
request but doesn't display the header in the response output.

```
http -b GET :8888/version
```

Once we know that our request is running OK, we can open a new terminal,
command-line or the GUI tool that we want to use to compose and send HTTP
requests from a computer or any device connected to the LAN. We just need to
use the IP address assigned to the board instead of localhost in our request
URLs. Don't forget to replace 192.168.1.107 with your board's IP address in
the next requests.

Now, we can run the following HTTPie command in a computer or device to use the
RESTful API to make the board turn on the five LEDs. After you enter the command,
you will notice the SSH terminal that displays the output for the Python code will
display a message indicating that it is turning on 5 LEDs and the additional messages
indicating the LEDs that are being turned on and off. In addition, you will see 5
LEDs turned on.

```
http -b PUT 192.168.1.107:8888/putnumberinleds/5
```

The previous command will compose and send the following HTTP request: PUT
http://192.168.1.107:8888/putnumberinleds/5. The request will match and run
the PutNumberInLedsHandler.put method that receives 5 in its number parameter.
The following lines show the response from the HTTP server with the number that
has been printed in LEDs, that is, the number of LEDs that have been turned on:

```
{
    "number": 5
}
```

The following image shows two Terminal windows side-by-side on OS X. The
Terminal window at the left-hand side is running on a computer that is generating
the HTTP requests and the Terminal window at the right-hand side is the SSH
terminal that is running the Tornado HTTP server in Yocto Linux and displays the
output for our Python code. It is a good idea to use a similar configuration to check
the output while we compose and send the HTTP requests.

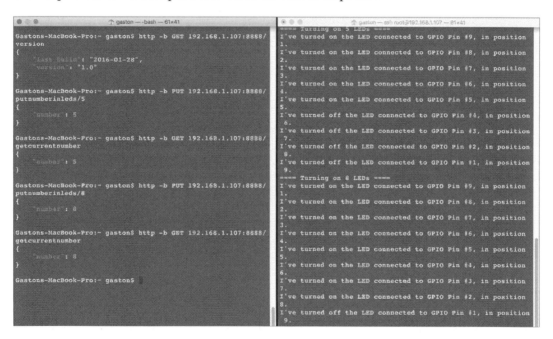

In Fiddler, click **Composer** or press *F9*, select **PUT** in the dropdown menu in the
Parsed tab, and enter 192.168.1.107:8888/putnumberinleds/5 in the textbox
at the right-hand side of the dropdown (don't forget to replace the IP with your
board's IP). Then, click **Execute** and double-click on the 200 result that appears on the
capture log. If you want to see the raw response, just click on the **Raw** button below
the **Request Headers** panel.

The following image shows a Fiddler window side-by-side with a Putty terminal window on Windows. The Fiddler window at the left-hand side is running on a computer that is generating the HTTP requests and the Putty terminal window at the right-hand side is the SSH terminal that is running the Tornado HTTP server in Yocto Linux and displays the output for our Python code.

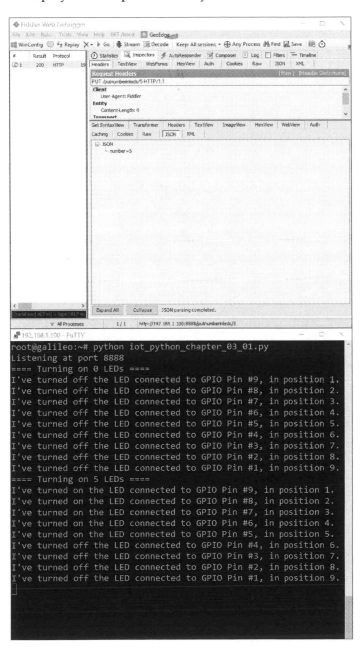

We can run the following HTTPie command in a computer or device to use the RESTful API to tell us how many LEDs are turned on.

```
http -b GET 192.168.1.107:8888/getcurrentnumber
```

The previous command will compose and send the following HTTP request: `GET` `http://192.168.1.107:8888/getcurrentnumber`. The request will match and run the `GetCurrentNumber.get` method. The following lines show the response from the HTTP server with the number that has been printed in LEDs, that is, the number of LEDs that have been turned on with the last API call:

```
{
    "number": 5
}
```

If we take a look again at the list of request handlers that make up the web application, we will notice that the entry for `putnumberinleds` specifies a regular expression that accepts numbers from 0 to 9 as its parameters:

```
(r"/putnumberinleds/([0-9])", PutNumberInLedsHandler)
```

If we run the following HTTPie command in a computer or device to use the RESTful API to make the board turn on twelve LEDs, the request won't match any regular expression in the list of request handlers.

```
http -b PUT 192.168.1.107:8888/putnumberinleds/12
```

Thus, Tornado will return a `404: Not found` error as a result.

```
<html><title>404: Not Found</title><body>404: Not Found</body></html>
```

The same will happen if we run the following HTTPie command in a computer or device because x isn't a number between 0 and 9.

```
http -b PUT 192.168.1.107:8888/putnumberinleds/x
```

The following HTTPie command will turn on 8 LEDs.

```
http -b PUT 192.168.1.107:8888/putnumberinleds/8
```

The previous command will compose and send the following HTTP request: PUT http://192.168.1.107:8888/putnumberinleds/8. The request will match and run the PutNumberInLedsHandler.put method that receives 8 in its number parameter. The following lines show the response from the HTTP server with the number that has been printed in LEDs, that is, the number of LEDs that have been turned on:

```
{
    "number": 8
}
```

The number of LEDs that are turned on changed from 5 to 8, and therefore, we can run the following HTTPie command in a computer or device to use the RESTful API to tell us how many LEDs are turned on.

```
http -b GET 192.168.1.107:8888/getcurrentnumber
```

The following lines show the response from the HTTP server with the number that has been printed in LEDs:

```
{
    "number": 8
}
```

We created a very simple RESTful API that allows us to turn on LEDs and check which is the number that is currently printed in LEDs. Of course, we should add authentication and overall security to the RESTful API in order to make it complete. Our RESTful API makes it possible for us to print numbers in LEDs with any application, mobile app or web application that can compose and send HTTP requests.

Wiring pins with PWM capabilities

We want to control the output voltage to make it possible to fade in and fade out three LEDs of three different colors: red, green and blue. The lower the output voltage, the lower the brightness level for the LEDs. The higher the output voltage, the higher the brightness level for the LEDs. Thus, as the output voltage is nearer to 0V, the brightness for the LEDs is lower and when the output voltage is nearer the IOREF voltage, that is, 5V in our actual configuration, the brightness is higher for the LEDs. Specifically, we want to be able to set 256 brightness levels for each LED, from 0 to 255. In this case, we will use three LEDs but we will move to a single RGB LED capable of mixing the three colors in a single electronic component later in this chapter.

When we worked with GPIO pins configured as digital outputs, we could set an output voltage of 0V (low value) or the IOREF voltage, that is, 5V in our actual configuration (high value). Thus, we could just turn off or turn on the LED with its maximum brightness level (without burning it).

If we connect our red, green and blue LEDs to three GPIO pins and we configure them as digital outputs, we won't be able to set 256 brightness levels. We have to connect the three LEDs to three of the digital I/O pins that we can use as **PWM** (short for **Pulse Width Modulation**) output pins. In *Chapter 1, Understanding and Setting up the Base IoT Hardware*, when we learned about the I/O pins included in the Intel Galileo Gen 2 board, we learned that the pins labeled with a tilde symbol (~) as a prefix for the number can be used as PWM output pins. Thus, we can use the following pins to connect the three LEDs:

- Pin ~**6** to connect the red LED
- Pin ~**5** to connect the green LED
- Pin ~**3** to connect the blue LED

After we finish the necessary wirings, we will write Python code to create another RESTful API that will allow us to set the brightness for each of the three LEDs. We need the following parts to work with this example:

- One red ultrabright 5mm LED
- One green ultrabright 5mm LED
- One blue ultrabright 5mm LED
- Three 270Ω resistors with 5% tolerance (red violet brown gold)

The following diagram shows the components connected to the breadboard, the necessary wirings and the wirings from the Intel Galileo Gen 2 board to the breadboard. The Fritzing file for the sample is `iot_fritzing_chapter_04_02.fzz` and the following image is the breadboard view:

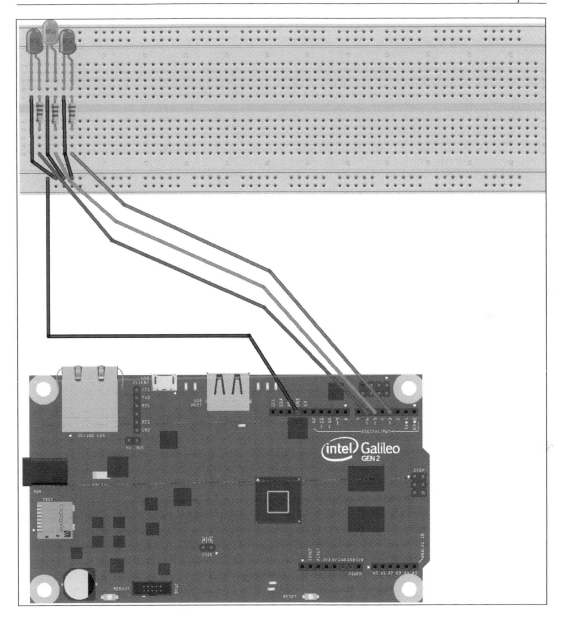

In this case, we wanted the three LEDs to be close to each other. This way, the three LEDs can project their light to a black surface and we can see how the intersection of the three colors generates a color that will be similar to a color selected in a color picker we will use later.

The following image shows the schematic with the electronic components represented as symbols.

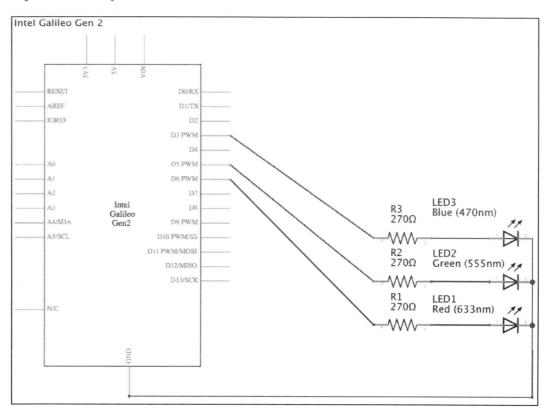

As seen in the previous schematic, three PWM capable GPIO pins labeled **D3 PWM**, **D5 PWM** and **D6 PWM** in the board's symbol is connected to a **270Ω** resistor, wired to an LED's anode, and each LED's cathode is connected to ground.

Now, it is time to insert the components in the breadboard and make all the necessary wirings. Don't forget to shutdown the Yocto Linux, wait for all the onboard LEDs to turn off, and unplug the power supply from the Intel Galileo Gen 2 board before adding or removing any wire from the board's pins.

Using PWM to generate analog values

Pulse width modulation, known as PWM, is a technique that makes it possible to generate an analog result with digital means through the usage of a digital on-off pattern. The pins that provide PWM capabilities use a digital control to create a square wave and it can simulate voltages between the configured **IOREF** voltage (5V in the default board configuration) and 0V by controlling the amount of time that the signal spends in the ON status (**IOREF** voltage) and the time the signal spends in the OFF status (0V). The pulse width is the duration of the signal in the ON status (**IOREF** voltage), and therefore, pulse width modulation means changing the pulse width to get perceived analog values.

When you repeat the signal in the ON status and the signal in the OFF status hundreds of times per second with a LED connected to the PWM pin, we can generate the same result as if the signal is a steady voltage between 0V and the **IOREF** voltage to control the LED's brightness level.

We can write floating point values from 0 to 1 to the PWM enabled pins configured as analog output, that is, from 0% duty cycle (always signal in the OFF status) to 100% duty cycle (always signal in the ON status). We want to represent 256 brightness values (from 0 to 255 inclusive), and therefore, the following graph shows the brightness values in the abscissa axis (*x*-axis) and the corresponding floating point values that have to be written to the pin in the ordinate axis (*y*-axis).

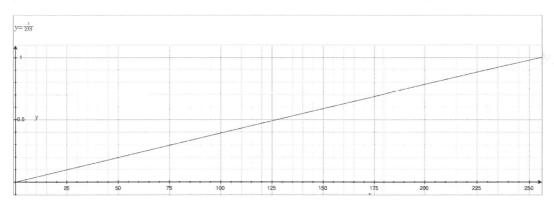

The equation for the previous graph is the following: `y = x / 255`, specifically `value = brightness / 255`. We can run the following code in our Python interpreter to see the output with all the values that will be written for each brightness level from 0 to 255 inclusive.

```
for brightness in range(0, 256):
    print(brightness / 255.0)
```

We can multiply the floating point values by 5 to calculate the voltage value for each brightness level. As we are working with the default settings for the board, the **IOREF** jumper is set to 5V, and therefore, a 1.0 value in the output means 5V (1.0 x 5 = 5). A value of 0.5 in the output means 2.5V (0.5 x 5 = 2.5). The following graph shows the brightness values in the abscissa axis (x-axis) and the corresponding voltage values in the output that will generate the corresponding brightness value in the LEDs in the ordinate axis (y-axis).

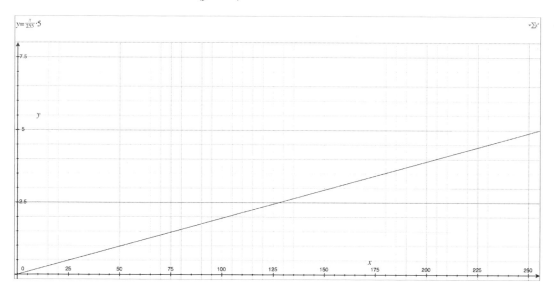

The equation for the previous graph is the following: y = x / 255 * 5, specifically voltage = brightness / 255 * 5. We can run the following code in our Python interpreter to see the output with all the voltages that will be generated for each brightness level from 0 to 255 inclusive.

```
for brightness in range(0, 256):
    print(brightness / 255.0 * 5)
```

We will create a new AnalogLed class to represent an LED connected to our board that can have a brightness level from 0 to 255 inclusive. The following lines show the code for the new AnalogLed class. The code file for the sample is iot_python_chapter_04_02.py.

```
import mraa
from datetime import date
import tornado.escape
import tornado.ioloop
```

```
import tornado.web


class AnalogLed:
    def __init__(self, pin, name):
        self.pin = pin
        self.name = name
        self.pwm = mraa.Pwm(pin)
        self.pwm.period_us(700)
        self.pwm.enable(True)
        self.brightness_value = 0
        self.set_bightness(0)


    def set_brightness(self, value):
        brightness_value = value
        if brightness_value > 255:
            brightness_value = 255
        elif brightness_value < 0:
            brightness_value = 0
        led_value = brightness_value / 255.0
        self.pwm.write(led_value)
        self.brightness_value = brightness_value
        print("{0} LED connected to PWM Pin #{1} set to brightness
{2}.".format(self.name, self.pin, brightness_value))
```

We have to specify the pin number to which the LED is connected when we create an instance of the AnalogLed class in the pin required argument, and a name for the LED in the name required argument. The constructor, that is, the __init__ method, creates a new mraa.Pwm instance with the received pin as its pin argument, saves its reference in the pwm attribute and calls its period_us method to configure the PWM period in 700 microseconds (700 μs). Thus, the output duty cycle will determine the percentage of the 700 microsecond period during which the signal is in the ON status. For example, a 0.5 (50%) output duty cycle means that the signal will be ON during 350 microseconds of the 700 microseconds period (700 * 0.5 = 350).

Then, the the code calls the pwm.enable method with True as a parameter to set the enable status of the PWM pin and allow us to start setting the output duty-cycle percentage for the PWM pin with calls to the pwm.write method.

The next line creates a brightness_value attribute initialized with 0 that will allow us to easily retrieve the last brightness value set to the LED connected to the pin. Finally, the constructor calls the set_brightness method with 0 as the value for the value argument to set the brightness level for the LED connected to the configured pin to 0.

The class defines a `set_brightness` method that receives a brightness level value in the `value` argument. The first lines of code make sure that we always set a brightness level between 0 and 255 (inclusive). In case the `value` argument has a value that isn't included in that range, the code assigns the lower-level (0) or upper-level value (255) to the `brightness_value` variable.

Then, the code calculates the necessary output duty-cycle percentage for the PWM pin to represent the brightness level as a floating point value between `1.0f` (100%) and `0.0f` (0%). The code saves the value in the `led_value` variable and then calls the `self.pwm.write` method with this variable for the percentage argument to set the output duty-cycle for the pin configured as PWM output to `led_value`. The next line saves the valid brightness level to the `brightness_value` attribute.

Finally, the code prints details about the LED name, the pin number and the brightness level that has been set. This way, the method translates a brightness level from 0 to 255 (inclusive) into the appropriate output duty-cycle value for the pin and writes the output to control the connected LED's brightness level.

Now, we can write code that uses the new `AnalogLed` class to create one instance for each of the three LEDs and easily control their brightness levels. The following lines show the code for the `BoardInteraction` class. The code file for the sample is `iot_python_chapter_04_02.py`.

```
class BoardInteraction:
    # The Red LED is connected to pin ~6
    red_led = AnalogLed(6, 'Red')
    # The Green LED is connected to Pin ~5
    green_led = AnalogLed(5, 'Green')
    # The Blue LED is connected to Pin ~3
    blue_led = AnalogLed(3, 'Blue')
```

The `BoardInteraction` class just declares three class attributes: `red_led`, `green_led` and `blue_led`. The three class attributes save new instances of the previously created `AnalogLed` class and represent the red, green and blue LEDs connected to pins ~**6**, ~**5** and ~**3**. Now, we will create other classes that define methods that work with these class attributes to access common `AnalogLed` instances.

The next lines show the code that adds the following classes: `VersionHandler`, `PutRedBrightnessHandler`, `PutGreenBrightnessHandler` and `PutBlueBrightnessHandler`. The code file for the sample is `iot_python_chapter_04_02.py`.

```
class VersionHandler(tornado.web.RequestHandler):
    def get(self):
        response = {'version': '1.0',
```

```
                        'last_build': date.today().isoformat()}
            self.write(response)


class PutRedBrightnessHandler(tornado.web.RequestHandler):
    def put(self, value):
        int_value = int(value)
        BoardInteraction.red_led.set_brightness(int_value)
        response = {'red': BoardInteraction.red_led.brightness_value}
        self.write(response)


class PutGreenBrightnessHandler(tornado.web.RequestHandler):
    def put(self, value):
        int_value = int(value)
        BoardInteraction.green_led.set_brightness(int_value)
        response = {'green': BoardInteraction.green_led.brightness_
value}
        self.write(response)


class PutBlueBrightnessHandler(tornado.web.RequestHandler):
    dcf put(self, value):
        int_value = int(value)
        BoardInteraction.blue_led.set_brightness(int_value)
        response = {'blue': BoardInteraction.blue_led.brightness_
value}
        self.write(response)
```

The code declares the following four subclasses of tornado.web.RequestHandler:

- VersionHandler: Defines the parameter less get method that returns a response with the version number and the last build date.

- PutRedBrightnessHandler: Defines the put method that requires a value argument that specifies the desired brightness level for the red LED. The method calls the set_brightness method for the AnalogNumber instance stored in the BoardInteraction.red_led class attribute with the desired brightness level specified in the value argument. Then, the code returns a response with the brightness level that has been translated to an output duty cycle percentage in the PWM pin to which the red LED is connected to.

- PutGreenBrightnessHandler: Defines the `put` method to set the desired brightness level for the green LED. It works as the previously described `PutRedBrightnessHandler` method but instead of using the `BoardInteraction.red_led` class attribute, the code uses `BoardInteraction.green_led` class attribute to control the brightness level for the green LED.

- PutBlueBrightnessHandler: Defines the `put` method to set the desired brightness level for the blue LED. It works as the previously described `PutRedBrightnessHandler` method but instead of using the `BoardInteraction.red_led` class attribute, the code uses `BoardInteraction.blue_led` class attribute to control the brightness level for the blue LED.

The next lines show the code that adds the following classes: GetRedBrightnessHandler, GetGreenBrightnessHandler and GetBlueBrightnessHandler. The code file for the sample is iot_python_chapter_04_02.py.

```python
class GetRedBrightnessHandler(tornado.web.RequestHandler):
    def get(self):
        response = {'red': BoardInteraction.red_led.brightness_value}
        self.write(response)


class GetGreenBrightnessHandler(tornado.web.RequestHandler):
    def get(self):
        response = {'green': BoardInteraction.green_led.brightness_
value}
        self.write(response)


class GetBlueBrightnessHandler(tornado.web.RequestHandler):
    def get(self):
        response = {'blue': BoardInteraction.blue_led.brightness_
value}
        self.write(response)
```

The code declares the following three subclasses of `tornado.web.RequestHandler`:

- `GetRedBrightnessHandler`: Defines the parameter less `get` method that returns a response with the value of the `BoardInteraction.red_led.brightness_value` attribute, that is, the brightness value set to the red LED

- `GetGREENBrightnessHandler`: Defines the parameter less `get` method that returns a response with the value of the `BoardInteraction.green_led.brightness_value` attribute, that is, the brightness value set to the green LED

- `GetBlueBrightnessHandler`: Defines the parameter less `get` method that returns a response with the value of the `BoardInteraction.blue_led.brightness_value` attribute, that is, the brightness value set to the blue LED

The following lines use the previously declared subclasses of `tornado.web.RequestHandler` to make up the web application with Tornado that represents a new RESTful API and the new `__main__` method. The code file for the sample is `iot_python_chapter_04_02.py`.

```python
application = tornado.web.Application([
    (r"/putredbrightness/([0-9]+)", PutRedBrightnessHandler),
    (r"/putgreenbrightness/([0-9]+)", PutGreenBrightnessHandler),
    (r"/putbluebrightness/([0-9]+)", PutBlueBrightnessHandler),
    (r"/getredbrightness", GetRedBrightnessHandler),
    (r"/getgreenbrightness", GetGreenBrightnessHandler),
    (r"/getbluebrightness", GetBlueBrightnessHandler),
    (r"/version", VersionHandler)])


if __name__ == "__main__":
    print("Listening at port 8888")
    application.listen(8888)
    tornado.ioloop.IOLoop.instance().start()
```

As happened in our previous example, the code creates an instance of the `tornado.web.Application` class named `application` with the list of request handlers that make up the web application, that is, the tuples of regular expressions and subclasses of `tornado.web.RequestHandler`.

The following table shows some HTTP requests that match the regular expressions defined in the preceding code. In this case, the HTTP requests use `192.168.1.107` because they are executed from a computer connected to our LAN. Don't forget to replace `192.168.1.107` with your board's IP address in the next requests.

HTTP verb and request URL	Tuple (regexp, request_class) that matches the request path	RequestHandler subclass and method that is called
PUT http:// 192.168.1.107:8888/ putredbrightness/30	(r"/putredbrightness/ ([0-9]+)", PutRedBrightnessHandler)	PutRedBrightnessHandler. put(30)
PUT http:// 192.168.1.107:8888/ putgreenbrightness/128	(r"/putgreenbrightness/ ([0-9]+)", PutGreenBrightnessHandler)	PutGreenBrightnessHandler. put(128)
PUT http:// 192.168.1.107:8888/ putbluebrightness/255	(r"/putbluebrightness/ ([0-9]+)", PutBlueBrightnessHandler)	PutGreenBrightnessHandler. put(255)
GET http:// 192.168.1.107:8888/ getredbrightness	(r"/getredbrightness", GetRedBrightnessHandler)	GetRedBrightnessHandler.get()
GET http:// 192.168.1.107:8888/ getgreenbrightness	(r"/getgreenbrightness", GetGreenBrightnessHandler)	GetGreenBrightnessHandler. get()
GET http:// 192.168.1.107:8888/ getbluebrightness	(r"/getbluebrightness", GetBlueBrightnessHandler)	GetBlueBrightnessHandler.get()

The following line will start the HTTP server and our RESTful API that allows us to control the brightness level for red, green and blue LEDs in the Yocto Linux running on the board. Don't forget that you need to transfer the Python source code file to the Yocto Linux with an SFTP client, as explained in the previous chapter.

```
python iot_python_chapter_04_02.py
```

After we start the HTTP server, we will see the following output and all the red, green and blue LEDs are going to be turned off.

```
Red LED connected to PWM Pin #6 set to brightness 0.
Green LED connected to PWM Pin #5 set to brightness 0.
Blue LED connected to PWM Pin #3 set to brightness 0.
Listening at port 8888
```

Generating analog values via HTTP requests

The HTTP server is running in Yocto Linux and waiting for our HTTP requests to control the LEDs on connected to the Intel Galileo Gen 2 board. Now, we will compose and send HTTP requests from other computer or devices connected to our LAN and we will control the brightness levels for the red, green and blue LEDs.

Open a new terminal, command-line or the GUI tool that we want to use to compose and send HTTP requests from a computer or any device connected to the LAN. Don't forget to replace `192.168.1.107` with your board's IP address in the next requests.

Run the following HTTPie command in a computer or device to use the RESTful API to make the board set the brightness level for the red LED to 30. After you enter the command, you will notice the SSH terminal that displays the output for the Python code will display the following message: **Red LED connected to PWM Pin #6 set to brightness 30**. In addition, you will see the red LED turned on with a very low brightness level.

```
http -b PUT 192.168.1.107:8888/putredbrightness/30
```

The previous command will compose and send the following HTTP request: `PUT http://192.168.1.107:8888/putredbrightness/30`. The request will match and run the `PutRedBrightnessHandler.put` method that receives `30` in its `value` parameter. The following lines show the response from the HTTP server with the brightness level that has been set for the red LED by taking advantage of PWM:

```
{
    "red": 30
}
```

We can run the following HTTPie command in a computer or device to use the RESTful API to tell us the current brightness level for the red LED.

```
http -b GET 192.168.1.107:8888/getredbrightness
```

The previous command will compose and send the following HTTP request: `GET http://192.168.1.107:8888/getredbrightness`. The request will match and run the `GetRedBrightnessHandler.get` method. The following lines show the response from the HTTP server with the brightness level that has been previously set for the red LED with the API call:

```
{
    "red": 30
}
```

Now, run the following HTTPie command in a computer or device to use the RESTful API to make the board set the brightness level for the green LED to 128. After you enter the command, you will notice the SSH terminal that displays the output for the Python code will display the following message: **Green LED connected to PWM Pin #5 set to brightness 128**. In addition, you will see the green LED turned on with a very low brightness level.

```
http -b PUT 192.168.1.107:8888/putredbrightness/128
```

The previous command will compose and send the following HTTP request: PUT
`http://192.168.1.107:8888/putgreenbrightness/128`. The request will match
and run the `PutGreenBrightnessHandler.put` method that receives `128` in its
`value` parameter. The following lines show the response from the HTTP server
with the brightness level that has been set for the green LED:

```
{
    "green": 128
}
```

Finally, we run the following HTTPie command in a computer or device to use the
RESTful API to make the board set the brightness level for the blue LED to `255`, that
is, its highest brightness level. After you enter the command, you will notice the
SSH terminal that displays the output for the Python code will display the following
message: **Blue LED connected to PWM Pin #3 set to brightness 255**. In addition,
you will see the blue LED turned on with its highest brightness level.

```
http -b PUT 192.168.1.107:8888/putbluebrightness/255
```

The previous command will compose and send the following HTTP request: PUT
`http://192.168.1.107:8888/putbluebrightness/255`. The request will match
and run the `PutBlueBrightnessHandler.put` method that receives 255 in its `value`
parameter. The following lines show the response from the HTTP server with the
brightness level that has been set for the blue LED:

```
{
    "blue": 255
}
```

Now, we can run the following two HTTPie commands to use the RESTful API to tell
us the current brightness levels for the green and blue LEDs.

```
http -b GET 192.168.1.107:8888/getgreenbrightness
http -b GET 192.168.1.107:8888/getbluebrightness
```

The following lines show the two responses from the HTTP server with the
brightness levels that had been set for the green and blue LEDs:

```
{
    "green": 128
}


{
    "blue": 255
}
```

We created a very simple RESTful API that allows us to set the desired brightness for red, green and blue LEDs, and check their current brightness levels. Our RESTful API makes it possible for us to generate different colors with the intersections of the three color and their different brightness levels with any application, mobile app or web application that can compose and send HTTP requests.

Preparing the RESTful API for Web application requirements

We want to develop a simple web application that displays a color picker to allow the user to choose a color. Once the user picks a color, we can obtain the red, green and blue components from 0 to 255 inclusive. We want to set the brightness level for the red, green and blue LEDs on the board based on the red, green and blue values for the selected color. Based on this requirement, it is convenient to add a new PUT method to our RESTful API to allow us to change the brightness levels for the three LEDs in single API call.

The next lines show the code that adds a new PutRGBBrightnessHandler class. The code file for the sample is iot_python_chapter_04_03.py.

```
class PutRGBBrightnessHandler(tornado.web.RequestHandler):
    def put(self, red, green, blue):
        int_red = int(red)
        int_green = int(green)
        int_blue = int(blue)
        BoardInteraction.red_led.set_brightness(int_red)
        BoardInteraction.green_led.set_brightness(int_green)
        BoardInteraction.blue_led.set_brightness(int_blue)
        response = dict(
            red=BoardInteraction.red_led.brightness_value,
            green=BoardInteraction.green_led.brightness_value,
            blue=BoardInteraction.blue_led.brightness_value)
        self.write(response)
```

The code declares a new subclass of tornado.web.RequestHandler named PutRGBBrightnessHandler. The class defines the put method that requires three arguments that specify the desired brightness for each of the three LEDs: red, green and blue. The method calls the set_brightness method for the AnalogNumber instances stored in the BoardInteraction.red_led, BoardInteraction.green_led and BoardInteraction.blue_led class attributes with the desired brightness levels specified in the arguments. Then, the code returns a response with the brightness levels that have been translated to output duty cycle percentages in the PWM pins to which the red, green and blue LEDs are connected to.

Now, it is necessary to add the highlighted lines to the code that creates an instance of the `tornado.web.Application` class named `application` with the list of request handlers that make up the web application, that is, the tuples of regular expressions and subclasses of `tornado.web.RequestHandler`. The code file for the sample is `iot_python_chapter_04_03.py`.

```
application = tornado.web.Application([
    (r"/putredbrightness/([0-9]+)", PutRedBrightnessHandler),
    (r"/putgreenbrightness/([0-9]+)", PutGreenBrightnessHandler),
    (r"/putbluebrightness/([0-9]+)", PutBlueBrightnessHandler),
    (r"/putrgbbrightness/r([0-9]+)g([0-9]+)b([0-9]+)",
     PutRGBBrightnessHandler),
    (r"/getredbrightness", GetRedBrightnessHandler),
    (r"/getgreenbrightness", GetGreenBrightnessHandler),
    (r"/getbluebrightness", GetBlueBrightnessHandler),
    (r"/version", VersionHandler)])
```

The following line will start the HTTP server and our new version of the RESTful API that allows us to control the brightness level for red, green and blue LEDs with a single API call in the Yocto Linux running on the board. Don't forget that you need to transfer the Python source code file to the Yocto Linux with an SFTP client, as explained in the previous chapter.

```
python iot_python_chapter_04_03.py
```

After we start the HTTP server, we will see the following output and all the red, green and blue LEDs are going to be turned off.

```
Red LED connected to PWM Pin #6 set to brightness 0.
Green LED connected to PWM Pin #5 set to brightness 0.
Blue LED connected to PWM Pin #3 set to brightness 0.
Listening at port 8888
```

With the new RESTful API we can compose the following HTTP verb and request URL:

```
PUT http://192.168.1.107:8888/putrgbbrightness/r30g128b255
```

The previous request path will match the previously added tuple (`regexp`, `request_class`) (`r"/putrgbbrightness/r([0-9]+)g([0-9]+)b([0-9]+)"`, `PutRGBBrightnessHandler`) and Tornado will call the `PutRGBBrightnessHandler.put` method with the values for `red`, `green` and `blue`, specifically `PutRGBBrightnessHandler.put(30, 128, 255)`.

Run the following HTTPie command in a computer or device to use the RESTful API to make the board set the brightness level for the three LEDs with the previously analyzed request path.

```
http -b PUT 192.168.1.107:8888/putrgbbrightness/r30g128b255
```

After you enter the command, you will notice the SSH terminal that displays the output for the Python code will display the following three messages:

- **Red LED connected to PWM Pin #6 set to brightness 30**
- **Green LED connected to PWM Pin #5 set to brightness 128**
- **Blue LED connected to PWM Pin #3 set to brightness 255**

In addition, you will see the three LEDs turned on with their different brightness levels. The following lines show the response from the HTTP server with the brightness levels that have been set for the three LEDs:

```
{
    "blue": 255,
    "green": 128,
    "red": 30
}
```

Using PWM plus a RESTful API to set colors for an RGB LED

Now, we will use the same source code to make it possible to change the color of an RGB LED, specifically, a common cathode RGB LED. This electronic component provides a common cathode and three anodes, that is, an anode for each of the three colors: red, green and blue. We can use our code to pulse width modulate the three colors and make the LED produce the mixed colors. We don't need to use a black surface to see the intersection of the three colors because the RGB LED mixes the three colors for us.

The following image shows a common cathode RGB LED with one of the most common configurations for the pins, where the common cathode is the second pin and the longest one.

The following table shows the pin configuration for the previous RGB LED, from left to right. However, always make sure that you check the datasheet for your RGB LED to check the right pins for the common cathode and the anode for each color.

Pin number	Description
1	Anode pin for red LED
2	Common cathode pin
3	Anode pin for green LED
4	Anode pin for blue LED

Based on the previous table, we will connect the three anode pins to three of the digital I/O pins that we can use as **PWM** (short for **Pulse Width Modulation**) output pins. We will use the same PWM output pins that we used in our previous example:

- Pin ~**6** to connect the anode pin for red LED
- Pin ~**5** to connect the anode pin for green LED
- Pin ~**3** to connect the anode pin for blue LED.

After we finish the necessary wirings, we will use the same Python code to run our RESTful API and mix colors by changing the brightness levels for red, green and blue. We need the following parts to work with this example:

- One common cathode 5mm RGB LED
- Three 270Ω resistors with 5% tolerance (red violet brown gold)

The following diagram shows the components connected to the breadboard, the necessary wirings and the wirings from the Intel Galileo Gen 2 board to the breadboard. The Fritzing file for the sample is `iot_python_chapter_04_03.fzz` and the following image is the breadboard view:

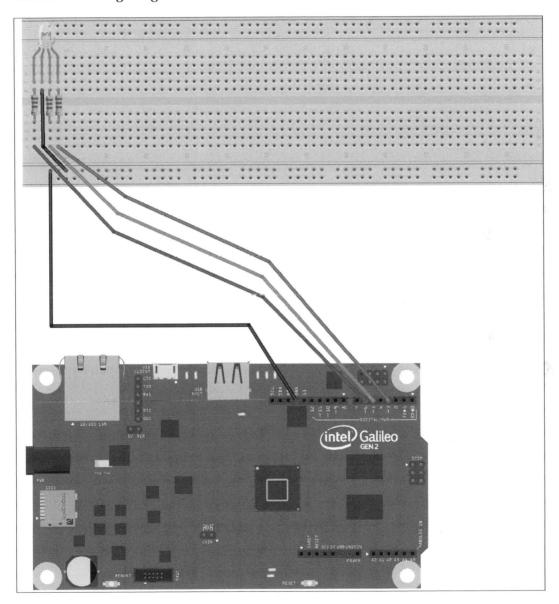

The following image shows the schematic with the electronic components represented as symbols:

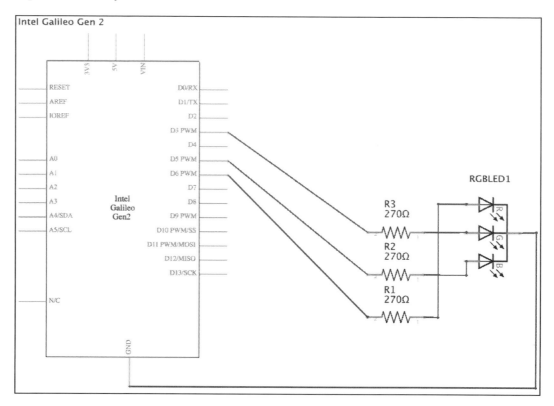

As seen in the previous schematic, three PWM capable GPIO pins labeled **D3 PWM**, **D5 PWM** and **D6 PWM** in the board's symbol is connected to a **270Ω** resistor, wired to an anode pin for each LED color, and the common cathode is connected to ground.

Now, it is time to insert the components in the breadboard and make all the necessary wirings. Don't forget to shutdown the Yocto Linux, wait for all the onboard LEDs to turn off, and unplug the power supply from the Intel Galileo Gen 2 board before adding or removing any wire from the board's pins.

After the board boots Yocto Linux, we have to start the HTTP server with our latest version of the RESTful API that allows us to control the brightness level for red, green and blue LEDs with a single API call.

```
python iot_python_chapter_04_03.py
```

Run the following HTTPie command in a computer or device to use the RESTful API to make the board set the brightness level for the colors included in the RGB LED.

```
http -b PUT 192.168.1.107:8888/putrgbbrightness/r255g255b0
```

After you enter the command, you will notice the RGB LED displays a yellow light because we set both red and green to its maximum brightness level while we turned off the blue component. The following lines show the response from the HTTP server with the brightness levels that have been set for the three colors:

```
{
    "blue": 0,
    "green": 255,
    "red": 255
}
```

Now, run the following HTTPie command.

```
http -b PUT 192.168.1.107:8888/putrgbbrightness/r255g0b128
```

After you enter the command, you will notice the RGB LED displays a pink or light magenta light because we set green to its maximum brightness level and blue to half its maximum brightness level while we turned off the green component. The following lines show the response from the HTTP server with the brightness levels that have been set for the three colors:

```
{
    "blue": 128,
    "green": 0,
    "red": 255
}
```

Now, run the following HTTPie command:

```
http -b PUT 192.168.1.107:8888/putrgbbrightness/r0g255b255
```

After you enter the command, you will notice the RGB LED displays a cyan light because we set both green and blue to its maximum brightness level while we turned off the red component. The following lines show the response from the HTTP server with the brightness levels that have been set for the three colors:

```
{
    "blue": 255,
    "green": 255,
    "red": 0
}
```

We can generate 256 * 256 * 256 different colors, which is 16,777,216 colors (more than 16 million colors) for the light generated by the RGB LED. We just need to use our RESTful API and change the values for the red, green and blue components.

Controlling PWM with the wiring-x86 library

So far, we have been using the `mraa` library to work with PWM and change the brightness level for the different LEDs and colors within an RGB LED. However, in the first chapter, we also installed the `wiring-x86` library. We can change just a few lines of our object-oriented code to replace the `mraa` library with the `wiring-x86` one to change the brightness levels for the red, green and blue components.

There is an important difference between the `mraa` library and the `wiring-x86` library when working with PWM. The former works with floating point values from 0.0f to 1.0f to set the output duty cycle percentage, but the latter works with values from 0 to 255 inclusive to set this value. Thus, when working with the `wiring-x86` library, we don't need to translate the desired brightness level to an output duty cycle percentage and we can use the brightness level value to specify the value for PWM. As a result, the code is simpler in this case.

The following lines shows the code for a `Board` class followed by the new version of the `AnalogLed` class that works with the `wiring-x86` library instead of using `mraa`. The code file for the sample is `iot_python_chapter_04_04.py`.

```python
from wiringx86 import GPIOGalileoGen2 as GPIO

class Board:
    gpio = GPIO(debug=False)


class AnalogLed:
    def __init__(self, pin, name):
        self.pin = pin
        self.name = name
        self.gpio = Board.gpio
        self.gpio.pinMode(pin, self.gpio.PWM)
        self.brightness_value = 0
        self.set_brightness(0)

    def set_brightness(self, value):
        brightness_value = value
```

Test your knowledge

1. PWM stands for:

    1. Pin Work Mode.

    2. Pulse Weight Modulation.

    3. Pulse Width Modulation.

2. In the Intel Galileo Gen 2 board, the pins labeled with the following symbol as a prefix for the number can be used as PWM output pins:

    1. Hash sign (#).

    2. Dollar sign ($).

    3. Tilde symbol (~).

3. A 100% duty cycle (always signal in the ON status) in a PWM pin will generate a steady voltage equal to:

    1. 0 V.

    2. The voltage specified in the position in which the IOREF jumper is located.

    3. 6 V.

4. A 0% duty cycle (always signal in the OFF status) in a PWM pin will generate a steady voltage equal to:

    1. 0 V.

    2. The voltage specified in the position in which the IOREF jumper is located.

    3. 6 V.

5. A 50% duty cycle in a PWM pin with a LED connected to it will generate the same result as a steady voltage equal to:

    1. 0 V.

    2. Half the voltage specified in the position in which the IOREF jumper is located.

    3. 6 V * 0.5 = 3 V.

Summary

In this chapter, we worked with Tornado web server, Python, the HTTPie command-line HTTP client, and the `mraa` and `wiring-x86` libraries. As in the previous chapters, we took advantage of Python's object-oriented features and we generated many versions of RESTful APIs that allowed us to interact with the board in computers and devices connected to the LAN.

We could compose and send HTTP requests that printed number in LEDs, changed the brightness levels for three LEDs and generated millions of colors with an RGB LED.

Now that we created our first RESTful APIs that made is possible for computers and devices to interact with our IoT device, we can take advantage of additional features that allow us to read digital inputs and analog values, which is the topic of the next chapter.

5
Working with Digital Inputs, Polling and Interrupts

In this chapter, we will use digital inputs to make it possible for users to interact with the board while we process the HTTP requests. We will:

- Understand the difference between pull-up and pull-down resistors to connect pushbuttons
- Wire digital input pins with pushbuttons
- Use polling to check the pushbutton status with the `mraa` and `wiring-x86` libraries
- Combine polling to read digital inputs while running a RESTful API
- Write code that maintains consistency when we provide shared features with electronic components and APIs
- Use interrupts and the `mraa` library to detect pressed pushbuttons
- Understand the differences, advantages, and trade-offs between polling and interrupts to detect changes in digital inputs

Understanding pushbuttons and pullup resistors

We controlled the brightness levels for red, green, and blue LEDs with a RESTful API. Then, we replaced the three LEDs with a single RGB LED and generated lights of different colors with the same RESTful API. Now, we want to make it possible for the users to change the brightness level for the three components with two pushbuttons added to the breadboard:

- A pushbutton to turn off all the colors, that is, to set all the colors to a brightness level equal to 0
- A pushbutton to set all the colors to their maximum brightness levels, that is, to set all the colors to a brightness level equal to 255

When the user presses the pushbutton, also known as a microswitch, it acts like a wire, and therefore, it lets the current flow through the circuit in which it is incorporated. When the pushbutton isn't pressed, the circuit in which it is incorporated is interrupted. Thus, whenever the user releases the pushbutton, the circuit is interrupted. Obviously, we don't want to short circuit the connection whenever the user presses a pushbutton, and therefore, we will analyze the different possible ways to safely connect a pushbutton to an Intel Galileo Gen 2 board.

The following picture shows one of the ways in which we can connect a pushbutton to an Intel Galileo Gen 2 board and uses the GPIO pin number **0** as an input to determine whether the pushbutton is pressed or not. The Fritzing file for the sample is `iot_fritzing_chapter_05_01.fzz` and the following picture is the breadboard view:

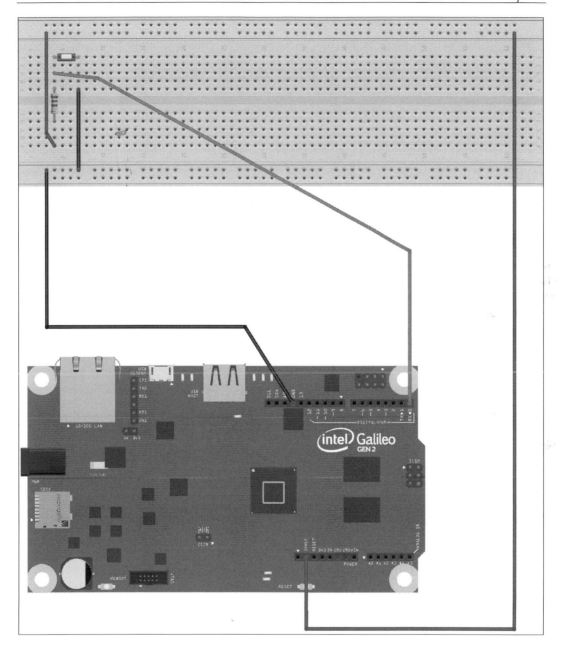

The following picture shows the schematic with the electronic components represented as symbols:

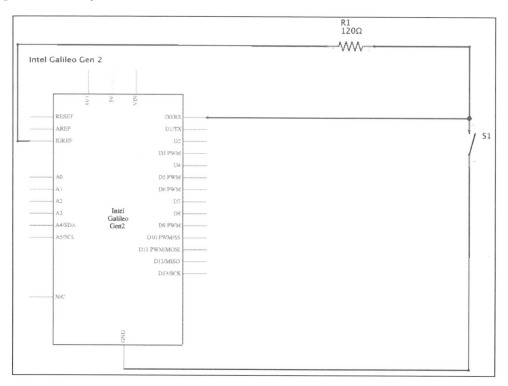

As seen in the previous schematic, the GPIO pin labeled **D0/RX**, in the board's symbol, is connected to a 120Ω resistor with 5% tolerance (brown red brown gold), and wired to the **IOREF** pin. We already know that the pin labeled **IOREF** provides us the IOREF voltage, that is, 5V in our actual configuration. As we might want to work with other voltage configuration in the future, we can always work with the IOREF pin instead of specifically using the **5V** or the **3V3** pins. The GPIO pin labeled **D0/RX** in the board's symbol is also connected to the **S1** pushbutton, wired to the 120Ω resistor and **GND** (ground).

 The configuration is known as a voltage divider and the 120Ω resistor is called a pull-up resistor.

The pull-up resistor limits the electric current when we press the **S1** pushbutton. As an effect of the pull-up resistor, if we press the **S1** pushbutton, we will read a low value (0V) in the GPIO pin labeled **D0/RX**. When we release the S1 pushbutton, we will read a high value, that is, the IOREF voltage (5V in our actual configuration).

The situation might be confusing because we read a low value when the button in pressed. However, we can write object-oriented code to encapsulate the behavior for a pushbutton and work with easier to understand states that isolate the way in which the pull-up resistor works.

It is also possible to work with a pull-down resistor. We can connect the 120Ω resistor to ground and transform it from a pull-up resistor into a pull-down resistor. The following picture shows how we can connect a pushbutton to an Intel Galileo Gen 2 board with a pull-down resistor and use the GPIO pin number **0** as an input to determine whether the pushbutton is pressed or not. The Fritzing file for the sample is `iot_fritzing_chapter_05_02.fzz` and the following picture is the breadboard view:

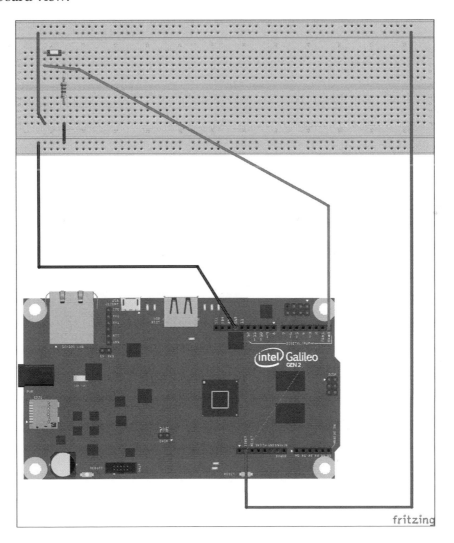

The following picture shows the schematic with the electronic components represented as symbols:

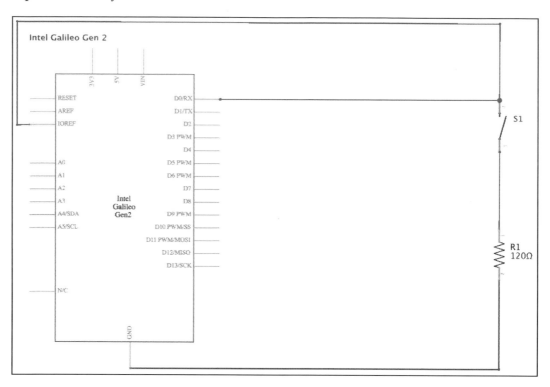

As seen in the previous schematic, in this case, the GPIO pin labeled **D0/RX** in the board's symbol is connected to the **S1** pushbutton and the **IOREF** pin. The other connector of the S1 pushbutton is wired to the 120Ω resistor and this resistor is wired to **GND** (ground).

> In this configuration, the 120Ω resistor is called a pull-down resistor.

The pull-down resistor limits the electric current when we press the **S1** pushbutton. As an effect of the pull-down resistor, if we press the **S1** pushbutton, we will read a high value, that is, the IOREF voltage (5V in our actual configuration) in the GPIO pin labeled **D0/RX**. When we release the **S1** pushbutton, we will read a low value (0V). Thus, the pull-down resistor works with the inverse values we read when we use a pull-up resistor.

Wiring digital input pins with pushbuttons

Now, we will use the following pins to connect the two pushbuttons and we will work with pull-up resistors:

- Pin **1** (labeled **D1/TX**) to connect the pushbutton that turns off the three colors
- Pin **0** (labeled **D0/RX**) to connect the pushbutton that sets the three colors to their maximum brightness levels

After we finish the necessary wirings, we will write the Python code to check whether each pushbutton was pressed while keeping our RESTful API working as expected. This way, we will make it possible for the user to interact with the RGB LED with the pushbuttons and also with the RESTful API. We need the following additional parts to work with this example:

- Two pushbuttons with two pins
- Two 120Ω resistors with 5% tolerance (brown red brown gold)

The following diagram shows the components connected to the breadboard, the necessary wirings and the wirings from the Intel Galileo Gen 2 board to the breadboard. The Fritzing file for the sample is `iot_fritzing_chapter_05_03.fzz` and the following picture is the breadboard view:

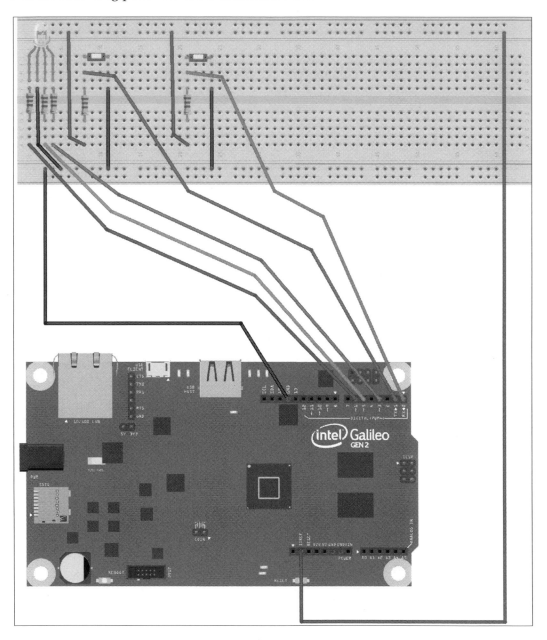

The following picture shows the schematic with the electronic components represented as symbols.

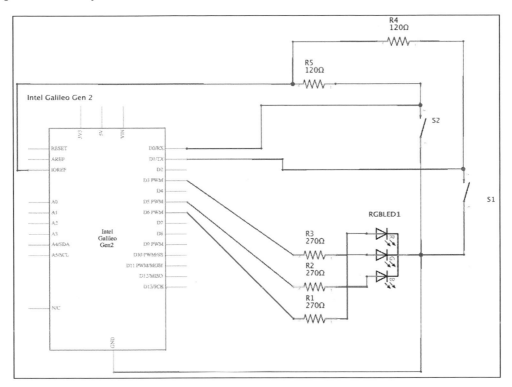

As seen in the previous schematic, we added two pushbuttons (**S1** and **S2**) and two 120Ω pull-up resistors (**R4** and **R5**). The GPIO pin labeled **D0/RX** in the board's symbol is connected to the **S2** pushbutton and the **R4** resistor is its pull-up resistor. The GPIO pin labeled **D1/TX** in the board's symbol is connected to the **S1** pushbutton and the **R5** resistor is its pull-up resistor. This way, GPIO pin number 0 will be low when the **S2** pushbutton is pressed and GPIO pin number 1 will be low when the **S1** pushbutton is pressed. The **S1** pushbutton is located at the left-hand side in the breadboard while the **S2** pushbutton is located at the right-hand side.

Now, it is time to insert the components in the breadboard and make all the necessary wirings. Don't forget to shutdown the Yocto Linux, wait for all the onboard LEDs to turn off, and unplug the power supply from the Intel Galileo Gen 2 board before adding or removing any wire from the board's pins.

Reading pushbutton statuses with digital inputs and the mraa library

We will create a new PushButton class to represent a pushbutton connected to our board that can use either a pull-up or a pull-down resistor. The following lines show the code for the new PushButton class that works with the mraa library. The code file for the sample is iot_python_chapter_05_01.py.

```python
import mraa
import time
from datetime import date

class PushButton:
    def __init__(self, pin, pull_up=True):
        self.pin = pin
        self.pull_up = pull_up
        self.gpio = mraa.Gpio(pin)
        self.gpio.dir(mraa.DIR_IN)

    @property
    def is_pressed(self):
        push_button_status = self.gpio.read()
        if self.pull_up:
            # Pull-up resistor connected
            return push_button_status == 0
        else:
            # Pull-down resistor connected
            return push_button_status == 1

    @property
    def is_released(self):
        return not self.is_pressed
```

We have to specify the pin number to which the pushbutton is connected when we create an instance of the PushButton class in the pin required argument. In case we don't specify additional values, the optional pull_up argument will be True and the instance will work as if the pushbutton were connected with a pull-up resistor. If we work with a pull-down resistor, we must pass False in the pull_up argument. The constructor, that is, the __init__ method, creates a new mraa.Gpio instance with the received pin as its pin argument, saves its reference in the gpio attribute and calls its dir method to configure the pin to be an input pin (mraa.DIR_IN).

The class defines the following two properties:

- is_pressed: Calls the read method for the related mraa.Gpio instance to retrieve the value from the pin and saved it in the push_button_status variable. If the pushbutton is connected with a pull-up resistor (self.pull_up is True), the code will return True, indicating that the pushbutton is pressed if the value in push_button_status is 0 (low value). If the pushbutton is connected with a pull-down resistor (self.pull_up is False), the code will return True, indicating that the pushbutton is pressed if the value in push_button_status is 1 (high value).

- is_released: Returns the inverted result of the is_pressed property.

Now, we can write code that uses the new PushButton class to create one instance for each of the two pushbuttons and easily check whether they are pressed or not. The new class handles whether the pushbuttons are connected with pull-up or pull-down resistors, and therefore, we just need to check the value of the is_pressed or is_released properties without worrying about the specific details about their connection.

We will integrate the code that considers the statuses of the two pushbuttons in our RESTful API later. First, we will isolate the two pushbuttons in a simple example to understand how we can read their statuses. In this case, we will use polling, that is, a loop that will check whether the pushbuttons are pressed or not. If a pushbutton is pressed, we want the code to print a message in the console output indicating the specific pushbutton that is being pressed.

The following lines show the Python code that performs the previously explained actions. The code file for the sample is iot_python_chapter_05_01.py.

```python
if __name__ == "__main__":
    s1_push_button = PushButton(1)
    s2_push_button = PushButton(0)
    while True:
        # Check whether the S1 pushbutton is pressed
        if s1_push_button.is_pressed:
            print("You are pressing S1.")
        # Check whether the S2 pushbutton is pressed
        if s2_push_button.is_pressed:
            print("You are pressing S2.")
        # Sleep 500 milliseconds (0.5 seconds)
        time.sleep(0.5)
```

The first two lines create two instances of the previously coded `PushButton` class. The **S1** pushbutton is connected to GPIO pin number 1 and the **S2** pushbutton is connected to GPIO pin number 0. In both cases, the code doesn't specify a value for the `pull_up` argument. Thus, the constructor, that is, the `__init__` method, will use the default value for this argument, `True`, and the instance will be configured for a pushbutton connected with a pull-up resistor. We need to worry about this when we create the two instances, and then, we work with the names of the variables that hold the instances: `s1_push_button` and `s2_push_button`.

Then, the code runs in a loop forever, that is, until you interrupt the execution by pressing *Ctrl* + *C* or the button to stop the process, in case you are using a Python IDE with remote development features to run the code in your board.

The first line within the `while` loop checks the value of the `is_pressed` property for the `PushButton` instance named `s1_push_button` is `True`. A `True` value means that the pushbutton is pressed at this time, and therefore, the code prints a message to the console output indicating that the S1 pushbutton is being pressed. The next lines within the while loop follow the same procedure for the `PushButton` instance named `s2_push_button`.

After we check the statuses for both the pushbuttons, a call to `time.sleep` with `0.5` as the value for the second argument delays the execution for 500 milliseconds, that is, 0.5 seconds.

The following line will start the example; don't forget that you need to transfer the Python source code file to the Yocto Linux with an SFTP client:

```
python iot_python_chapter_05_01.py
```

After you run the example, perform the following actions:

- Press the S1 pushbutton for 1 second
- Press the S2 pushbutton for 1 second
- Press both the S1 and S2 pushbuttons for one second

As a result of the previous actions, you will see the following output:

```
You are pressing S1.
You are pressing S2.
You are pressing S1.
You are pressing S2.
```

In this case, we are reading digital inputs with polling. The `mraa` library also allows us to work with interrupts and declare interrupt handlers with Python. This way, whenever a user presses a button, the event generates an interrupt and the `mraa` library calls the specified interrupt handler. If you have ever worked with event-based programming, you can think about events and event handlers instead of interrupts and interrupt handlers and you will easily understand how things work.

The interrupt handlers run in a different thread, and the code you can write for them has many limitations. For example, you cannot use the basic types within interrupt handlers. Thus, in this case, it doesn't make sense to work with interrupts and polling makes things easier for us due to the tasks that we have to execute when the user presses any of the two buttons.

Reading digital inputs with polling as in the previous example has the following advantages compared with the usage of interrupts for the same task:

- The code is easy to understand and read
- The flow is easy to understand and we don't have to worry about code running in callbacks
- We can write all the necessary code to perform actions when the button is pressed without worrying about specific limitations related to interrupt callbacks
- We don't have to worry about code running in multiple threads

However, reading digital inputs with polling has the following disadvantages compared with the usage of interrupts for the same task:

- If we don't keep the pushbutton pressed for a specific amount of time, the code might not detect that the pushbutton has been pressed.
- If we keep the pushbutton pressed for a long time, the code will behave as if the pushbutton was pressed many times. Sometimes, we don't want this situation to happen.
- The loop consumes more resources that we can require for other tasks compared with an interrupt triggered event.

In this case, we want users to keep any of the two buttons pressed for at least half a second, and therefore, we don't need the advantages of interrupts. However, we will use interrupts later in this chapter.

Reading pushbutton statuses and running a RESTful API

Now, we will integrate the code that checks the statuses of the two pushbuttons in our RESTful API. We want to be able to make HTTP requests to the RESTful API and we also want to be able to use the two buttons we have added to the breadboard.

We have to make Tornado run a periodic callback and write the code that checks the statuses of the two pushbuttons in this callback. We will take the code we wrote in the previous chapter when we created the last version of our RESTful API with the mraa library and we will use this code as a baseline to add the new features. The code file for the sample was iot_python_chapter_04_03.py.

We will add two class attributes and three class methods to the existing BoardInteraction class. The code file for the sample is iot_python_chapter_05_02.py.

```python
class BoardInteraction:
    # The Red LED is connected to pin ~6
    red_led = AnalogLed(6, 'Red')
    # The Green LED is connected to Pin ~5
    green_led = AnalogLed(5, 'Green')
    # The Blue LED is connected to Pin ~3
    blue_led = AnalogLed(3, 'Blue')
    # The push button to reset colors
    reset_push_button = PushButton(1)
    # The push button to set colors to their maximum brightness
    max_brightness_push_button = PushButton(0)

    @classmethod
    def set_min_brightness(cls):
        cls.red_led.set_brightness(0)
        cls.green_led.set_brightness(0)
        cls.blue_led.set_brightness(0)

    @classmethod
    def set_max_brightness(cls):
        cls.red_led.set_brightness(255)
        cls.green_led.set_brightness(255)
        cls.blue_led.set_brightness(255)

    @classmethod
    def check_push_buttons_callback(cls):
        # Check whether the reset push button is pressed
```

```
if cls.reset_push_button.is_pressed:
    print("You are pressing the reset pushbutton.")
    cls.set_min_brightness()

# Check whether the maximum brightness push button is pressed
if cls.max_brightness_push_button.is_pressed:
    print("You are pressing the maximum brightness
pushbutton.")
    cls.set_max_brightness()
```

The previous code adds two class attributes to the BoardInteraction class: reset_push_button and max_brightness_push_button. The reset_push_button class attribute is an instance of PushButton with its pin attribute set to 1. This way, the instance can check the status of the pushbutton connected to GPIO pin number 1. The max_brightness_push_button class attribute is an instance of PushButton with its pin attribute set to 0, and therefore, this instance can check the status of the pushbutton connected to GPIO pin number 0. In addition, the previous code adds the following class methods to the BoardInteraction class:

- set_min_brightness: Calls the set_brightness method with 0 as an argument for the three AnalogLed instances saved in the red_led, green_led and blue_led class attributes. This way, the three components of the RGB LED will be turned off.

- set_max_brightness: Calls the set_brightness method with 255 as an argument for the three AnalogLed instances saved in the red_led, green_led and blue_led class attributes. This way, the three components of the RGB LED will be turned on with their maximum brightness levels.

- check_push_buttons_callback: First, checks whether the reset pushbutton is pressed by evaluating the value of the is_pressed property for the PushButton instance that represents the reset pushbutton, that is, cls.reset_push_button. In case the value for the property is True, the code prints a message indicating that you are pressing the reset pushbutton and calls the previously described cls.set_min_brightness class method to turn off the three components of the RGB LED. Then, the code checks whether the maximum brightness pushbutton is pressed by evaluating the value of the is_pressed property for the PushButton instance that represents the maximum brightness pushbutton, that is, cls.max_brightness_push_button. In case the value for the property is True, the code prints a message indicating that you are pressing the maximum brightness pushbutton and calls the previously described cls.set_max_brightness class method to turn on the three components of the RGB LED with their maximum brightness levels.

It is necessary to add the @classmethod decorator before the class method header to declare class methods in Python. Instance methods receive self as the first argument, but class methods receive the current class as the first argument and the parameter name is usually called cls. In the previous code, we have been using cls to access the class attributes and class methods for the BoardInteraction class.

The following lines show the new classes that we must add to our existing code to make it possible to set the minimum and maximum brightness with HTTP requests. We want to be able to have the same features we can command with pushbuttons available in our RESTful API. The code adds the following two classes: PutMinBrightnessHandler and PutMaxBrightnessHandler. The code file for the sample is iot_python_chapter_05_02.py.

```
class PutMinBrightnessHandler(tornado.web.RequestHandler):
    def put(self):
        BoardInteraction.set_min_brightness()
        response = dict(
            red=BoardInteraction.red_led.brightness_value,
            green=BoardInteraction.green_led.brightness_value,
            blue=BoardInteraction.blue_led.brightness_value)
        self.write(response)


class PutMaxBrightnessHandler(tornado.web.RequestHandler):
    def put(self):
        BoardInteraction.set_max_brightness()
        response = dict(
            red=BoardInteraction.red_led.brightness_value,
            green=BoardInteraction.green_led.brightness_value,
            blue=BoardInteraction.blue_led.brightness_value)
        self.write(response)
```

The code declares the following two subclasses of tornado.web.RequestHandler:

- PutMinBrightnessHandler: Defines the put method that calls the set_min_brightness class method for the BoardInteraction class. Then, the code returns a response with the minimum brightness levels that have been translated to output duty cycle percentages in the PWM pins to which the red, green and blue anodes of the RGB LED are connected to.

- **PutMaxBrightnessHandler**: Defines the `put` method that calls the `set_max_brightness` class method for the `BoardInteraction` class. Then, the code returns a response with the maximum brightness levels that have been translated to output duty cycle percentages in the PWM pins to which the red, green and blue anodes of the RGB LED are connected to.

Now, it is necessary to add the highlighted lines to the code that creates an instance of the `tornado.web.Application` class named `application` with the list of request handlers that make up the Web application, that is, the tuples of regular expressions and subclasses of `tornado.web.RequestHandler`. The code file for the sample is `iot_python_chapter_05_02.py`.

```
application = tornado.web.Application([
    (r"/putredbrightness/([0-9]+)", PutRedBrightnessHandler),
    (r"/putgreenbrightness/([0-9]+)", PutGreenBrightnessHandler),
    (r"/putbluebrightness/([0-9]+)", PutBlueBrightnessHandler),
    (r"/putrgbbrightness/r([0-9]+)g([0-9]+)b([0-9]+)",
     PutRGBBrightnessHandler),
    (r"/putminbrightness", PutMinBrightnessHandler),
    (r"/putmaxbrightness", PutMaxBrightnessHandler),
    (r"/getredbrightness", GetRedBrightnessHandler),
    (r"/getgreenbrightness", GetGreenBrightnessHandler),
    (r"/getbluebrightness", GetBlueBrightnessHandler),
    (r"/version", VersionHandler)])
```

As shown in our previous example, the code creates an instance of the `tornado.web.Application` class named `application` with the list of request handlers that make up the Web application, that is, the tuples of regular expressions and subclasses of `tornado.web.RequestHandler`.

Finally, it is necessary to replace the `__main__` method with a new one because we want to run a periodic callback to check whether any of the two pushbuttons was pressed. The code file for the sample is `iot_python_chapter_05_02.py`.

```
if __name__ == "__main__":
    print("Listening at port 8888")
    application.listen(8888)
    ioloop = tornado.ioloop.IOLoop.instance()
    periodic_callback = tornado.ioloop.PeriodicCallback(BoardInteraction.check_push_buttons_callback, 500, ioloop)
    periodic_callback.start()
    ioloop.start()
```

As happened in the previous examples, the __main__ method calls the application.listen method to build an HTTP server for the application with the defined rules on the port number 8888. Then, the code retrieves the global IOLoop instance and saves it in the ioloop local variable. We have to use the instance as one of the arguments to create a tornado.ioloop.PeriodicCallback instance named periodic_callback.

The PeriodicCallback instance allows us to schedule a specified callback to be called periodically. In this case, we specify the BoardInteraction.check_push_buttons_callback class method as the callback that will be called every 500 milliseconds. This way, we instruct Tornado to run the BoardInteraction.check_push_buttons_callback class method every 500 milliseconds. In case the method takes more than 500 milliseconds to complete its execution, Tornado will skip subsequent invocations to get back on schedule. After the code creates the PeriodicCallback instance, the next line calls its start method.

Finally, the call to ioloop.start() starts the server created with application.listen. This way, the Web application will process the received requests and will also run a callback to check whether the buttons are pressed.

The following line will start the HTTP server and our new version of the RESTful API. Don't forget that you need to transfer the Python source code file to the Yocto Linux with an SFTP client.

```
python iot_python_chapter_05_02.py
```

After you run the example, press the pushbutton that sets the colors to their maximum brightness for one second. The RGB LED will display a white light and you will see the following output:

```
You are pressing the maximum brightness pushbutton.
Red LED connected to PWM Pin #6 set to brightness 255.
Green LED connected to PWM Pin #5 set to brightness 255.
Blue LED connected to PWM Pin #3 set to brightness 255.
```

Now, press the pushbutton that sets the colors to their minimum brightness for one second. The RGB LED will turn off and you will see the following output:

```
You are pressing the reset pushbutton.
Red LED connected to PWM Pin #6 set to brightness 0.
Green LED connected to PWM Pin #5 set to brightness 0.
Blue LED connected to PWM Pin #3 set to brightness 0.
```

With the new RESTful API we can compose the following HTTP verb and request URL:

```
PUT http://192.168.1.107:8888/putmaxbrightness
```

The previous request path will match the previously added tuple (`regexp`, `request_ class`) (`r"/putmaxbrightness"`, `PutMaxBrightnessHandler`) and Tornado will call the `PutMaxBrightnessHandler.put` method. The RGB LED will display a white light, as happened when you pressed the maximum brightness button. The following lines show the response from the HTTP server with the brightness levels that have been set for the three LEDs:

```
{
    "blue": 255,
    "green": 255,
    "red": 255
}
```

The following HTTP verb and request URL will turn off the RGB LED, as happened when we pressed the pushbutton that sets the colors to their minimum brightness:

```
PUT http://192.168.1.107:8888/putminbrightness
```

The following lines show the response from the HTTP server with the brightness levels that have been set for the three LEDs:

```
{
    "blue": 0,
    "green": 0,
    "red": 0
}
```

Now, press the pushbutton that sets the colors to their maximum brightness for one second. The RGB LED will display a white light. Then, the following three HTTP verbs and request URLs will retrieve the brightness level for each of the colors. All the requests will return 255 as the current value. We set the brightness level with the pushbutton, but the code has the same effect as if we were making API calls to change the colors. We kept the consistency for our application.

```
GET http://192.168.1.107:8888/getredbrightness
GET http://192.168.1.107:8888/getgreenbrightness
GET http://192.168.1.107:8888/getbluebrightness
```

If we work with HTTPie, the following commands will do the job:

```
http –b GET http://192.168.1.107:8888/getredbrightness
http –b GET http://192.168.1.107:8888/getgreenbrightness
http –b GET http://192.168.1.107:8888/getbluebrightness
```

The following lines show the responses from the three requests:

```
{
    "red": 255
}
{
    "green": 255
}
{
    "blue": 255
}
```

We created methods that we could use in both an API call and when the user presses the pushbuttons. We can process HTTP requests and run actions when the user presses pushbuttons. As we build our RESTful API with Tornado, we had to create and configure a `PeriodicCallback` instance to make it possible to check whether the pushbuttons are pressed every 500 milliseconds.

> It is very important to take into account consistency when we add features that we can control with pushbuttons or other electronic components that interact with the board. In this case, we made sure that when the user pressed the pushbuttons and changed the brightness values for the three colors, the brightness values read with API calls were exactly the values set. We worked with object-oriented code and with the same methods, and therefore, it was easy to keep consistency.

Reading digital inputs with the wiring-x86 library

So far, we have been using the `mraa` library to read digital inputs. However, in the first chapter, we also installed the `wiring-x86` library. We can change just a few lines of our object-oriented code to replace the `mraa` library with the `wiring-x86` one to check whether the pushbuttons were pressed.

We will take the code we wrote in the previous chapter when we created the last version of our RESTful API with the `wiring-x86` library and we will use this code as a baseline to add the new features. The code file for the sample was `iot_python_chapter_04_04.py`.

First, we will create a new version of the `PushButton` class to represent a pushbutton connected to our board that can use either a pull-up or a pull-down resistor. The following lines show the code for the new `PushButton` class that works with the `wiring-x86` library. The code file for the sample is `iot_python_chapter_05_03.py`.

```python
from wiringx86 import GPIOGalileoGen2 as GPIO

class PushButton:
    def __init__(self, pin, pull_up=True):
        self.pin = pin
        self.pull_up = pull_up
        self.gpio = Board.gpio
        pin_mode = self.gpio.INPUT_PULLUP if pull_up else self.gpio.INPUT_PULLDOWN
        self.gpio.pinMode(pin, pin_mode)

    @property
    def is_pressed(self):
        push_button_status = self.gpio.digitalRead(self.pin)
        if self.pull_up:
            # Pull-up resistor connected
            return push_button_status == 0
        else:
            # Pull-down resistor connected
            return push_button_status == 1

    @property
    def is_released(self):
        return not self.is_pressed
```

We just needed to change a few lines from the previous code of the PushButton class, that is, the version that worked with the mraa library. The new lines that interact with the wiring-x86 library are highlighted in the previous code. The constructor, that is, the __init__ method receives the same argument as the PushButton class that worked with the mraa library. In this case, this method saves a reference to the Board.gpio class attribute in self.gpio. Then, the code determines the value of the pin_mode local variable based on the value of the pull_up parameter. If pull_up is true, the value will be self.gpio.INPUT_PULLUP and self.gpio.INPUT_PULLDOWN otherwise. Finally, the constructor calls the self.gpio.pinMode method with the received pin as its pin argument and pin_mode as its mode argument. This way, we configure the pin to be a digital input pin with the appropriate pull-up or pull-down resistor. All the PushButton instances will save a reference to the same Board.gpio class attribute that created an instance of the GPIO class, specifically, the wiringx86.GPIOGalileoGen2 class with its debug argument set to False to avoid unnecessary debug information for the low-level communications.

The is_pressed property calls the digitalRead method for the GPIO instance (self.gpio) to set retrieve the digital value for the pin configured as a digital input. The self.pin attribute specifies the pin value for the analogRead method call. The rest of the code for the is_pressed property and the PushButton class remains the same as the version that works with the mraa library.

Then, it is necessary to make the same edits we made in the previous example to create the new version of the BoardInteraction class, add the PutMinBrightnessHandler and PutMaxBrightnessHandler classes, create the tornado.web.Application instance and the new version of the __main__ method that created and configured the PeriodicCallback instance. Thus, the rest of the code for our RESTful API remains the same one that we have used for the previous example. There is no need to make changes to the rest of the code because it will automatically work with the new PushButton class and there were no changes in the arguments for its constructor or its properties.

The following line will start the HTTP server and our new version of the RESTful API that works with the `wiring-x86` library. Don't forget that you need to transfer the Python source code file to the Yocto Linux with an SFTP client, as explained in the previous chapter.

```
python iot_python_chapter_05_03.py
```

 We can press the pushbuttons and then make the same HTTP requests we made in our previous example to check that we can achieve exactly the same results with the `wiring-x86` library.

Using interrupts to detect pressed pushbuttons

Previously, we analyzed the advantages of disadvantages of reading digital inputs with polling as in the previous examples compared with the usage of interrupts for the same task. If we keep any of the pushbuttons pressed for a long time, the code behaves as if the pushbutton was pressed many times. Now, we don't want this situation to happen, and therefore, we will use interrupts instead of polling to detect when the pushbuttons are pressed.

Before we start editing our code, it is necessary to make changes to our existing wirings. The problem is that not all the GPIO pins support interrupts. In fact, pins number 0 and 1 don't support interrupts and we have our pushbuttons connected to them. In *Chapter 1, Understanding and Setting up the Base IoT Hardware* when we learned about the I/O pins included in the Intel Galileo Gen 2 board, we understood that the pins labeled with a tilde symbol (~) as a prefix for the number can be used as PWM output pins. The fact is that the pins labeled with a tilde symbol (~) as a prefix for the number also supports interrupts.

Thus, we can move the wire that connects the reset pushbutton that turns off the three colors from pin **1** to pin **~11**, and move the wire that connects the pushbutton that sets the three colors to their maximum brightness from pin **0** to pin **~10**.

The following diagram shows the components connected to the breadboard, the necessary wirings and the wirings from the Intel Galileo Gen 2 board to the breadboard. The Fritzing file for the sample is `iot_fritzing_chapter_05_04.fzz` and the following picture is the breadboard view:

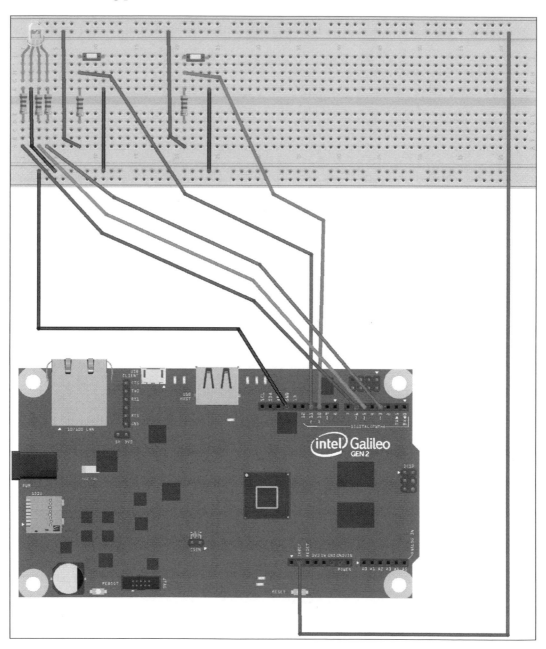

The following picture shows the schematic with the electronic components represented as symbols:

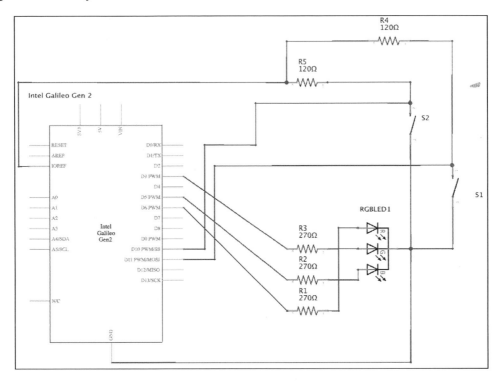

The GPIO pin labeled **D10 PWM/SS** in the board's symbol is connected to the **S2** pushbutton and the **R4** resistor is its pull-up resistor. The GPIO pin labeled **D11 PWM/MOSI** in the board's symbol is connected to the **S1** pushbutton and the **R5** resistor is its pull-up resistor. This way, GPIO pin number 10 will be low when the **S2** pushbutton is pressed and GPIO pin number 11 will be low when the **S1** pushbutton is pressed.

> The signal will fall from high to low when the pushbutton is pressed, and therefore, we are interested in the interrupt that is generated when the signal falls because it indicates that the pushbutton has been pressed. If the user keeps the pushbutton pressed, the signal won't fall many times, and the GPIO pin will stay in the low level. Thus, only one interrupt will be fired when we are observing the fall from high to low and we won't have multiple calls to the interrupt handler code even if the user keeps the button pressed for a long time.

Remember that the **S1** pushbutton is located at the left-hand side in the breadboard while the **S2** pushbutton is located at the right-hand side. Now, it is time to make the changes to the wirings. Don't forget to shutdown the Yocto Linux, wait for all the onboard LEDs to turn off, and unplug the power supply from the Intel Galileo Gen 2 board before removing any wire from the board's pins. After we finish the changes in the wirings, we will write the Python code to detect when the user presses the pushbuttons with interrupts instead of working with polling.

We will take the code we wrote in the previous example when we created the last version of our RESTful API with the mraa library and we will use this code as a baseline to add the new features. The code file for the sample was iot_python_chapter_05_02.py.

We will create a new PushButtonWithInterrupt class to represent a pushbutton connected to our board that can use either a pull-up or a pull-down resistor and will specify the callback that needs to be called when the button is pressed, that is, the interrupt handler. When the button is pressed, an interrupt will occur and the specified callback will be executed as the interrupt handler. The following lines show the code for the new PushButtonWithInterrupt class that works with the mraa library. The code file for the sample is iot_python_chapter_05_04.py.

```python
import mraa
import time
from datetime import date


class PushButtonWithInterrupt:
    def __init__(self, pin, pyfunc, args, pull_up=True):
        self.pin = pin
        self.pull_up = pull_up
        self.gpio = mraa.Gpio(pin)
        self.gpio.dir(mraa.DIR_IN)
        mode = mraa.EDGE_FALLING if pull_up else mraa.EDGE_RISING
        result = self.gpio.isr(mode, pyfunc, args)
        if result != mraa.SUCCESS:
            raise Exception("I could not configure ISR on pin {0}".
format(pin))

    def __del__(self):
        self.gpio.isrExit()
```

We have to specify the following arguments when we create an instance of the
`PushButtonWithInterrupt` class:

- The pin number to which the pushbutton is connected in the `pin` argument
- The function that will be called when the interrupt is triggered, that is,
  the interrupt handler function, in the `pyfunc` argument
- The arguments that will be passed to the interrupt handler function, in the
  `args` argument

In case we don't specify additional values, the optional `pull_up` argument will
be `True` and the instance will work as if the pushbutton were connected with a
pull-up resistor. If we work with a pull-down resistor, we must pass `False` in the
`pull_up` argument.

The constructor, that is, the __init__ method, creates a new `mraa.Gpio` instance
with the received `pin` as its `pin` argument, saves its reference in the `gpio` attribute
and calls its `dir` method to configure the pin to be an input pin (`mraa.DIR_IN`). Then,
the code determines the value of the `mode` local variable based on the value of the
`pull_up` parameter. If `pull_up` is true, the value will be `mraa.EDGE_FALLING` and
`mraa.EDGE_RISING` otherwise. The `mode` local variable holds the edge mode that
will trigger the interrupt. When we work with pull-up resistors and the user presses
a pushbutton, the signal will fall from high to low, and therefore, we want an edge
falling scenario to trigger the interrupt that indicates the button has been pressed.

Then, the code calls the `self.gpio.isr` method with the received `pin` as its `pin`
argument, the local `mode` variable as its `mode` argument, and the received `pyfunc` and
`args` as its `pyfunc` and `args` arguments. This way, we set the callback to be called
when the pin value changes because a pushbutton was pressed. As we determined
the appropriate value for the `mode` local variable before, we will configure the
appropriate edge mode that will trigger an interrupt when the button is pressed
based on the usage of pull-up or pull-down resistors. As previously explained,
not all the GPIO pins support interrupts, and therefore, it is necessary to check
the results of calling the `self.gpio.isr` method. In case an interrupt handler has
already been set to the pin with a previous call to the `self.gpio.isr` method
wouldn't return an `mraa.SUCCESS` value.

The `PushButtonWithInterrupt` class also declares a __del__ method that will
be called before Python removes an instance of this class from memory, that is,
when the object becomes inaccessible and gets deleted by the garbage-collection
mechanism. The method just calls the `self.gpio.isrExit` method to remove the
interrupt handler associated to the pin.

We will replace the two class attributes in the existing `BoardInteraction` class. Instead of working with `PushButton` instances, we will work with `PushButtonWithInterrupt` instances. The class methods declared in the class remain the same as in the code we are using as a baseline but they aren't included in the next lines. The code file for the sample is `iot_python_chapter_05_04.py`.

```
class BoardInteraction:
    # The Red LED is connected to pin ~6
    red_led = AnalogLed(6, 'Red')
    # The Green LED is connected to Pin ~5
    green_led = AnalogLed(5, 'Green')
    # The Blue LED is connected to Pin ~3
    blue_led = AnalogLed(3, 'Blue')
    # The push button to reset colors
    reset_push_button = PushButtonWithInterrupt(11,
    set_min_brightness_callback, set_min_brightness_callback)
    # The push button to set colors to their maximum brightness
    max_brightness_push_button = PushButtonWithInterrupt(10,
    set_max_brightness_callback, set_max_brightness_callback)
```

The highlighted lines of code declare two class attributes for the `BoardInteraction` class: `reset_push_button` and `max_brightness_push_button`. The `reset_push_button` class attribute is an instance of `PushButtonWithInterrupt` with its `pin` attribute set to `11` and its interrupt handler set to the `set_min_brightness_callback` function that we will declare later. This way, the instance will make all the necessary configurations to call the `set_min_brightness_callback` function when the user presses the pushbutton connected to GPIO pin number 11. The `max_brightness_push_button` class attribute is an instance of `PushButtonWithInterrupt` with its `pin` attribute set to `10`, and therefore, will make all the necessary configurations to call the `set_max_brightness_callback` function when the user presses the pushbutton connected to GPIO pin number 10.

Now, it is necessary to declare the functions that will be called when the interrupts are triggered: `set_min_brightness_callback` and `set_max_brightness_callback`. Notice that the functions are declared as functions and they aren't methods of any class.

```
def set_max_brightness_callback(args):
    print("You have pressed the maximum brightness pushbutton.")
    BoardInteraction.set_max_brightness()


def set_min_brightness_callback(args):
    print("You have pressed the reset pushbutton.")
    BoardInteraction.set_min_brightness()
```

Both functions declared in the previous code print a message indicating that a specific button has been pressed and call either the `BoardInteraction.set_max_brightness` or the `BoardInteraction.set_min_brightness` class method. We already know these class methods from our previous examples and we didn't have to make any changes to them.

Finally, it is necessary to replace the `__main__` method with a new one because we don't need to run a periodic callback anymore. Now, our `PushButtonWithInterrupt` instances configure the interrupt handlers that will be called whenever a pushbutton is pressed. The code file for the sample is `iot_python_chapter_05_04.py`.

```
if __name__ == "__main__":
    print("Listening at port 8888")
    application.listen(8888)
    ioloop = tornado.ioloop.IOLoop.instance()
    ioloop.start()
```

When the `__main__` method starts running, the `BoardInteraction` class already executed the code that creates the two `PushButtonWithInterrupt` instances, and therefore, the interrupt handlers will run whenever we press a pushbutton. The `__main__` method just builds and starts the HTTP server.

The following line will start the HTTP server and our new version of the RESTful API. Don't forget that you need to transfer the Python source code file to the Yocto Linux with an SFTP client.

```
python iot_python_chapter_05_04.py
```

After you run the example, press the pushbutton that sets the colors to their maximum brightness for 5 seconds. The RGB LED will display a white light and you will see the following output:

```
You are pressing the maximum brightness pushbutton.
Red LED connected to PWM Pin #6 set to brightness 255.
Green LED connected to PWM Pin #5 set to brightness 255.
Blue LED connected to PWM Pin #3 set to brightness 255.
```

You were pressing the pushbutton for 5 seconds but the output displayed the messages indicating that you were pressing the button just once. The GPIO pin number 10 signal went from high to low once when you pressed the button, and therefore, the `mraa.EDGE_FALLING` interrupt was fired and the configured interrupt handler (`set_max_brightness_callback`) was executed. You kept the pushbutton pressed, but the signal stayed in the low value, and therefore, the interrupt wasn't triggered again.

Obviously, when you want to run code just once when a pushbutton is pressed even for a long time, the usage of interrupt handlers provides the necessary precision that polling makes more complex to achieve.

Now, press the pushbutton that sets the colors to their minimum brightness for 10 seconds. The RGB LED will turn off and you will see the following output:

```
You are pressing the reset pushbutton.
Red LED connected to PWM Pin #6 set to brightness 0.
Green LED connected to PWM Pin #5 set to brightness 0.
Blue LED connected to PWM Pin #3 set to brightness 0.
```

As happened with the other pushbutton, you were pressing the pushbutton for many seconds but the output displayed the messages indicating that you were pressing the button just once. The GPIO pin number 11 signal went from high to low once when you pressed the button, and therefore, the `mraa.EDGE_FALLING` interrupt was fired and the configured interrupt handler (`set_min_brightness_callback`) was executed.

 We can make the same HTTP requests we made in our previous examples to check that we can achieve exactly the same results with the new code that works with interrupt handlers while running the HTTP server.

We can process HTTP requests and run interrupt handlers when the user presses pushbuttons. We improved accuracy compared with the previous version in which the code acted as if the pushbuttons were pressed many times when the user kept the pushbuttons for a long time. In addition, we removed the periodic callback.

 Whenever we have to read digital inputs, we can decide between working with polling or interrupt handlers based on the specific requirements we have for our projects. Sometimes, interrupt handlers are the best solution but in other cases polling is more suitable. It is very important to know that the `wiring-x86` library doesn't allow us to work with interrupt handlers for digital inputs, and therefore, in case we decide to use them, we have to work with the `mraa` library.

Test your knowledge

1. As an effect of using a pull-up resistor with a pushbutton, we will read the following value when the pushbutton is pressed in the GPIO pin to which it is connected:

    1. A low value (0V).

    2. A high value, that is, the IOREF voltage.

    3. A value between 1V and 3.3V.

2. As an effect of using a pull-up resistor with a pushbutton, we will read the following value when the pushbutton is released in the GPIO pin to which it is connected:

    1. A low value (0V).

    2. A high value, that is, the IOREF voltage.

    3. A value between 1V and 3.3V.

3. If we check a pushbutton status by reading the GPIO pin value to which it is connected with polling, the loop runs every 0.5 seconds and the user keeps the pushbutton pressed for 3 seconds:

    1. The code will behave as if the pushbutton was pressed more than once.

    2. The code will behave as if the pushbutton was pressed just once.

    3. The code will behave as if the pushbutton was never pressed.

4. We have an interrupt handler for a pushbutton with the interrupt edge mode set to `mraa.EDGE_FALLING`, and the pushbutton is connected with a pull-up resistor. If the user keeps the pushbutton pressed for 3 seconds:

    1. The code will behave as if the pushbutton was pressed more than once.

    2. The code will behave as if the pushbutton was pressed just once.

    3. The code will behave as if the pushbutton was never pressed.

5. In the Intel Galileo Gen 2 board, the pins labeled with the following symbol as a prefix for the number can be configured with interrupt handlers for digital inputs in the `mraa` library:

    1. Hash sign (#).

    2. Dollar sign ($).

    3. Tilde symbol (~).

Summary

In this chapter, we understood the difference between pull-up and pull-down resistors to wire pushbuttons and read their status with the mraa and wiring-x86 libraries. We understood the difference between reading the pushbutton statuses with polling and working with interrupts and interrupt handlers.

We created consistent code that allowed the user to perform the same actions with either pushbuttons in the breadboard or HTTP request. We combined code that reacts to changes in the statuses of the pushbuttons with a RESTful API built with Tornado Web server. As in the previous chapters, we took advantage of Python's object-oriented features and we created classes to encapsulate pushbuttons and the necessary configurations with the mraa and wiring-x86 libraries. Our code is easy to read and understand and we can easily switch the underlying low-level library.

Now that we were able to read digital inputs in different ways and configurations that made is possible for users to interact with our IoT device while it processed HTTP requests, we can work with more complex communications capabilities included in the board and take advantage of its storage, which are the topics of the next chapter.

6
Working with Analog Inputs and Local Storage

In this chapter, we will work with analog inputs to transform quantitative values retrieved from the real environment into qualitative values that we will use to fire actions. We will:

- Understand how analog inputs work
- Learn about the impact of the resolution of analog to digital converters
- Measure a voltage with an analog pin and the `mraa` library
- Include a photoresistor in a voltage divider and wire an analog input pin with a voltage source
- Transform a variable resistor into a voltage source
- Determine the darkness level with analog input and the `mraa` library
- Fire actions when the environment light changes
- Control analog inputs with the wiring-x86 library
- Work with different local storage options to log events

Understanding the analog inputs

In *Chapter 1, Understanding and Setting up the Base IoT Hardware*, we learned that the Intel Galileo Gen 2 board provides six analog input pins numbered from **A0** to **A5** and located in the lower-right corner of the front-side of the board. It is possible to measure from 0V (ground) to the value configured with the **IOREF** jumper position (5V by default) and the board provides 12 bits of resolution for the analog to digital converter. Thus, we can detect 4096 different values ($2^{12} = 4096$), or 4096 units, with values ranging from zero to 4095 (inclusive), where 0 represents 0V and 4095 means 5V.

In case you have an experience with other Arduino boards, you must take into account that the Intel Galileo Gen 2 board does not use the pin labeled **AREF**. In other Arduino boards, you can use this pin to set the analog reference voltage for the analog to digital conversion process. When we work with the Intel Galileo Gen 2 board, the maximum value for the analog pins is always going to be controlled by the **IOREF** jumper position (5V or 3.3V) and it is not possible to use any external reference for an analog input. In all our examples, we will work with the default position for the **IOREF** jumper, and therefore, the maximum value will be always 5V.

We just need to apply a linear function to convert the raw values read from the analog pin and map them to the input voltage values. If we use 12 bits of resolution, the detected values will have a minimum difference or step of 5V / 4095 = 0.001220012 V, approximately 1.22 mV (milliVolts) or 1.22E-03 V. We just need to multiply the raw value read from the analog pin by five and divide it by 4095.

The following graph shows the read values from an analog pin in the abscissa axis (*x*-axis) and the corresponding floating-point voltage value that it represents in the ordinate axis (*y*-axis).

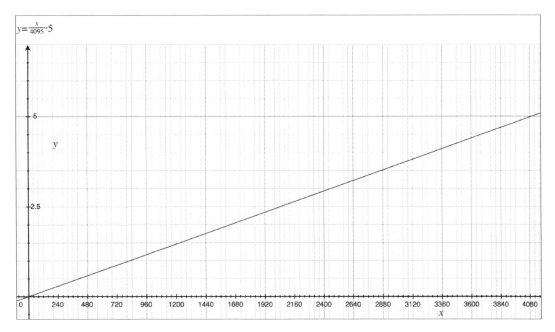

The equation for the previous graph is $y = x / 4095 * 5$, specifically `voltage_value = analog_pin_read_value / 4095 * 5`. We can run the following code in our Python interpreter to see the output with all the voltage values that can be generated with the formula for each raw value read from the analog pin from `0` to `4095` (inclusive).

```
for analog_pin_read_value in range(0, 4096):
    print(analog_pin_read_value / 4095.0 * 5.0)
```

We can also work with a lower resolution, such as 10 bits of resolution and we would be able to detect less different values, specifically 1024 different values (2^{10} = 1024), or 1024 units, from 0 to 1023 (inclusive). In this case, the values will have a minimum difference or step of 5V / 1023 = 0.004887585V, approximately 4.89mV (milliVolts) or 4.89E-03 V. In case we decide to work with this lower resolution, we just need to multiply the raw value read from the analog pin by five and divide it by 1023.

Wiring an analog input pin with a voltage source

The easiest way to understand how to read the values from analog pins and map these values back to voltage values is to work with a very simple example. We will connect a power source to one of the analog input pins, specifically a pack with two AA or AAA 1.25 V rechargeable batteries in series. It is also possible to use AA or AAA 1.5 V standard batteries in series. Note that the maximum voltage with the two rechargeable batteries in series will be 2.5 V (1.25 V * 2), while the maximum voltage with the two standard batteries in series will be 3 V (1.5 V * 2).

We will use the analog pin labeled **A0** to connect to the positive side (+) of the battery pack. Don't forget that the positive side (+) of the batter pack is connected to the battery's nipple. After we finish the necessary wirings, we will write Python code to measure the batteries pack voltage. This way, we will read the result of converting an analog value to its digital representation and we will map it to the voltage value. We need the following parts to work with this example:

- Two AA or AAA 1.25 V rechargeable batteries or two AA or AAA 1.5 V standard batteries.

- An appropriate battery holder to plug the two selected batteries in series and simplify wirings. For example, in case you use two AA 1.25 rechargeable batteries, you will need a 2 x AA battery holder.

- A 2200Ω (2k2Ω) resistor with 5% tolerance (red red red gold).

The following image shows the battery holder, the resistor connected to the breadboard, the necessary wirings, and the wirings from the Intel Galileo Gen 2 board to the breadboard. The Fritzing file for the sample is iot_fritzing_ chapter_06_01.fzz and the following image is the breadboard view:

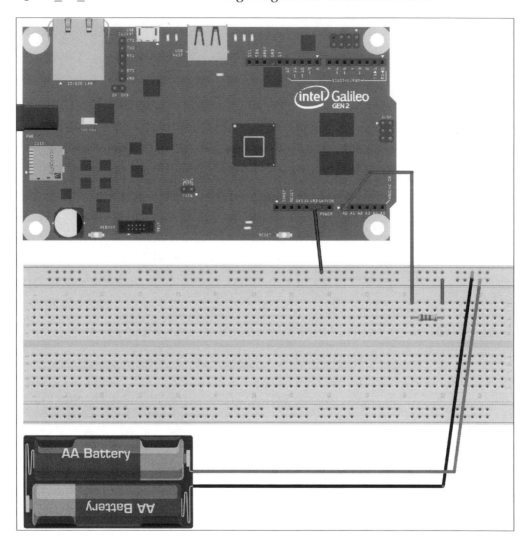

The following schematic shows the schematic with the electronic components represented as symbols:

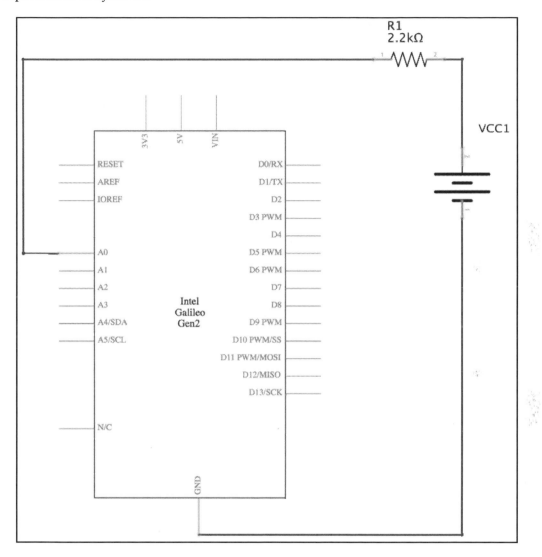

As seen in the previous schematic, the analog input pin labeled **A0** in the board's symbol, is connected to the positive terminal of the power source through the resistor. The negative terminal of the power source is connected to the ground.

Now, it's time to make all the necessary wirings. Don't forget to shutdown the Yocto Linux, wait for all the onboard LEDs to turn off, and unplug the power supply from the Intel Galileo Gen 2 board before adding or removing any wire from the board's pins.

Measuring voltage with analog inputs and the mraa library

We will create a new VoltageInput class to represent a voltage source connected to our board, specifically, to an analog input pin. The following lines show the code for the new VoltageInput class that works with the mraa library. The code file for the sample is iot_python_chapter_06_01.py.

```python
import mraa
import time


class VoltageInput:
    def __init__(self, analog_pin):
        self.analog_pin = analog_pin
        self.aio = mraa.Aio(analog_pin)
        # Configure ADC resolution to 12 bits (0 to 4095)
        self.aio.setBit(12)

    @property
    def voltage(self):
        raw_value = self.aio.read()
        return raw_value / 4095.0 * 5.0
```

We have to specify the analog pin number to which the voltage source is connected when we create an instance of the VoltageInput class in the analog_pin required argument. The constructor, that is, the __init__ method, creates a new mraa.Aio instance with the received analog_pin as its pin argument, saves its reference in the aio attribute and calls its setBit method to configure the analog to digital converter resolution to be of 12 bits, that is, to provide 4096 possible values to represent from 0 to 5V.

The class defines a voltage property that calls the read method for the related mraa.Aio instance (self.aio) to retrieve the raw value from the analog pin and saves it in the raw_value variable. Then, the code returns the result of dividing raw_value by 4095 and multiplying it by 5. This way, the property returns the voltage value, converted from the raw value returned by the read function.

Now, we can write code that uses the new `VoltageInput` class to create an instance for the battery pack and easily retrieve the voltage value. The new class makes the necessary calculations to map the read value into a voltage value, and therefore, we just need to check the value of the `voltage` property without worrying about the specific details about the analog to digital converter and its resolution.

Now, we will write a loop that will retrieve the voltage value every second. The code file for the sample is `iot_python_chapter_06_01.py`.

```
if __name__ == "__main__":
    v0 = VoltageInput(0)
    while True:
        print("Voltage at pin A0: {0}".format(v0.voltage))
        # Sleep 1 second
        time.sleep(2)
```

The first line creates an instance of the previously coded `VoltageInput` class with 0 as the value of the `analog_pin` argument. This way, the instance will read the analog values from the pin labeled **A0**, that is connected to the positive terminal of the power source through the resistor.

Then, the code runs a loop forever, that is, until you interrupt the execution by pressing *Ctrl* + *C* or the button to stop the process in case you are using a Python IDE with remote development features to run the code in your board. The loop prints the voltage value at pin **A0** every two seconds. The following lines show a sample output line generated when the code is executed with two rechargeable batteries that have lost a bit of their charge:

```
Voltage at pin A0: 2.47130647131
```

Wiring a photoresistor to an analog input pin

Now, we will use a photoresistor, that is, a light sensor, specifically, an electronic component that provides a variable resistor that changes the resistor value based on the incident light intensity. As the incident light intensity increases, the resistance of the photoresistor decreases, and vice versa.

A photoresistor is also known as an **LDR** (short for **Light-Dependent Resistor**) or photocell. Bear in mind that pohotoresistors are not the best components to sense light with great accuracy. However, they are extremely useful to easily determine whether we are in a dark environment when we don't have problems with latencies that can reach one second.

We cannot measure a resistance value with our board. However, we can read voltage values, and therefore, we will use a voltage divider configuration that will include the photoresistor as one of its two resistors. The voltage divider will output a high voltage value when the photoresistor receives a high amount of light and it will output a low voltage value when the photoresistor is in a dark zone, that is, when it receives little or no light at all.

We learned how to read values from analog pins and map these values back to voltage values in the previous examples. We will use this knowledge to determine when it becomes dark using the photoresistor. Once we understand how the sensor works, we will react to the changes in the light conditions and we will log data about specific scenarios.

We will use the analog pin labeled **A0** to connect the positive side (+) of the voltage divider that includes a photoresistor. After we finish the necessary wirings, we will write Python code to determine whether we are in a dark environment or not. This way, we will read the result of converting a resistance value into a voltage, and then converting this analog value into its digital representation. As we learned in our previous example, we will map the read digital value to a voltage value and then we will map this voltage value to a darkness measurement value. It sounds like a big mess, but it is really easier than it sounds. We need the following parts to work with this example:

- A photoresistor
- A 10,000Ω (10kΩ) resistor with 5% tolerance (brown black orange gold)

The following diagram shows the photoresistor and the resistor connected to the breadboard, the necessary wirings and the wirings from the Intel Galileo Gen 2 board to the breadboard. The Fritzing file for the sample is `iot_fritzing_chapter_06_02.fzz` and the following picture is the breadboard view:

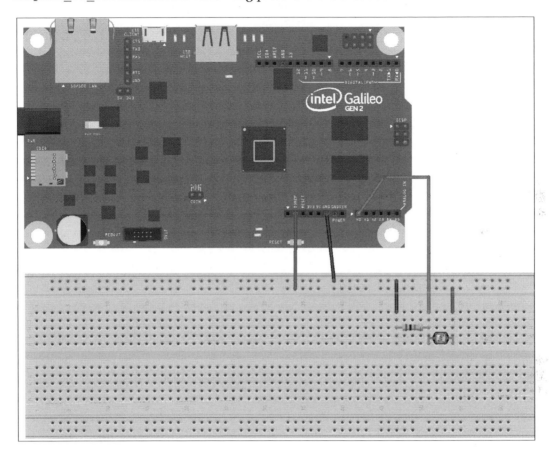

The following picture shows the schematic with the electronic components represented as symbols:

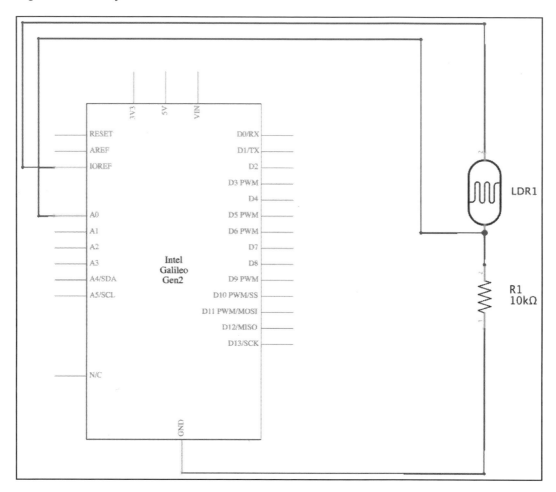

As seen in the previous schematic, the GPIO pin labeled **A0** in the board's symbol is connected to the voltage divider built with the photoresistor named **LDR1** and a 10kΩ resistor with 5% tolerance named **R1**. The **LDR1** photoresistor is wired to the **IOREF** pin. We already know that the pin labeled **IOREF** provides us the IOREF voltage, that is, 5V in our actual configuration. The **R1** resistor is wired to **GND** (ground).

Now, it is time make all the necessary wirings. Don't forget to shutdown the Yocto Linux, wait for all the onboard LEDs to turn off, and unplug the power supply from the Intel Galileo Gen 2 board before adding or removing any wire from the board's pins.

Determining the darkness level with analog inputs and the mraa library

We will create a new `DarknessSensor` class to represent the photoresistor included in the voltage divider and connected to our board, specifically, to an analog input pin. As we already wrote code to read and transform an analog input, we will use the previously created `VoltageInput` class. The following lines show the code for the new `DarknessSensor` class that works with the `mraa` library. The code file for the sample is `iot_python_chapter_06_02.py`.

```python
import mraa
import time


class DarknessSensor:
    # Light level descriptions
    light_extremely_dark = "extremely dark"
    light_very_dark = "very dark"
    light_dark = "just dark"
    light_no_need_for_a_flashlight = \
        "there is no need for a flashlight"
    # Maximum voltages that determine the light level
    extremely_dark_max_voltage = 2.0
    very_dark_max_voltage = 3.0
    dark_max_voltage = 4.0

    def __init__(self, analog_pin):
        self.voltage_input = VoltageInput(analog_pin)
        self.voltage = 0.0
        self.ambient_light = self.__class__.light_extremely_dark
        self.measure_light()

    def measure_light(self):
        self.voltage = self.voltage_input.voltage
        if self.voltage < self.__class__.extremely_dark_max_voltage:
            self.ambient_light = self.__class__.light_extremely_dark
        elif self.voltage < self.__class__.very_dark_max_voltage:
            self.ambient_light = self.__class__.light_very_dark
        elif self.voltage < self.__class__.dark_max_voltage:
            self.ambient_light = self.__class__.light_dark
        else:
            self.ambient_light = self.__class__.light_no_need_for_a_
flashlight
```

We have to specify the analog pin number to which the voltage divider, which includes the photoresistor, is connected when we create an instance of the DarknessSensor class in the analog_pin required argument. The constructor, that is, the __init__ method, creates a new VoltageInput instance with the received analog_pin as its analog_pin argument and saves its reference in the voltage_input attribute. Then, the constructor creates and initializes two attributes: voltage and ambient_light. Finally, the constructor calls the measure_light method.

The class defines a measure_light method that saves the voltage value retrieved by checking the self.voltage_input.voltage property in the voltage attribute (self.voltage). This way, the code can check whether the value stored in the voltage attribute is lower than the three maximum voltage values that determine the light level and sets the appropriate value for the ambient_light attribute (self.ambient_light).

The class defines the following three class attributes that determine the maximum voltage values that determine each light level:

- extremely_dark_max_voltage: If the retrieved voltage is lower than 2V, it means that the environment is extremely dark
- very_dark_max_voltage: If the retrieved voltage is lower than 3V, it means that the environment is very dark
- dark_max_voltage. If the retrieved voltage is lower than 4V, it means that the environment is just dark

The values are configured for a specific photoresistor and environment conditions. You might need to set different values based on the voltage values retrieved with the photoresistor included in the voltage divider. Once you run the sample, you can check the voltage values and make the necessary adjustments to the voltage values stored in the previously explained class attributes. Remember that the voltage value will be higher, that is, closer to 5V, when the incident light increases. Thus, the darkest environment, the lower the measured voltage.

Our goal is to convert a quantitative value, specifically, a voltage value, into a qualitative value, that is, a value that explains the real situation in a real environment. The class defines the following four class attributes that specify the light level descriptions and determine one of the four light levels in which a voltage value will be converted after we call the `measure_light` method:

- `light_extremely_dark`
- `light_very_dark`
- `light_dark`
- `light_no_need_for_a_flashlight`

Now, we can write the code that uses the new `DarkSensor` class to create an instance for the photoresistor included in the voltage divider and easily print a description of the light conditions. The new class uses the previously created `VoltageInput` class to make the necessary calculations to map the read value into a voltage value, and then, transforms it into a qualitative value that provides us with a description of the light conditions. Now, we will write a loop that will check whether the light conditions changed every two seconds. The code file for the sample is `iot_python_chapter_06_02.py`.

```
if __name__ == "__main__":
    darkness_sensor = DarknessSensor(0)
    last_ambient_light = ""
    while True:
        darkness_sensor.measure_light()
        new_ambient_light = darkness_sensor.ambient_light
        if new_ambient_light != last_ambient_light:
            # The ambient light value changed
            last_ambient_light = new_ambient_light
            print("Darkness level: {0}".format(new_ambient_light))
        # Sleep 2 seconds
        time.sleep(2)
```

The first line creates an instance of the previously coded `DarknessSensor` class with 0 as the value of the `analog_pin` argument and saves the instance in the `darkness_sensor` local variable. This way, the instance will use an instance of the `VoltageInput` class to read the analog values from the pin labeled **A0**. Then, the code initializes the `last_ambient_light` local variable with an empty string.

Then, the code runs a loop forever, that is, until you interrupt the execution by pressing *Ctrl + C* or the button to stop the process in case you are using a Python IDE with remote development features to run the code in your board. The loop calls the `darkness_sensor.measure_light` method to retrieve the current light conditions and saves the updated `darkness_sensor.ambient_light` value in the `new_ambient_light` local variable. Then, the code checks whether the `new_ambient_light` value is different from `last_ambient_light`. In case they are different, it means that the ambient light has changed, and therefore, it sets the value for `last_ambient_light` equal to `new_ambient_light`, and prints the ambient light description stored in `new_ambient_light`.

The loop prints the ambient light description only when it changes from the last printed value, and checks the ambient light every two seconds. The following line will start the example. Don't forget that you need to transfer the Python source code file to the Yocto Linux with an SFTP client.

```
python iot_python_chapter_06_02.py
```

After you run the example, perform the following actions:

- Use a smartphone or a flashlight to induce light over the photoresistor
- Use your hand to generate a shadow over the photoresistor
- Reduce the light in the environment, but not the minimum, just make it a bit dark
- Reduce the light in the environment to the minimum, a complete dark environment with no light at all

As a result of the previous actions, you should see the following output:

```
Darkness level: there is no need for a flashlight
Darkness level: just dark
Darkness level: very dark
Darkness level: extremely dark
```

Firing actions when the environment light changes

In previous examples, we worked with PWM to set the brightness level for the red, green, and blue components of an RGB LED. Now, we will add an RGB LED and we will set the brightness level for its three components based on the ambient light detected with the photoresistor. We will wire the RGB LED as we did in the example in which we worked with this component in *Chapter 4, Working with a RESTful API and Pulse Width Modulation*. We will use the following PWM output pins:

- Pin ~**6** to connect the anode pin for red LED
- Pin ~**5** to connect the anode pin for green LED
- Pin ~**3** to connect the anode pin for blue LED.

We need the following additional parts to work with this example:

- One common cathode 5mm RGB LED
- Three 270Ω resistors with 5% tolerance (red violet brown gold)

The following diagram shows the components connected to the breadboard, the necessary wirings and the wirings from the Intel Galileo Gen 2 board to the breadboard. The Fritzing file for the sample is `iot_fritzing_chapter_06_03.fzz` and the following picture is the breadboard view:

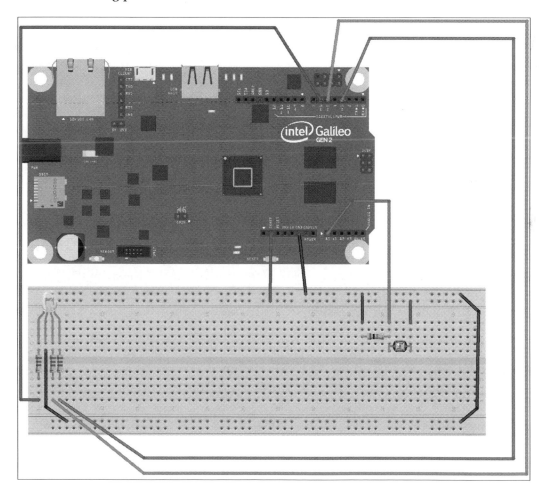

The following picture shows the schematic with the electronic components represented as symbols:

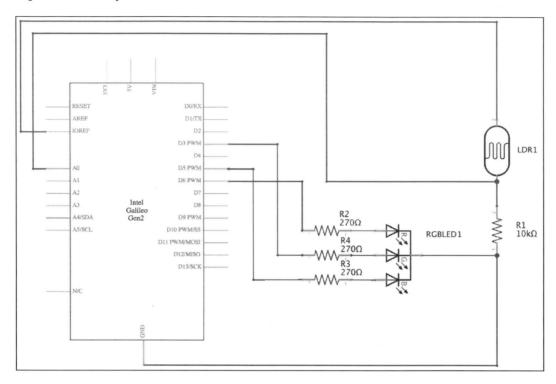

As seen in the previous schematic, three PWM capable GPIO pins labeled **D3 PWM**, **D5 PWM**, and **D6 PWM** in the board's symbol is connected to a 270Ω resistor, wired to an anode pin for each LED color, and the common cathode is connected to ground.

Now, it is time to insert the components in the breadboard and make all the necessary wirings. Don't forget to shutdown the Yocto Linux, wait for all the onboard LEDs to turn off, and unplug the power supply from the Intel Galileo Gen 2 board before adding or removing any wire from the board's pins.

We will add the code for the AnalogLed class that represent an LED connected to our board that can have a brightness level from 0 to 255 inclusive. We created this class in *Chapter 4, Working with a RESTful API and Pulse Width Modulation* and the code file for the sample was iot_python_chapter_04_02.py.

We will create a new `BoardInteraction` class to create an instance of our `DarknessSensor` class and one instance for each component of the RGB LED and easily control their brightness levels. The following lines show the code for the `BoardInteraction` class. The code file for the sample is `iot_python_chapter_06_03.py`:

```python
class BoardInteraction:
    # The photoresistor included in the voltage divider
    # is connected to analog PIN A0
    darkness_sensor = DarknessSensor(0)
    # The Red LED is connected to GPIO pin ~6
    red_led = AnalogLed(6, 'Red')
    # The Green LED is connected to GPIO Pin ~5
    green_led = AnalogLed(5, 'Green')
    # The Blue LED is connected to GPIO Pin ~3
    blue_led = AnalogLed(3, 'Blue')

    @classmethod
    def set_rgb_led_brightness(cls, brightness_level):
        cls.red_led.set_brightness(brightness_level)
        cls.green_led.set_brightness(brightness_level)
        cls.blue_led.set_brightness(brightness_level)

    @classmethod
    def update_leds_brightness(cls):
        if cls.darkness_sensor.ambient_light == DarknessSensor.light_extremely_dark:
            cls.set_rgb_led_brightness(255)
        elif cls.darkness_sensor.ambient_light == DarknessSensor.light_very_dark:
            cls.set_rgb_led_brightness(128)
        elif cls.darkness_sensor.ambient_light == DarknessSensor.light_dark:
            cls.set_rgb_led_brightness(64)
        else:
            cls.set_rgb_led_brightness(0)
```

The BoardInteraction class declares four class attributes: darkness_sensor, red_led, green_led and blue_led. The first class attribute saves a new instance of the DarknessSensor class and the last three class attributes save new instances of the previously imported AnalogLed class and represent the red, green, and blue LEDs connected to pins ~**6**, ~**5**, and ~**3**. Then, the BoardInteraction class declares the following two class methods:

- set_rgb_led_brightness: Sets the same brightness level received in the brightness_level argument to the three components of the RGB LED.

- update_leds_brightness: Sets the brightness level for the three components of the RGB LED based on the ambient_light value of the DarknessSensor instance (cls.darkness_sensor). If it is extremely dark, the brightness level will be 255. If it is very dark, the brightness level will be 128. If it is dark, the brightness level will be 64. Otherwise, the RGB LED will be completely turned off.

Now, we can write a code that uses the new BoardInteraction class to measure the ambient light and set the brightness for the RGB LED based on the retrieved value. As in our previous example, we will only make changes when the ambient light value changes from the current value. We will write a loop that will check whether the light conditions changed every two seconds. The code file for the sample is iot_python_chapter_06_03.py.

```
last_ambient_light = ""
while True:
    BoardInteraction.darkness_sensor.measure_light()
    new_ambient_light = BoardInteraction.darkness_sensor.ambient_
light
    if new_ambient_light != last_ambient_light:
        # The ambient light value changed
        last_ambient_light = new_ambient_light
        print("Darkness level: {0}".format(new_ambient_light))
        BoardInteraction.update_leds_brightness()
    # Sleep 2 seconds
    time.sleep(2)
```

The first line initializes the `last_ambient_light` local variable with an empty string. Then, the code runs a loop forever, that is, until you interrupt the execution. The loop calls the `BoardInteraction.darkness_sensor.measure_light` method to retrieve the current light conditions and saves the updated `BoardInteraction.darkness_sensor.ambient_light` value in the `new_ambient_light` local variable. Then, the code checks whether the `new_ambient_light` value is different from `last_ambient_light`. In case they are different, it means that the ambient light has changed, and therefore, it sets the value for `last_ambient_light` equal to `new_ambient_light`, prints the ambient light description stored in `new_ambient_light` and calls the `BoardInteraction.update_leds_brightness` method to set the brightness for the RGB LED based on the ambient light.

The following line will start the example. Don't forget that you need to transfer the Python source code file to the Yocto Linux with an SFTP client.

```
python iot_python_chapter_06_03.py
```

After you run the example, perform the following actions, and you will see the RGB LED changing its brightness level as explained:

- Use a smartphone or a flashlight to induce light over the photoresistor. The RGB LED will stay turned off.

- Use your hand to generate a shadow over the photoresistor. The RGB LED will turn on with a dimmed light.

- Reduce the light in the environment, but not the minimum, just make it a bit dark. The RGB LED will increase its brightness.

- Reduce the light in the environment to the minimum, a complete dark environment with no light at all. The RBG LED will increase its brightness to the maximum level.

- Use a smartphone or a flashlight to induce light over the photoresistor, again. The RGB LED will turn off.

As a result of the previous actions, you should see the following output:

```
Darkness level: there is no need for a flashlight
Red LED connected to PWM Pin #6 set to brightness 0.
Green LED connected to PWM Pin #5 set to brightness 0.
Blue LED connected to PWM Pin #3 set to brightness 0.
Darkness level: just dark
Red LED connected to PWM Pin #6 set to brightness 64.
Green LED connected to PWM Pin #5 set to brightness 64.
Blue LED connected to PWM Pin #3 set to brightness 64.
Darkness level: very dark
Red LED connected to PWM Pin #6 set to brightness 128.
Green LED connected to PWM Pin #5 set to brightness 128.
Blue LED connected to PWM Pin #3 set to brightness 128.
Darkness level: extremely dark
Red LED connected to PWM Pin #6 set to brightness 255.
Green LED connected to PWM Pin #5 set to brightness 255.
Blue LED connected to PWM Pin #3 set to brightness 255.
Darkness level: there is no need for a flashlight
Red LED connected to PWM Pin #6 set to brightness 0.
Green LED connected to PWM Pin #5 set to brightness 0.
Blue LED connected to PWM Pin #3 set to brightness 0.
```

We wrote object-oriented Python code that is easy to read and understand. With the help of the mraa library, we could easily fire actions when the environment light changes. We could control the brightness for an RGB LED when the ambient light changed. We worked with an analog input to determine the ambient light level and we used PWM to generate an analog output and control the RGB LED brightness level.

Controlling analog inputs with the wiring-x86 library

So far, we have been using the mraa library to work with analog inputs and retrieve the ambient light level. However, we have also been working with the wiring-x86 library in our previous examples. We can change just a few lines of our object-oriented code to replace the mraa library with the wiring-x86 one to read analog values.

First, we have to replace the code for the AnalogLed class with the version that works with the wiring-x86 library. We created this version in *Chapter 4, Working with a RESTful API and Pulse Width Modulation,* and the code file for the sample was iot_python_chapter_04_04.py. When we grab the code for the AnalogLed class, we will also have the Board class.

The following lines shows the new version of the VoltageInput class that works with the wiring-x86 library instead of using mraa. The code file for the sample is iot_python_chapter_06_04.py.

```python
from wiringx86 import GPIOGalileoGen2 as GPIO


class VoltageInput:
    initial_analog_pin_number = 14

    def __init__(self, analog_pin):
        self.analog_pin = analog_pin
        self.gpio = Board.gpio
        self.gpio.pinMode(
            analog_pin + self.__class__.initial_analog_pin_number,
            self.gpio.ANALOG_INPUT)

    @property
    def voltage(self):
        raw_value = self.gpio.analogRead(
            self.analog_pin +
            self.__class__.initial_analog_pin_number)
        return raw_value / 1023.0 * 5.0
```

We created a new version of the VoltageInput class that declares an initial_analog_pin_number class attribute set to 14. The wiring-x86 library uses Arduino compatible numbers to reference the analog input pins or ADC pins. Thus, analog input pin 0 is known as 14, analog input pin 1 as 15, and so on. As we don't want to make changes to the rest of our code, we use a class attribute to specify the number that we must sum to the received analog_pin value to convert it to a wiring-x86 analog pin number.

The constructor, that is, the __init__ method, saves a reference to the Board.gpio class attribute in self.gpio and calls its pinMode method with the received analog_ pin and the value specified in initial_analog_pin_number class attribute as its pin argument, and self.gpio.ANALOG_INPUT as its mode argument. This way, we configure the pin to be an analog input pin converting the analog input pin number into a wiring-x86 compatible analog input pin number. The wiring-x86 library doesn't make a difference between GPIO and analog I/O pins, and we can manage all of them through the Board.gpio class attribute.

All the VoltageInput instances will save a reference to the same Board.gpio class attribute that created an instance of the GPIO class, specifically, the wiringx86. GPIOGalileoGen2 class with its debug argument set to False to avoid unnecessary debug information for the low-level communications.

The class defines a voltage property that calls the analogRead method for the GPIO instance (self.gpio) to retrieve the raw value from the analog pin and saves it in the raw_value variable. The result of the self.analog_pin attribute plus the value specified in initial_analog_pin_number class attribute specifies the pin value for the analogRead method call. Then, the code returns the result of dividing raw_value by 1023 and multiplying it by 5. This way, the property returns the voltage value, converted from the raw value returned by the analogRead function.

> Unluckily, the wiring-x86 library doesn't support 12 bit of resolution for the analog to digital converter. The library works with a fixed 10 bit of resolution, and therefore, we are only able to detect 1024 different values (2^{10} = 1024), or 1024 units, with values ranging from 0 to 1023 (inclusive), where 0 represents 0V and 1023 means 5V. For this reason, we have to divide raw_value by 1023 instead of 4095 within the voltage property.

The rest of the code remains the same one that we have used for the previous example. There is no need to make changes to the DarknessSensor class, the BoardInteraction class or the main loop because they will automatically work with the new VoltageInput class and there were no changes in the arguments for its constructor or its voltage property.

The following line will start the new version of the example that works with the `wiring-x86` library:

```
python iot_python_chapter_06_04.py
```

 We can make the same changes in the incident light over the photoresistor that we made in our previous example to check that we can achieve exactly the same results with the `wiring-x86` library. The only difference will be in the precision of the voltage values retrieved because we are working with 10 bits of resolution in the analog to digital converter in this case.

Logging to files in the local storage

Python provides a powerful and flexible logging API provided by a standard library module. We can use the logging module to track events that happen when our IoT applications run on the board and save them on a log file by taking advantage of the local storage options.

Now, we will make changes to our last version of our previous example that worked with the `mraa` library to log the voltage values read from the ambient light sensor. We only want to log the new voltage value when the ambient light changes, that is, when the value for `BoardInteraction.darkness_sensor.ambient_light` mutates. We will use the previous code as a baseline to add the new logging features. The code file for the sample was `iot_python_chapter_06_03.py`.

We will replace the `__main__` method. The following lines show the new version that adds logging capabilities. The new lines of code are highlighted and the code file for the sample is `iot_python_chapter_06_05.py`.

```
import logging

if __name__ == "__main__":
    logging.basicConfig(
        filename="iot_python_chapter_06_05.log",
        level=logging.INFO,
        format="%(asctime)s %(message)s",
        datefmt="%m/%d/%Y %I:%M:%S %p")
    logging.info("Application started")
```

```
        last_ambient_light = ""
        last_voltage = 0.0
        while True:
            BoardInteraction.darkness_sensor.measure_light()
            new_ambient_light = BoardInteraction.darkness_sensor.ambient_
light
            if new_ambient_light != last_ambient_light:
                # The ambient light value changed
                logging.info(
                    "Ambient light value changed from {0} to {1}".format(
                        last_voltage, BoardInteraction.darkness_sensor.
voltage))
                last_ambient_light = new_ambient_light
                last_voltage = BoardInteraction.darkness_sensor.voltage
                print("Darkness level: {0}".format(new_ambient_light))
                BoardInteraction.update_leds_brightness()
            # Sleep 2 seconds
            time.sleep(2)
```

The first line calls the `logging.basicConfig` method to do the basic configuration for the logging system. The `fileName` argument specifies `"iot_python_chapter_06_05.log"` as the file name we want to use for logging. As we don't specify a value for the `fileMode` argument, the default `'a'` mode is used and the messages from successive runs will be appended to the specified log file name, that is, the file will never be overwritten.

> We didn't specify any path in the `fileName` argument, and therefore, the log file will be created in the same folder in which the Python script runs, that is, the `/home/root` folder. In this case, the log file will be using the storage space available in the microSD card that boots the Yocto Linux distribution.

The `format` argument specifies `"%(asctime)s %(message)s"` because we want to store the date and time followed by a message. The `datefmt` argument specifies `"%m/%d/%Y %I:%M:%S %p"` as the date and time format we want to use for the date and time that will be included as a prefix for all the lines appended to the log. We want a short date (month/date/year) followed by a short time (hours/minutes/seconds AM/PM). We just want to log the information logs to the file, and therefore, the `level` argument specifies `logging.INFO` to set the root logger level to this value.

The next line calls the `logging.info` method to log the first event: the application that has started its execution. Before entering into the loop, the code declared a new `last_voltage` local variable and initializes it to `0.0`. We want to log the previous voltage and the new voltage whenever the ambient light changes, and therefore, it is necessary to save the last voltage in a new variable. When the ambient light changes, a call to the `logging.info` method logs the transition from the previous voltage to the new voltage value. However, it is very important to notice that the first time this method is called, the previous voltage will be equal to `0.0`. The next line saves the value for the `BoardInteraction.darkness_sensor.voltage` in the `last_voltage` variable.

The following line will start the new version of the example that will create the `iot_python_chapter_06_05.log` file:

```
python iot_python_chapter_06_05.py
```

Keep the Python script running for a few minutes and make many changes in the incident light over the photoresistor. This way, you will generate many lines in the log file. Then, you can use your favorite SFTP client to download the log file from `/home/root` and read it.

The following lines show some sample lines generated in the log file after executing the application:

```
03/08/2016 04:54:46 PM Application started
03/08/2016 04:54:46 PM Ambient light value changed from 0.0 to
4.01953601954
03/08/2016 04:55:20 PM Ambient light value changed from 4.01953601954
to 3.91208791209
03/08/2016 04:55:26 PM Ambient light value changed from 3.91208791209
to 2.49572649573
03/08/2016 04:55:30 PM Ambient light value changed from 2.49572649573
to 3.40903540904
03/08/2016 04:55:34 PM Ambient light value changed from 3.40903540904
to 2.19291819292
03/08/2016 04:55:38 PM Ambient light value changed from 2.19291819292
to 3.83394383394
03/08/2016 04:55:42 PM Ambient light value changed from 3.83394383394
to 4.0
03/08/2016 04:55:48 PM Ambient light value changed from 4.0 to
3.40903540904
```

```
03/08/2016 04:55:50 PM Ambient light value changed from 3.40903540904
to 2.89133089133
03/08/2016 04:55:56 PM Ambient light value changed from 2.89133089133
to 3.88278388278
03/08/2016 04:55:58 PM Ambient light value changed from 3.88278388278
to 4.69841269841
03/08/2016 04:56:00 PM Ambient light value changed from 4.69841269841
to 3.93650793651
```

Working with USB attached storage

Log files that record events related to sensors can grow really fast, and therefore, storing log files in the the microSD storage space might become a problem. We can work with microSD cards up to 32 GB. Thus, one option is to create the Yocto Linux image on a bigger microSD card and continue working with a single storage. This would require us to expand the partition from the default image. The other option is to take advantage of the cloud and just keep a constrained log in our local storage. However, we will work with this option later. Now, we want to explore the additional options we have to use local storage.

As we learned in *Chapter 1, Understanding and Setting up the Base IoT Hardware*, The Intel Galileo Gen 2 board provides a USB 2.0 host connector, labeled **USB HOST**. We can use this connector to plug a USB thumb drive for additional storage and save the log file in this new storage.

Before you plug any USB thumb drive, run the following command in the SSH terminal to list the partition tables:

```
fdisk -l
```

The following lines show an example of the output generated by the previous command. Your output might be different because it depends on the microSD card that you are using to boot Yocto Linux. Notice that the /dev/mmcblk0 disk identifies the microSD card and you have two partitions: /dev/mmcblk0p1 and /dev/mmcblk0p2.

```
Disk /dev/mmcblk0: 7.2 GiB, 7746879488 bytes, 15130624 sectors
Units: sectors of 1 * 512 = 512 bytes
Sector size (logical/physical): 512 bytes / 512 bytes
I/O size (minimum/optimal): 512 bytes / 512 bytes
Disklabel type: dos
Disk identifier: 0x000a69e4

Device         Boot    Start      End  Blocks  Id System
/dev/mmcblk0p1 *        2048   106495   52224  83 Linux
/dev/mmcblk0p2        106496  2768895 1331200  83 Linux
```

Now, we will plug a USB thumb drive to the board's USB 2.0 host connector, we will run the necessary commands to mount it, and then we will make change to the code to save the log in a folder within the USB thumb drive. You will need a preformatted USB thumb drive compatible with USB 2.0 to run this example.

The following picture shows a USB thumb drive plugged to the board's USB 2.0 host connector, labeled **USB HOST**. Wait a few seconds after you plug the USB thumb drive.

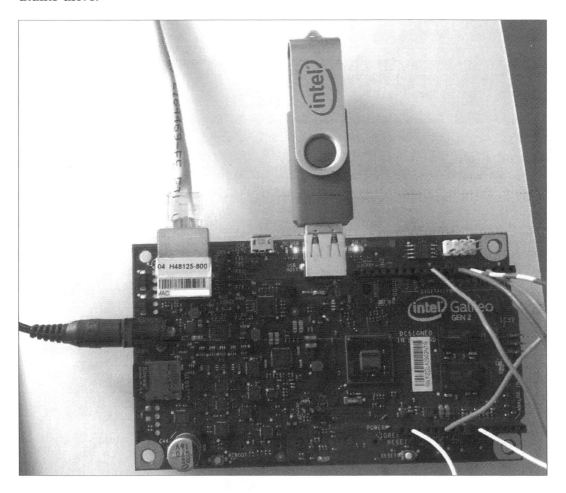

Yocto Linux will add a new block device to the /dev folder. Run the following command in the SSH terminal to list the partition tables:

```
fdisk -l
```

The following lines show an example of the output generated by the previous command. Your output might be different because it depends on the USB drive and also on the microSD card that you are using. Compare the output with the output generated when you executed the same command before you plugged the USB thumb drive. The additional lines provide information about the USB thumb drive, its disk name, and its partitions. The highlighted lines show the partition details for the USB thumb, identified as the /dev/sda disk and with a FAT32 partition /dev/sda1. We will use this partition name for one of our next steps.

```
Disk /dev/mmcblk0: 7.2 GiB, 7746879488 bytes, 15130624 sectors
Units: sectors of 1 * 512 = 512 bytes
Sector size (logical/physical): 512 bytes / 512 bytes
I/O size (minimum/optimal): 512 bytes / 512 bytes
Disklabel type: dos
Disk identifier: 0x000a69e4


Device          Boot    Start      End  Blocks  Id System
/dev/mmcblk0p1  *        2048   106495   52224  83 Linux
/dev/mmcblk0p2          106496  2768895 1331200 83 Linux


Disk /dev/sda: 3.8 GiB, 4026531840 bytes, 7864320 sectors
Units: sectors of 1 * 512 = 512 bytes
Sector size (logical/physical): 512 bytes / 512 bytes
I/O size (minimum/optimal): 512 bytes / 512 bytes
Disklabel type: dos
Disk identifier: 0x02bb0a1a

Device     Boot Start      End  Blocks  Id System
/dev/sda1  *       64  7864319 3932128   b W95 FAT32
```

Now, it is necessary to create a mount point. We have to create a new sub-folder in the /media folder. We will use usb as the name for the sub-folder, and therefore, the folder in which we will mount the drive will be /media/usb. Run the following command to create the folder:

```
mkdir /media/usb
```

Run the following command to mount the partition in the recently created /media/usb folder. In the previous steps we retrieved the partition name and it was named /dev/sda1. Your partition name might be different, and therefore, you just need to replace /dev/sda1 with your partition name listed when you executed the fdisk command that listed the disks and their partitions.

```
mount /dev/sda1 /media/usb
```

Now, we can access the contents of the USB thumb drive through the `/media/usb` folder, that is, whenever we create a folder or file in this folder, we are writing to the USB thumb drive partition.

Run the following command to create a new `/media/usb/log` folder in which we will store the log for our IoT application:

```
mkdir /media/usb/log
```

Now, we will change the value we pass to the filename argument when we call the `logging.basicConfig` method within the __main__ method. We want to save the log file within the `/media/usb/log` folder. This way, we will store it in the USB thumb drive, in the `log` folder. We will use the previous code as a baseline to change the log file name and its path. The code file for the sample was `iot_python_chapter_06_05.py`.

The following lines show the new code that calls the `logging.basicConfig` method and the code file for the sample is `iot_python_chapter_06_06.py`. The rest of the code remains the same we have used in our previous example.

```python
import logging


if __name__ == "__main__":
    logging.basicConfig(
        filename="/media/usb/log/iot_python_chapter_06_06.log",
        level=logging.INFO,
        format="%(asctime)s %(message)s",
        datefmt="%m/%d/%Y %I:%M:%S %p")
```

The following line will start the new version of the example that will create the `iot_python_chapter_06_06.log` file in the `/media/usb/log` folder:

```
python iot_python_chapter_06_06.py
```

Keep the Python script running for a few minutes and make many changes in the incident light over the photoresistor. This way, you will generate many lines in the log file. Then, you can use your favorite SFTP client to download the log file from `/media/usb/log` and read it. However, don't forget to go back to the `home/root` folder in your SFTP client because this is the folder in which you upload the Python scripts.

If you need to unplug the USB thumb drive to plug it on another computer or device, first you must interrupt the execution of the Python script, and then, you must run the following command to unmount the partition. In the previous steps we retrieved the partition name and it was named /dev/sda1. Your partition name might be different, and therefore, you just need to replace /dev/sda1 with your partition name listed when you executed the fdisk command that listed the disks and their partitions. Be careful and make sure you run this command on the terminal that is running the shell on the Yocto Linux. Make sure you see the root@galileo:~# prompt before you execute it. If you run the command in a computer that runs Linux or OS X, you might unmount one of your drives.

```
umount /dev/sda1
```

Now, you can remove the USB thumb drive from the USB 2.0 host connector.

Test your knowledge

1. The Intel Galileo Gen 2 board provides the following resolution for the analog to digital converter:

    1. 32 bits.

    2. 64 bits.

    3. 12 bits.

2. The analog pins allow us to detect a maximum of:

    1. 4,096 different values, with values ranging from 0 to 4095 (inclusive).

    2. 16,384 different values, with values ranging from 0 to 16,383 (inclusive).

    3. 256 different values, with values ranging from 0 to 255 (inclusive).

3. We can configure the number of bits we want to use as the resolution by calling the following method of an mraa.Aio instance:

    1. setADCResolution.

    2. setBit.

    3. setResolutionBits.

4. A call to the `read` method for a `mraa.Aio` instance returns:

    1. A raw number of units based on the number of the resolution bits configured for the instance.

    2. A voltage value automatically converted from the raw number of units.

    3. A resistance value measured in Ohms (Ω).

5. We can use analog pins to read:

    1. Resistance values.

    2. Current values.

    3. Voltage values.

Summary

In this chapter, we learned how to work with analog inputs to measure voltage values. We understood the impact of the different bits of resolution for the analog to digital converter and we wrote code that converted the raw units read into voltage values.

We measure voltages with an analog pin and both the mraa and the wiring-x86 library. We were able to transform a variable resistor into a voltage source and make it possible to measure the darkness level with an analog input, a photoresistor and a voltage divider.

As in the previous chapters, we continued taking advantage of Python's object-oriented features and created classes to encapsulate voltage inputs, darkness sensors, and the necessary configurations with the mraa and wiring-x86 libraries. Our code is easy to read and understand and we can easily switch the underlying low-level library.

We fired actions when the environment light changed and we were able to work with both analog inputs and analog outputs. Finally, we registered events by taking advantage of the logging features included in the Python standard library. We also learned to take advantage of the USB 2.0 host connector included in the Intel Galileo Gen 2 board to plug a USB thumb and use it as an additional storage.

Now that we were able to read the analog inputs in different ways and configurations that made it possible for our IoT device to read analog values generated by changed in the environment, we can work with a wider variety of sensors to retrieve data from the real world, which is the topic of the next chapter.

7
Retrieving Data from the Real World with Sensors

In this chapter, we will work with a variety of sensors to retrieve data from the real world. We will cover the following topics:

- Understanding sensors and their connection types
- Learn the most important things we must consider when choosing sensors
- Take advantage of the upm library with many different sensors
- Measure the magnitude and direction of proper acceleration or g-force with an accelerometer
- Work with a three axis analog accelerometer
- Use a digital accelerometer that works with the I²C bus
- Work with the mraa library and the I²C bus to control a digital accelerometer
- Measure ambient temperature with an analog sensor
- Use a digital temperature and humidity sensor that works with the I²C bus

Understanding sensors and their connection types

In *Chapter 6, Working with Analog Inputs and Local Storage*, we used a photoresistor that is included in a voltage divider and we connected it to an analog input pin. We were able to measure the ambient light and we determined different darkness levels and change the brightness levels of an RGB LED. The photoresistor, also known as **LDR** (short for **Light-Dependent Resistor**) or photocell, is a sensor. We just needed to include it in a voltage divider to make the changes in the resistance value of the photoresistor via the ambient light. These variations in the resistance value will generate changes in the voltage value in our analog pin. Thus, we worked with a configuration of electronic components that generated an analog sensor, capable of transforming changes in the environment light into voltage values.

There are a huge number of sensors that allow us to retrieve data from the real world and convert it into analog or digital values that we can collect with the different communications ports included in the Intel Galileo Gen 2 board and process with Python and different libraries. When we worked with the photoresistor to measure the environment light, we wired the configuration to an analog pin and we worked with the mraa library and then the wiring-x86 library to take advantage of the analog to digital converter to retrieve the values.

In *Chapter 2, Working with Python on Intel Galileo Gen 2*, we installed the latest available version of the upm library. This library provides high level interfaces for sensors and actuators. Whenever we work with a sensor, it is usually convenient to check whether the upm library includes support for it because the high level interface can save us a lot of time and make it easier for us to start retrieving the values from the sensor and perform the necessary conversions to the different measuring units.

In this chapter, we will take advantage of the upm library with many different sensors. However, we must take into account that sometimes the features included in the upm library for a specific sensor might not be enough and we might need to write our own low level code to interact with the sensor with either the mraa or the wiring-x86 library. As we will analyze later, depending on the connection type, only the mraa will provide us with all the necessary features when the sensor is not supported in the upm library.

Obviously, the first thing that we must consider when selecting a sensor is what we want to measure, for example, temperature. However, that is not the only thing we have to consider to select a specific sensor. When we select sensors, we must take into account their features, their measurement range, their precision and their connection types, among other things. The following list enumerates the most important things we must consider and their explanation:

- **Compatibility with Intel Galileo Gen 2 board and the voltage supply that we are using (5V or 3.3V)**: Sometimes, we have to wire more than one sensor to the board, and therefore, it is important to check whether all the sensors we are selecting can work with the voltage configuration we have for the board. Some sensors are only capable to work with the board if we have a specific setting.

- **Power consumption**: We must take into account that some sensors have different working modes. For example, some sensors have a high performance mode that requires more power than a normal mode. As we might work with more than one sensor wired to the board, it is also important to consider the overall power consumption with all the sensors connected to the board and in the modes in which we will use them. In addition, some sensors switch to power saving modes when we don't use them.

- **Connection type**: We need to answer a few questions in order to decide the most convenient connection type. Do we have the necessary connections, communications or interface ports? Are they available? Do the connection type and the distance we need have any impact on the accuracy for the measured values? In addition, when we select the first sensor for our board, all the connections might be available, but the situation changes as we add more sensors and it can force the decision to select a sensor with a different connection type. Let's consider the following situation, we are already measuring ambient light in 6 different positions. We have 6 photoresistors connected with 6 voltage divider configurations and wired to the 6 available analog input pins, and therefore, we don't have additional analog pins available. If we have to add a temperature sensor, we cannot add an analog sensor that requires an analog input pin because all of them are wired to the light sensors. In this case, we have to use a digital temperature sensor that we can wire to either the I²C or the SPI buses. Another option is to use a digital temperature sensor that we can wire to the UART port. We will dive deep on the different connection types for the sensors later.

- **Measurement ranges**: The specifications for the sensors indicate their measurement ranges. For example, a temperature sensor measuring ambient temperature can have a measurement range of -40°F to 185°F (equivalent to -40°C to 85°C). In case we need to measure ambient temperatures that can reach 90°C, we have to select a temperature sensor with a higher upper range. For example, another sensor that measuring ambient temperature provides a measurement range of -40°F to 257°F (equivalent to -40°C to 125°C) will be suitable for this job.

- **Sensitivity and precision**: Each sensor is sensitive and might offer different configurable precision levels. We have to make sure the accuracy provided by the sensor is compatible with our needs. As the measured value changes, it is important to consider the sensitivity, also known as measurement resolution. For example, if we have to measure temperature and we must be able to determine changes of at least 2°F or 1°C based on the unit of measure we are using, we have to make sure that the sensor is capable providing the required sensitivity.

 When we start the process of selecting the appropriate sensor, it is very important to pay attention to the units of measure when we analyze measurement ranges, sensitivity and precision. A typical example is a temperature sensor that can express the values in either degrees Celsius (°C) or degrees Fahrenheit (°F).

- **Latency**: It is very important to determine how much can we wait for the sensor to gather a new value and whether it is capable of providing us with a real new value in this amount of time. When the measure value changes in the real environment or object that we are measuring, the sensor takes some time to be able to provide us with the new measured value. Sometimes, they are microseconds but in other cases, they can be milliseconds or even seconds. It depends on the sensor and we have to take it into account when selecting the appropriate sensor for our project. For example, we might need a temperature sensor to allow us to measure 2 temperature values per second, and therefore, we must work with a sensor with a latency lower than 500 milliseconds (0.5 seconds) to achieve our goal. Specifically, we can select a temperature sensor with a latency of 200 milliseconds. Unluckily, sometimes we have to dive deep on the datasheets to check the latency value for some sensors and the electronic components that it uses.

- **Operating range and special environment requirements**: It is very important to consider the operating range for the sensor. Sometimes, the sensors have to work in specific environment conditions that might not be suitable for all of the available sensors. The following are some examples of rough environment requirements: high shock survivability, water resistance, extremely high temperatures, and very high humidity levels.

- **Dimensions**: Sensors come with different dimensions. Sometimes only specific dimensions are suitable for our project.

- **Protocol, support in the upm library and Python bindings**: We will end up processing the data retrieved from the sensor with Python code, and therefore, it is very important to make sure that we can work with the sensor in Python. In some cases, we don't want to write low-level code and we want to make sure that the sensor is supported in the upm library. In other cases, we have to make sure that we have the necessary Python libraries to work with the protocols that some digital sensors use. For example, many temperature sensors that work with the UART port use the MODBUS serial communications protocol. If they aren't supported in the upm library, we have to work with specific Python libraries to establish communications using the MODBUS serial communications protocol and it might require additional work on our side in case we don't have previous experience with this protocol.

- **Cost**: Obviously, we have to take into account the sensor's cost. Perhaps the best sensor that complies with all our requirements is extremely expensive and we might decide to use another sensor with less features or less precision but with a lower cost. We have a huge number of cheap sensors with impressive features that are compatible with the Intel Galileo Gen 2 board. However, we always have to take into account how much each sensor costs to select it according to our needs and our budget.

The sensors or modules that include sensors that we can wire to an Intel Galileo Gen 2 board can use the following connection types. The list enumerates the acronym that manufacturers usually use to describe the connection type for the modules and their explanation:

- **AIO**: The module requires one or more analog input pins. The sensors that require analog input pins are known as analog sensors.

- **GPIO**: The module requires one or more GPIO pins.

- **I²C**: The module requires two wires to connect to the two I²C bus lines: **SCL** (short for **S**erial **CL**ock) and **SDA** (short for **S**erial **DA**ta). We can connect many devices to this bus as long as each of them have a different I²C address.

- **SPI**: The module requires three wires to connect to the three SPI bus lines: **MISO** (short for **Master In Slave Out**), **MOSI** (short for **Master Out Slave In**) and **SCK** (short for **Serial Clock**).

- **UART**: The module works with a serial connection (RX/TX), and therefore, requires two wires to connect to the two pins for the UART port: **TX->1** and **RX<-0**. An **UART** port stands for **Universal Asynchronous Receiver/ Transmitter**.

The modules that work with the I²C bus, the SPI bus or an UART port are known as **digital sensors** because they use a digital interface. Some modules combine one of the buses or an UART port with GPIO pins.

We already worked with analog inputs and the analog to digital converter with both the `mraa` and `wiring-x86` libraries. We also worked with GPIO pins configured as input pins with these libraries. However, we still didn't work with the I²C bus, the SPI bus or the UART ports.

The `mraa` library provides the following classes that allow us to work with the previously mentioned serial buses and the UART ports:

- `mraa.I2c`: The class represents an I²C bus master device (the board) that can talk to multiple I²C bus slave devices by selecting their address. It is possible to create many instances of this class to interact with many slave devices. The class allows us to write data to and read data from slave devices connected to the I²C bus.

- `Mraa.Spi`: The class represents an SPI bus and its chip select. The class allows us to write data to and read data from devices connected to the SPI bus.

- `mraa.UART`: The class represents an UART port and allow us to configure, send data to and receive data from an UART port.

> We can use the previously explained classes provided by the `mraa` library to interact with any of the digital modules. However, this would require us to spend some time reading the datasheets for the modules, understanding their working modes, writing code that writes data to and reads data from the appropriate bus or UART port. Each module has its own API and we have to compose requests and process responses through the serial buses or the UART port.

First, we will take advantage of the upm library for each of the modules. In a few cases, we will also use the appropriate classes in the mraa library to understand how to interact with the sensors with a lower level interface. This way, in case we have to work with a module that isn't supported in the upm library, we can analyze the information provided in the datasheets and write code to interact with the module.

Working with accelerometers

An accelerometer allows us to measure the magnitude and direction of proper acceleration or g-force. Tablets and smartphones use accelerometers to automatically switch between portrait and landscape modes depending on the direction in which we hold the device. In addition, the built-in accelerometer allows us to control apps by making small movements of different intensity with the device in the different directions.

An accelerometer allows us to detect how an object is oriented with respect to the Earth's surface by measuring acceleration due to gravity. In addition, an accelerometer is extremely useful when we want to detect when an object starts or stops moving. Accelerometers are also capable of detecting vibration and when an object is falling down.

Accelerometers usually measure proper acceleration in g-force, abbreviated with a g. It is important to avoid the confusion generated by the force word included in the name of the unit of measure because we are measuring proper acceleration and not a force. Some accelerometers use meters per second squared (m/s^2) as their unit of measure instead of g-force.

Nowadays, most accelerometers are capable of measuring acceleration in three axes and are known as 3-axis accelerometers or triple axis accelerometers. A 3-axis accelerometer can measure acceleration for the x, y and z axis. If we want to measure small accelerations or vibrations, it will be more convenient to work with a small range 3-axis accelerometer because they provide the necessary sensitivity.

Wiring an analog accelerometer to the analog input pins

The easiest way to understand how an accelerometer works is to use it in a simple example. Now, we will work with an analog 3-axis accelerometer with a full sensing range from -3g to +3g. This kind of accelerometer requires three analog input pins, one for each measured axes. The accelerometer supplies voltage levels based on the measured acceleration for each axes.

We will use the three analog pins labeled **A0**, **A1** and **A2** to connect the positive voltage outputs of an analog accelerometer breakout board. After we finish the necessary wirings, we will write Python code to measure and display the acceleration for the three axis: x, y and z. This way, we will read the result of converting an analog value to its digital representation and we will map it to the acceleration value.

We need a SparkFun triple axis accelerometer breakout ADXL335 to work with this example. The following URL provides detailed information about this breakout board: `https://www.sparkfun.com/products/9269`. The breakout board incorporates the ADXL335 accelerometer sensor from Analog Devices.

The power supplied to the breakout board should be between 1.8VDC and 3.6VDC, and therefore, we will use the power pin labeled **3V3** as the power supply to make sure we supply 3.3V and we never supply **5V** to the breakout board.

It is also possible to use a Seeedstudio Grove 3-axis analog accelerometer to work with this example. The following URL provides detailed information about this module: `http://www.seeedstudio.com/depot/Grove-3Axis-Analog-Accelerometer-p-1086.html`. If you use this module, you can use either the power pin labeled **3V3** or **5V** as the power supply because the breakout board is capable of working with voltage supplies from 3V to 5V. The full sensing range is the same than the SparkFun breakout board and both use the same accelerometer sensor. The wirings are compatible for both modules.

The following diagram shows a SparkFun triple axis accelerometer breakout ADXL335, the necessary wirings and the wirings from the Intel Galileo Gen 2 board to the breadboard. The Fritzing file for the sample is `iot_fritzing_chapter_07_01.fzz` and the following picture is the breadboard view:

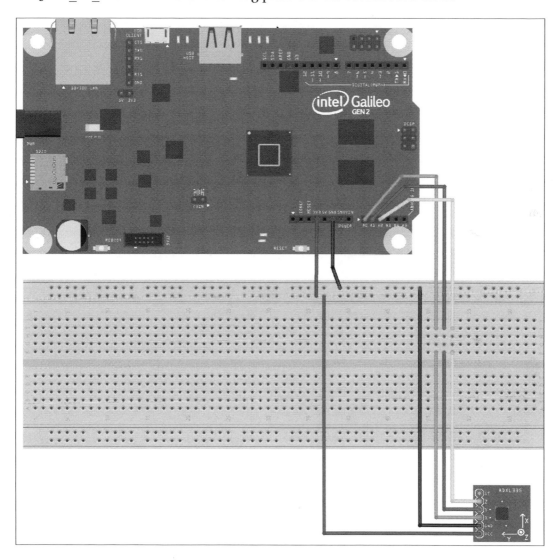

The following picture shows the schematic with the electronic components represented as symbols:

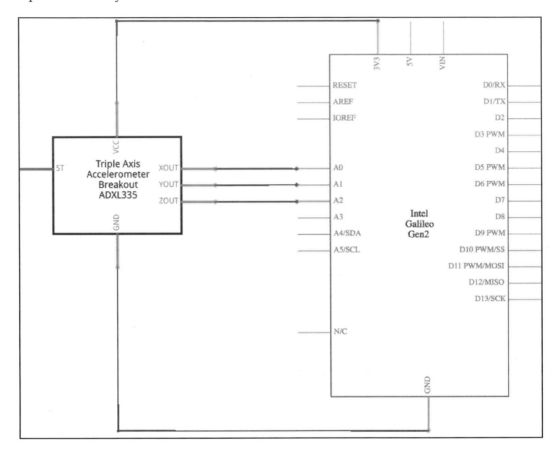

As seen in the previous schematic, we have the following connections:

- The analog input pin labeled **A0** is connected to the accelerometer output pin labeled **X** (**XOUT** in the breakout board's symbol)

- The analog input pin labeled **A1** is connected to the accelerometer output pin labeled **Y** (**YOUT** in the breakout board's symbol)

- The analog input pin labeled **A2** is connected to the accelerometer output pin labeled **Z** (**ZOUT** in the breakout board's symbol)

- The power pin labeled **3V3** is connected to the accelerometer power pin labeled **VCC**

- The ground pin labeled **GND** is connected to the accelerometer ground pin labeled **GND**

Now, it is time make all the necessary wirings. Don't forget to shutdown the Yocto Linux, wait for all the onboard LEDs to turn off, and unplug the power supply from the Intel Galileo Gen 2 board before adding or removing any wire from the board's pins. Make sure you use large wires to allow you to move the accelerometer breakout board in different directions without accidentally unplugging cables.

Measuring three axis acceleration with an analog accelerometer

The upm library includes support for the three axis analog accelerometer breakout board in the pyupm_adxl335 module. The ADXL335 class declared in this module represents a three axis analog accelerometer connected to our board. The class makes it easy to calibrate the accelerometer and convert the raw values read from the analog inputs into values expressed in the g unit.

We will create a new Accelerometer class to represent the accelerometer and make it easier for us to retrieve the acceleration values without worrying about type conversion that are necessary when working with an instance of the ADXL335 class. We will use the ADXL335 class to interact with the accelerometer. The following lines show the code for the new Accelerometer class that works with the upm library, specifically with the pyupm_adxl335 module. The code file for the sample is iot_python_chapter_07_01.py.

```python
import pyupm_adxl335 as upmAdxl335
import time


class Accelerometer:
    def __init__(self, pinX, pinY, pinZ):
        self.accelerometer = upmAdxl335.ADXL335(
            pinX, pinY, pinZ)
        self.accelerometer.calibrate()
        self.x_acceleration_fp = upmAdxl335.new_floatPointer()
        self.y_acceleration_fp = upmAdxl335.new_floatPointer()
        self.z_acceleration_fp = upmAdxl335.new_floatPointer()
        self.x_acceleration = 0.0
        self.y_acceleration = 0.0
        self.z_acceleration = 0.0

    def calibrate(self):
        self.accelerometer.calibrate()
```

```
def measure_acceleration(self):
    # Retrieve the acceleration values for the three axis
    self.accelerometer.acceleration(
        self.x_acceleration_fp,
        self.y_acceleration_fp,
        self.z_acceleration_fp)
    self.x_acceleration = upmAdxl335.floatPointer_value(
        self.x_acceleration_fp)
    self.y_acceleration = upmAdxl335.floatPointer_value(
        self.y_acceleration_fp)
    self.z_acceleration = upmAdxl335.floatPointer_value(
        self.z_acceleration_fp)
```

We have to specify the analog pin numbers to which each axes pin is connected when we create an instance of the Accelerometer class in the pinX, pinY, and pinZ required arguments. The constructor, that is, the __init__ method, creates a new upmAdxl335.ADXL335 instance with the received pinX, pinY, and pinZ arguments and saves its reference in the accelerometer attribute.

The upmAdxl335.ADXL335 instance requires working with floating point pointers to retrieve the acceleration values for the three axis. Thus, the constructor saves the three objects of type float * (float pointers) in the following three attributes by calling upmAdxl335.new_floatPointer().

- x_acceleration_fp
- y_acceleration_fp
- z_acceleration_fp

Finally, the constructor creates and initializes three attributes with 0.0: x_acceleration, y_acceleration and z_acceleration. After the constructor is executed, we must calibrate the accelerometer and then, we will be ready to retrieve acceleration values for the three axis: *x*, *y* and *z*.

The class defines the following two methods:

- calibrate: Calls the calibrate method for self.accelerometer to calibrate the analog accelerometer.

- measure_acceleration: Retrieves the acceleration values for the three axis and saves them in the following three attributes: x_acceleration, y_acceleration and z_acceleration. The acceleration values are expressed in g-force (g). First, the code calls the acceleration method for self.accelerometer with the three objects of type float * as arguments. The method reads the raw values retrieved from the three analog pins, converts them to the appropriate values in g-force (g) and changes the floating point values for the objects of type float* received as arguments with the updated values. Then, the code calls the upmAdxl335.floatPointer_value method to retrieve the floating point values from the objects of type float* and update the three attributes: x_acceleration, y_acceleration and z_acceleration.

Now, we will write a loop that will run a calibration, retrieve and display the acceleration values for the three axis expressed in g-force (g) every 500 milliseconds, that is, twice per second. The code file for the sample is iot_python_chapter_07_01.py.

```python
if __name__ == "__main__":
    # The accelerometer is connected to analog pins A0, A1 and A2
    # A0 -> x
    # A1 -> y
    # A2 -> z
    accelerometer = Accelerometer(0, 1, 2)
    # Calibrate the accelerometer
    accelerometer.calibrate()

    while True:
        accelerometer.measure_acceleration()
        print("Acceleration for x:
            {0}g".format(accelerometer.x_acceleration))
        print("Acceleration for y:
            {0}g".format(accelerometer.y_acceleration))
        print("Acceleration for z:
            {0}g".format(accelerometer.z_acceleration))
        # Sleep 0.5 seconds (500 milliseconds)
        time.sleep(0.5)
```

The first line creates an instance of the previously coded `Accelerometer` class with 0, 1 and 2 as the values of the `pinX`, `pinY` and `pinZ` arguments. This way, the instance will read the analog values from the pins labeled **A0**, **A1** and **A2**. Then, the code calls the `calibrate` method for the `Accelerometer` instance to calibrate the analog accelerometer.

 The calibration measures the *x*, *y* and *z* axis values while the sensor is still, and then, the sensor uses these values as the zero values, that is, as a baseline. The default sensitivity for this analog sensor is 0.25V/g.

Then, the code runs a loop forever, that is, until you interrupt the execution by pressing *Ctrl + C* or the button to stop the process, in case you are using a Python IDE with remote development features to run the code in your board. The loop calls the `measure_acceleration` method to update the acceleration values and then prints them, expressed in g-force (g).

The following line will start the example. Don't forget that you need to transfer the Python source code file to the Yocto Linux with an SFTP client. Before you start the example, make sure that the accelerometer breakout board is located on stable surface that doesn't vibrate. This way, the calibration will work OK.

```
python iot_python_chapter_07_01.py
```

After you run the example, perform the following actions:

- Make small movements to the accelerometer breakout board in different directions
- Make large movements to the accelerometer breakout board in specific directions
- Leave the accelerometer breakout board on a stable surface that doesn't vibrate

As a result of the previous actions, you will see the different acceleration values measured for the three axis. The following lines show some sample output lines generated when we make large movements with the breakout board:

```
Acceleration for x: 0.0g
Acceleration for y: 0.4296875g
Acceleration for z: 0.0g
Acceleration for x: 0.0g
```

```
Acceleration for y: 0.52734375g
Acceleration for z: 0.0g
Acceleration for x: 0.0g
Acceleration for y: 0.60546875g
Acceleration for z: 0.0g
Acceleration for x: 0.01953125g
Acceleration for y: 0.68359375g
Acceleration for z: 0.0g
```

Wiring a digital accelerometer to the I²C bus

Digital accelerometers usually provide a better precision, higher resolution and more sensitivity than analog accelerometers. Now, we will work with a digital 3-axis accelerometer with a full sensing range from -16g to +16g. We will use a breakout board that uses the I²C bus to allow the board to communicate with the accelerometer.

We will use the two pins labeled **SDA** and **SCL** to connect the data and clock lines of the I²C bus to the corresponding pins in the digital accelerometer breakout board. After we finish the necessary wirings, we will write Python code to measure and display the acceleration for the three axis: *x*, *y* and *z*. This way, we will read the result of sending commands to the accelerometer through the I²C bus, reading the responses and decoding them into the appropriate acceleration values expressed in g-force (g).

We need a SparkFun triple axis accelerometer breakout ADXL345 to work with this example. The following URL provides detailed information about this breakout board: https://www.sparkfun.com/products/9836. The breakout board incorporates the ADXL345 digital accelerometer sensor from Analog Devices and provides support for both the SPI and I²C buses. In this case, we will only use the I²C bus.

 The power supplied to the breakout board should be between 2.0VDC and 3.6VDC, and therefore, we must use the power pin labeled **3V3** as the power supply to make sure we supply 3.3V and we never supply **5V** to the breakout board.

It is also possible to use a Seeedstudio Grove 3-axis digital accelerometer to work with this example. The following URL provides detailed information about this module: `http://www.seeedstudio.com/depot/Grove-3Axis-Digital-Accelerometer16g-p-1156.html`. If you use this module, you can use either the power pin labeled **3V3** or **5V** as the power supply because the breakout board is capable of working with voltage supplies from 3V to 5V. The full sensing range is the same than the SparkFun breakout board and both use the same accelerometer sensor. The wirings are compatible for both modules.

The Seeedstudio Grove 3-axis digital accelerometer is prepared to use cables to plug it into a Grove base shield. The Grove base shield is a board that you can plug in your Intel Galileo Gen 2 board and provides digital, analog and I²C ports that you can use with the appropriate cables to easily wire Grove sensors to the underlying Intel Galileo Gen 2 board. In our examples, we won't be using the Grove base shield and we will continue to use wirings to connect each different sensor. However, you will achieve the same results if you decide to use the Grove base shield in combination with Grove sensors. Other Grove sensors that we will use in the next examples will also be prepared to work with the Grove base shield. The latest version of the Grove base shield is V2 and you can gather more information about it in the following URL: `http://www.seeedstudio.com/depot/Base-Shield-V2-p-1378.html`

The following diagram shows a Seeedstudio Grove 3-axis digital accelerometer breakout ADXL345, the necessary wirings and the wirings from the Intel Galileo Gen 2 board to the breadboard. The Fritzing file for the sample is `iot_fritzing_chapter_07_02.fzz` and the following picture is the breadboard view.

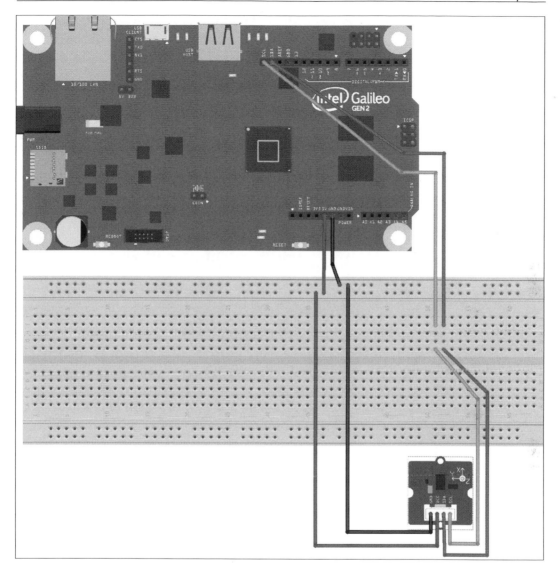

The following picture shows the schematic with the electronic components represented as symbols.

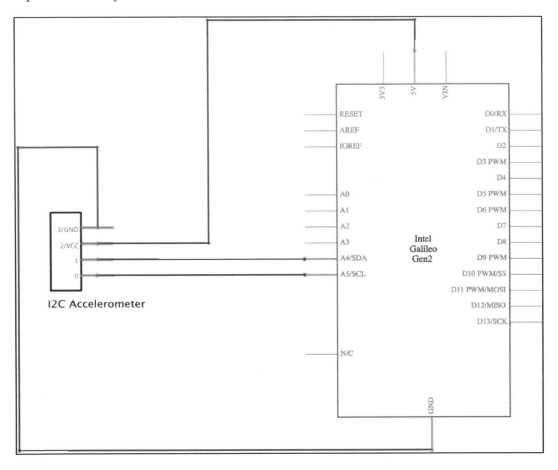

As seen in the previous schematic, we have the following connections:

- The **SDA** pin is connected to the accelerometer pin labeled **SDA**. This way, we connect the digital accelerometer to the serial data line for the I²C bus. The **SDA** pin in the Intel Galileo Gen 2 board is connected to the analog input pin labeled **A4**, and therefore, the board's symbol uses the **A4/SDA** label. The pin labeled **SDA** is in a different location than the pin labeled **A4**, but they are internally connected.

- The **SCL** pin is connected to the accelerometer pin labeled **SCL**. This way, we connect the digital accelerometer to the serial clock line for the I²C bus. The **SCL** pin in the Intel Galileo Gen 2 board is connected to the analog input pin labeled **A5**, and therefore, the board's symbol uses the **A5/SCL** label. The pin labeled **SCL** is in a different location than the pin labeled **A5**, but they are internally connected.

- The power pin labeled **5V** is connected to the accelerometer power pin labeled **VCC**. In case you work with the SparkFun triple axis accelerometer breakout ADXL345, the power pin labeled **3V3** is connected to the accelerometer power pin labeled **VCC**.

- The ground pin labeled **GND** is connected to the accelerometer ground pin labeled **GND**.

Now, it is time make all the necessary wirings. Don't forget to shutdown the Yocto Linux, wait for all the onboard LEDs to turn off, and unplug the power supply from the Intel Galileo Gen 2 board before adding or removing any wire from the board's pins. As you did with the analog accelerometer, make sure you use large wires to allow you to move the accelerometer breakout board in different directions without accidentally unplugging cables.

Measuring three axis acceleration with a digital accelerometer

The upm library includes support for the three axis digital accelerometer breakout board ADXL345 in the `pyupm_adxl345` module. The `Adxl345` class declared in this module represents a three axis digital accelerometer based on the ADXL345 sensor, connected to our board. The class makes it easy to initialize the sensor, update and retrieve the acceleration values for the three axis through the I²C bus. The class works with the `mraa.I2c` class under the hoods to talk with the sensor, that is, to write data to and read data from the ADXL345 sensor that acts as a slave device connected to the I²C bus.

 Unluckily, each module in the upm library doesn't follow the same naming conventions we should expect for Python code. For example, in our previous example, that class name was `ADXL335`, with capital letters, while in this example the class name is `Adxl345`.

We will create a new version of the `Accelerometer` class to represent the accelerometer and make it easier for us to retrieve the acceleration values without worrying about specific methods and arrays when working with an instance of the `Adxl345` class. We will use the `Adxl345` class to interact with the accelerometer. The following lines show the code for the new `Accelerometer` class that works with the `upm` library, specifically with the `pyupm_adxl345` module. The code file for the sample is `iot_python_chapter_07_02.py`.

```python
import pyupm_adxl345 as upmAdxl345
import time


class Accelerometer:
    def __init__(self, bus):
        self.accelerometer = upmAdxl345.Adxl345(bus)
        self.x_acceleration = 0.0
        self.y_acceleration = 0.0
        self.z_acceleration = 0.0

    def measure_acceleration(self):
        # Update the acceleration values for the three axis
        self.accelerometer.update()
        # Retrieve the acceleration values for the three axis
        acceleration_array = \
            self.accelerometer.getAcceleration()
        self.x_acceleration = acceleration_array[0]
        self.y_acceleration = acceleration_array[1]
        self.z_acceleration = acceleration_array[2]
```

We have to specify the I²C bus number to which the digital accelerometer is wired when we create an instance of the `Accelerometer` class in the `bus` required argument. The constructor, that is, the `__init__` method, creates a new `upmAdxl345.Adxl345` instance with the received `bus` argument and saves its reference in the `accelerometer` attribute.

The `upmAdxl345.Adxl345` instance requires working with an array of floating point pointers to retrieve the acceleration values for the three axis. We want to work with easy to understand attributes, and therefore, the constructor creates and initializes three attributes with `0.0`: `x_acceleration`, `y_acceleration`, and `z_acceleration`. After the constructor is executed, we have an initialized digital accelerometer ready to retrieve acceleration values for the three axis: x, y and z.

The class defines a `measure_acceleration` method that updates the acceleration values for the three axes in the sensor, retrieves these acceleration values from the sensor, and finally saves them in the following three attributes: `x_acceleration`, `y_acceleration` and `z_acceleration`. The acceleration values are expressed in g-force (g).

First, the code within the `measure_acceleration` method calls the `update` method for `self.accelerometer` to request the sensor to update the read values. Then, the code calls the `getAcceleration` method for `self.accelerometer` to retrieve the acceleration values for the three axis and saves the returned array in the `acceleration_array` local variable. The first element in the array has the acceleration value for x, the second for y and the third for z. Thus, the code updates the following three attributes with the values in the `acceleration_array` array: `x_acceleration`, `y_acceleration`, and `z_acceleration`. This way, we can easily access each acceleration value by accessing the appropriate attribute instead of working with elements of an array that might lead to confusion.

Now, we will write a loop that will run a calibration, retrieve and display the acceleration values for the three axis expressed in g-force (g) every 500 milliseconds, that is, twice per second. The code file for the sample is `iot_python_chapter_07_02.py`.

```
if __name__ == "__main__":
    accelerometer = Accelerometer(0)
    while True:
        accelerometer.measure_acceleration()
        print("Acceleration for x: {:5.2f}g".
            format(accelerometer.x_acceleration))
        print("Acceleration for y: {:5.2f}g".
            format(accelerometer.y_acceleration))
        print("Acceleration for z: {:5.2f}g".
            format(accelerometer.z_acceleration))
        # Sleep 0.5 seconds (500 milliseconds)
        time.sleep(0.5)
```

The first line creates an instance of the previously coded `Accelerometer` class with `0` as the values of the `bus` argument. The `mraa.I2c` class identifies the I²C bus to which we wired the accelerometer with number `0`. This way, the instance will establish a communication with the digital accelerometer through the I²C bus. The Intel Galileo Gen 2 board is the master in the bus and the digital accelerometer, as any other device connected to this bus, acts as a slave.

Then, the code runs a loop forever that calls `measure_acceleration` method to update the acceleration values and then prints them, expressed in g-force (g).

The following line will start the example:

```
python iot_python_chapter_07_02.py
```

After you run the example, perform the same actions done with the previous example. As a result of these actions, you will see the different acceleration values measured for the three axis. The following lines show some sample output lines generated when we make small movements with the breakout board:

```
Acceleration for x: 0.000g
Acceleration for y: 0.056g
Acceleration for z: 0.000g
Acceleration for x: 0.000g
Acceleration for y: 0.088g
Acceleration for z: 0.000g
Acceleration for x: 0.000g
Acceleration for y: 0.872g
Acceleration for z: 0.056g
```

Using the I²C bus to control a digital accelerometer with the mraa library

Sometimes, the features included in the `upm` library for a specific sensor do not include all of its possible usages and configurations. An example of this situation is the `upmAdxl345.Adxl345` class that we used in our previous example. This class doesn't allow us to configure the desired scale for the accelerometer while the sensor supports the following four selectable measurement ranges: ±2g, ±4g, ±8g and ±16g. If we want to use specific features that aren't included in the `upm` module, we can use the appropriate `mraa` class to interact with the sensor, in this case, we can use `mraa.I2c` to control the digital accelerometer through the I²C bus.

We will use the C++ source code for the upm module as a baseline to write our own Python code that controls the accelerometer through the I²C bus using the `mraa.I2c` class. The C++ source code file is `adxl1345.cxx` and it can be found in the following GitHub URL: `http://github.com/intel-iot-devkit/upm/blob/master/src/adxl345/adxl345.cxx`. As we use the C++ source code as a baseline, we will use the same naming convention (capital letters) for the constants declared with `#define`, but we will convert them into class attributes.

The following lines show the code for the new `Adxl1345` class that works with an instance of the `mraa.I2c` class to communicate with the digital accelerometer. The code file for the sample is `iot_python_chapter_07_03.py`.

```python
class Adxl345:
    # Read buffer length
    READ_BUFFER_LENGTH = 6
    # I2C address for the ADXL345 accelerometer
    ADXL345_I2C_ADDR = 0x53
    ADXL345_ID = 0x00
    # Control registers
    ADXL345_OFSX = 0x1E
    ADXL345_OFSY = 0x1F
    ADXL345_OFSZ = 0x20
    ADXL345_TAP_THRESH = 0x1D
    ADXL345_TAP_DUR = 0x21
    ADXL345_TAP_LATENCY = 0x22
    ADXL345_ACT_THRESH = 0x24
    ADXL345_INACT_THRESH = 0x25
    ADXL345_INACT_TIME = 0x26
    ADXL345_INACT_ACT_CTL = 0x27
    ADXL345_FALL_THRESH = 0x28
    ADXL345_FALL_TIME = 0x29
    ADXL345_TAP_AXES = 0x2A
    ADXL345_ACT_TAP_STATUS = 0x2B
    # Interrupt registers
    ADXL345_INT_ENABLE = 0x2E
    ADXL345_INT_MAP = 0x2F
    ADXL345_INT_SOURCE = 0x30
    # Data registers (read only)
    ADXL345_XOUT_L = 0x32
    ADXL345_XOUT_H = 0x33
    ADXL345_YOUT_L = 0x34
    ADXL345_YOUT_H = 0x35
    ADXL345_ZOUT_L = 0x36
    ADXL345_ZOUT_H = 0x37
    DATA_REG_SIZE = 6
    # Data and power management
    ADXL345_BW_RATE = 0x2C
    ADXL345_POWER_CTL = 0x2D
    ADXL345_DATA_FORMAT = 0x31
    ADXL345_FIFO_CTL = 0x38
    ADXL345_FIFO_STATUS = 0x39
    # Useful values
```

```
ADXL345_POWER_ON = 0x08
ADXL345_AUTO_SLP = 0x30
ADXL345_STANDBY = 0x00
# Scales and resolution
ADXL345_FULL_RES = 0x08
ADXL345_10BIT = 0x00
ADXL345_2G = 0x00
ADXL345_4G = 0x01
ADXL345_8G = 0x02
ADXL345_16G = 0x03


def __init__(self, bus):
    # Init bus and reset chip
    self.i2c = mraa.I2c(bus)
    # Set the slave to talk to
    if self.i2c.address(self.__class__.ADXL345_I2C_ADDR) != mraa.
SUCCESS:
        raise Exception("i2c.address() failed")
    message = bytearray(
        [self.__class__.ADXL345_POWER_CTL,
         self.__class__.ADXL345_POWER_ON])
    if self.i2c.write(message) != mraa.SUCCESS:
        raise Exception("i2c.write() control register failed")
    if self.i2c.address(self.__class__.ADXL345_I2C_ADDR) != mraa.
SUCCESS:
        raise Exception("i2c.address() failed")
    message = bytearray(
        [self.__class__.ADXL345_DATA_FORMAT,
         self.__class__.ADXL345_16G | self.__class__.ADXL345_FULL_
RES])
    if self.i2c.write(message) != mraa.SUCCESS:
        raise Exception("i2c.write() mode register failed")
    # 2.5V sensitivity is 256 LSB/g = 0.00390625 g/bit
    # 3.3V x and y sensitivity is 265 LSB/g = 0.003773584 g/bit, z
is the same
    self.x_offset = 0.003773584
    self.y_offset = 0.003773584
    self.z_offset = 0.00390625
    self.x_acceleration = 0.0
    self.y_acceleration = 0.0
    self.z_acceleration = 0.0
    self.update()
```

```
def update(self):
    # Set the slave to talk to
    self.i2c.address(self.__class__.ADXL345_I2C_ADDR)
    self.i2c.writeByte(self.__class__.ADXL345_XOUT_L)
    self.i2c.address(self.__class__.ADXL345_I2C_ADDR)
    xyz_raw_acceleration = self.i2c.read(self.__class__.DATA_REG_
SIZE)
    x_raw_acceleration = (xyz_raw_acceleration[1] << 8) |
                          xyz_raw_acceleration[0]
    y_raw_acceleration = (xyz_raw_acceleration[3] << 8) |
                          xyz_raw_acceleration[2]
    z_raw_acceleration = (xyz_raw_acceleration[5] << 8) |
                          xyz_raw_acceleration[4]
    self.x_acceleration = x_raw_acceleration * self.x_offset
    self.y_acceleration = y_raw_acceleration * self.y_offset
    self.z_acceleration = z_raw_acceleration * self.z_offset
```

First, the class declares many constants that make it easier for us to understand the code that interacts with the accelerometer through the I²C bus. For example, the ADXL345_I2C_ADDR constant specifies the address for the ADXL345 accelerometer in the I²C bus, which is 53 in hexadecimal (0x53). If we just see a 0x53 within the code, we don't understand that it is an I²C bus address for the sensor. We imported all the constants defined in the C++ version so that we have all the necessary values in case we want to add additional features not included in the initial version. The datasheet provided by the manufacturer provides the necessary details to know the addresses for each register and the way in which the commands work in the I²C bus.

We have to specify the I²C bus number to which the digital accelerometer is wired when we create an instance of the Adxl345 class in the bus required argument. The constructor, that is, the __init__ method, creates a new mraa.I2c instance with the received bus argument and saves its reference in the i2c attribute.

```
self.i2c = mraa.I2c(bus)
```

Before performing any read or write operation in the I²C bus, it is a good practice to call the address method for the mraa.I2c instance to indicate the slave device to which we want to talk to. In this case, the address for the slave device is specified in the ADXL345_I2C_ADDR constant.

```
if self.i2c.address(self.__class__.ADXL345_I2C_ADDR) != mraa.SUCCESS:
    raise Exception("i2c.address() failed")
```

Then, the code builds a message by creating a `bytearray` with the two hexadecimal values that we want to write to the slave: `ADXL345_POWER_CTL` and `ADXL345_POWER_ON`. We can read the message as `write turn on to the power control register`. The call to the `write` method for the `mraa.I2c` instance with this message will turn on the accelerometer.

```
message = bytearray(
    [self.__class__.ADXL345_POWER_CTL,
     self.__class__.ADXL345_POWER_ON])
if self.i2c.write(message) != mraa.SUCCESS:
    raise Exception("i2c.write() control register failed")
```

We declared the following constants related to resolutions:

- `ADXL345_FULL_RES`: Work with full resolution, where resolution increases with the g range up to 13-bit resolution
- `ADXL345_10BIT`: Work with a fixed 10-bit resolution

We declared the following constants related to scales:

- `ADXL345_2G`: Sets the g range to ±2g
- `ADXL345_4G`: Sets the g range to ±4g
- `ADXL345_8G`: Sets the g range to ±8g
- `ADXL345_16G`: Sets the g range to ±16g

The code makes another call to the `address` method for the `mraa.I2c` instance before it makes another write to configure the desired resolution and scale for the sensor. The code builds another message by creating a `bytearray` with the two hexadecimal values that we want to write to the slave: `ADXL345_DATA_FORMAT` and the result of applying a bitwise or operator (`|`) for `ADXL345_16G` and `ADXL345_FULL_RES`. We can read the message as `write ±16g + full resolution to the data format register`. It is necessary to combine the desired resolution and the range in a single byte value, and therefore, we have to use the bitwise or operator (`|`).

```
if self.i2c.address(self.__class__.ADXL345_I2C_ADDR) != mraa.SUCCESS:
    raise Exception("i2c.address() failed")
message = bytearray(
    [self.__class__.ADXL345_DATA_FORMAT,
     self.__class__.ADXL345_16G | self.__class__.ADXL345_FULL_RES])
if self.i2c.write(message) != mraa.SUCCESS:
    raise Exception("i2c.write() mode register failed")
```

The call to the write method for the `mraa.I2c` instance with this message will configure the accelerometer to work with a ±16g range for g and with the full resolution. As we have access to this call, we can make changes to the code to change the desired resolution or the scale for our acceleration measures. For example, the following lines that compose the message will change the configuration to make the accelerometer work with a g range of ±4g:

```
message = bytearray(
    [self.__class__.ADXL345_DATA_FORMAT,
     self.__class__.ADXL345_4G | self.__class__.ADXL345_FULL_RES])
```

Then, the code declares offset attributes for x, y, and z that is necessary to convert the raw acceleration values retrieved from the accelerometer into the appropriate values expressed in g. We want to work with easy to understand attributes instead, and therefore, the constructor creates and initializes three attributes with `0.0`: `x_acceleration`, `y_acceleration`, and `z_acceleration`. Finally, the constructor calls the `update` method to retrieve the first values from the accelerometer.

The `update` method makes a call to the `address` method for the `mraa.I2c` instance and then calls its `writeByte` method with `ADXL345_XOUT_L` as its argument, that is, the first data register that we want to read.

```
self.i2c.address(self.__class__.ADXL345_I2C_ADDR)
self.i2c.writeByte(self.__class__.ADXL345_XOUT_L)
```

The accelerometer values are stored in six data registers. There are two bytes per axis: the low byte (eight least significant bits) and the high byte (eight most significant bits), and therefore, we can read the six bytes with a single I²C read operation, starting with the address of the first byte for the x axis. Then, we have to compose each pair of bytes into a single value. The call to the `read` method for the `mraa.I2c` instance passes the `DATA_REG_SIZE` constant as an argument to indicate that we want to read six bytes and the code saves the resulting `bytearray` in the `xyz_raw_acceleration` local variable.

```
self.i2c.address(self.__class__.ADXL345_I2C_ADDR)
xyz_raw_acceleration = self.i2c.read(self.__class__.DATA_REG_SIZE)
```

Then, the code combines the low bytes and the high bytes to compose a single value for each raw acceleration pair of bytes retrieved from the accelerometer and saves them in three local variables: `x_raw_acceleration`, `y_raw_acceleration`, and `z_raw_acceleration`. The code uses the binary left shift (<<) bitwise operator to move the high byte (the eight most significant bits) to the left by 8 places and make the new bits on the right-hand side zeros. Then, it applies a binary or (|) to build the entire word (two bytes). The `x_raw_acceleration` value is the result of joining the high byte and the low byte to compose a word of two bytes.

The first element in the `xyz_raw_acceleration` array (`xyz_raw_acceleration[0]`) includes the low byte for the x raw acceleration and the second element in the `xyz_raw_acceleration` array (`xyz_raw_acceleration[1]`) includes the high byte for the x raw acceleration. Thus, it is necessary to add 8 binary zeros to the high byte (`xyz_raw_acceleration[1]`) and replace those eight zeros with the low byte (`xyz_raw_acceleration[0]`). The same has to be done for the y and z raw acceleration bytes.

```
x_raw_acceleration = (xyz_raw_acceleration[1] << 8) | xyz_raw_
acceleration[0]
y_raw_acceleration = (xyz_raw_acceleration[3] << 8) | xyz_raw_
acceleration[2]
z_raw_acceleration = (xyz_raw_acceleration[5] << 8) | xyz_raw_
acceleration[4]
```

Finally, it is necessary to multiply each value by the offsets defined in the constructor to obtain the appropriate values for x, y, and z expressed in g and save them in the three attributes: `x_acceleration`, `y_acceleration`, and `z_acceleration`.

```
self.x_acceleration = x_raw_acceleration * self.x_offset
self.y_acceleration = y_raw_acceleration * self.y_offset
self.z_acceleration = z_raw_acceleration * self.z_offset
```

Now, we have a class that represents the ADXL345 accelerometer entirely written in Python and we can make any necessary changes to make different configurations for the accelerometer.

We just need to create a new version of the `Accelerometer` class to use the recently created `Adxl345` class instead of the `pyupm_adxl345.Adxl345` class. The following lines show the code for the new `Accelerometer` class. The code file for the sample is `iot_python_chapter_07_03.py`.

```
class Accelerometer:
    def __init__(self, bus):
        self.accelerometer = Adxl345(bus)
        self.x_acceleration = 0.0
        self.y_acceleration = 0.0
        self.z_acceleration = 0.0

    def measure_acceleration(self):
        # Update the acceleration values for the three axis
        self.accelerometer.update()
```

```
self.x_acceleration = self.accelerometer.x_acceleration
self.y_acceleration = self.accelerometer.y_acceleration
self.z_acceleration = self.accelerometer.z_acceleration
```

Now, we can use the same code that we have in the previous example for the
__main__ method and perform the same operations to check the values retrieved
from the accelerometer.

 Writing code that interacts with the I²C bus and a specific
sensor requires a big effort because we have to read the detailed
specifications from the manufacturer's datasheet. Sometimes, we
won't be able to use all the features included in a sensor if we
don't write our own code. In other cases, the features included in
the upm library will be enough for our projects.

Wiring an analog temperature sensor

In *Chapter 6*, *Working with Analog Inputs and Local Storage*, we used a photoresistor
included in a voltage divider and we connected it to an analog input pin. We can use
a similar configuration and replace the photoresistor with a thermistor to measure
ambient temperature. A thermistor changes its resistance value with temperature,
and therefore, we can convert resistance changes into voltage value changes.

We can also work with an analog sensor breakout board that includes a thermistor
in the necessary configuration to provide us with voltage levels to an analog pin that
represent temperature values. In this case, we will work with an analog temperature
sensor supported in the upm library to measure ambient temperature.

We will use the the analog pin labeled **A0** to connect the voltage output of an
analog accelerometer breakout board. After we finish the necessary wirings, we
will write Python code to measure and display the ambient temperature in both
degrees Celsius (°C) and degrees Fahrenheit (°F). This way, we will read the result
of converting an analog value to its digital representation and we will map it to the
temperature value in the appropriate measurement unit.

We need a Seeedstudio Grove temperature sensor to work with this example. The following URL provides detailed information about this module: `http://www.seeedstudio.com/depot/Grove-Temperature-Sensor-p-774.html`. The following diagram shows the sensor breakout board, the necessary wirings, and the wirings from the Intel Galileo Gen 2 board to the breadboard. The Fritzing file for the sample is `iot_fritzing_chapter_07_04.fzz` and the following picture is the breadboard view. Don't forget that you can also decide to use the Grove base shield to plug this sensor to the Intel Galileo Gen 2 board.

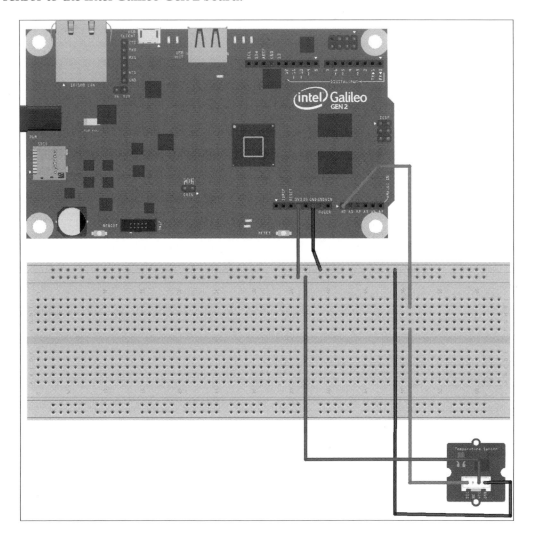

The following picture shows the schematic with the electronic components represented as symbols:

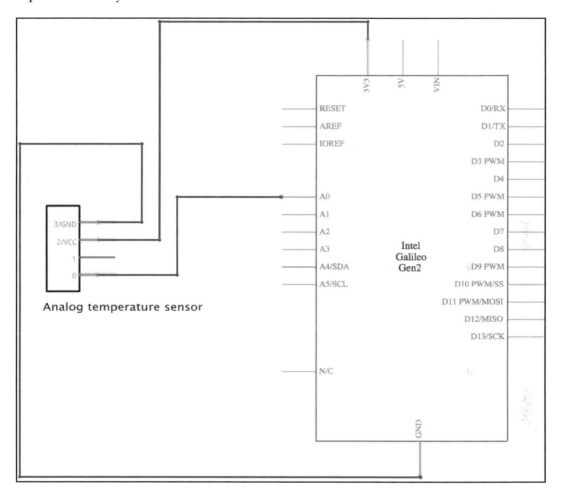

As seen in the previous schematic, we have the following connections:

- The analog input pin labeled **A0** is connected to the temperature output pin labeled **SIG** (0 in the breakout board's symbol)

- The power pin labeled **3V3** is connected to the temperature sensor power pin labeled **VCC**

- The ground pin labeled **GND** is connected to the temperature sensor ground pin labeled **GND**

Now, it is time make all the necessary wirings. Don't forget to shutdown the Yocto Linux, wait for all the onboard LEDs to turn off, and unplug the power supply from the Intel Galileo Gen 2 board before adding or removing any wire from the board's pins.

Measuring ambient temperature with an analog sensor

The upm library includes support for the Grove analog temperature sensor breakout board in the pyupm_grove module. The GroveTemp class declared in this module represents the analog temperature sensor connected to our board. The class makes it easy to retrieve the raw values read from the analog input into values expressed in degrees Celsius (°C).

We will create a new TemperatureSensor class to represent the temperature sensor and make it easier for us to retrieve the ambient temperature values without worrying about unit conversions that are necessary when working with an instance of the GroveTemp class. We will use the GroveTemp class to interact with the analog temperature sensor. The following lines show the code for the new TemperatureSensor class that works with the upm library, specifically with the pyupm_grove module. The code file for the sample is iot_python_chapter_07_04.py.

```python
import pyupm_grove as upmGrove
import time


class TemperatureSensor:
    def __init__(self, analog_pin):
        self.temperature_sensor = upmGrove.GroveTemp(analog_pin)
        self.temperature_celsius = 0.0
        self.temperature_fahrenheit = 0.0

    def measure_temperature(self):
        # Retrieve the temperature expressed in Celsius degrees
        temperature_celsius = self.temperature_sensor.value()
        self.temperature_celsius = temperature_celsius
        self.temperature_fahrenheit = \
            (temperature_celsius * 9.0 / 5.0) + 32.0
```

We have to specify the analog pin to which the sensor is connected when we create an instance of the `TemperatureSensor` class in the `analog_pin` required arguments. The constructor, that is, the `__init__` method, creates a new `upmGrove`. `GroveTemp` instance with the received `analog_pin` argument and saves its reference in the `temperature_sensor` attribute. Finally, the constructor instance creates and initializes two attributes with `0.0`: `temperature_celsius`, and `temperature_fahrenheit`.

The class defines the `measure_temperature` method that retrieves the current ambient temperature measured in degrees Celsius (°C) by calling the value method for `self.temperature_sensor` and saves the value in the `temperature_celsius` local variable. The next line assigns the value to the `temperature_celsius` attribute. Finally, the code assigns the result of converting the the temperature measured in degrees Celsius (°C) to the equivalent value in degrees Fahrenheit (°F). The formula is easy to read because it is just necessary to multiply the temperature measured in degrees Celsius (°C) by 9, divide the result by 5 and sum 32. This way the `TemperatureSensor` class updates two attributes with the ambient temperature measured by the sensor in degrees Celsius (°C) and degrees Fahrenheit (°F).

Now, we will write a loop that will retrieve and display the ambient temperature in degrees Celsius (°C) and degrees Fahrenheit (°F), every 10 seconds. The code file for the sample is `iot_python_chapter_07_04.py`.

```
if __name__ == "__main__":
    # The temperature sensor is connected to analog pin A0
    temperature_sensor = TemperatureSensor(0)

    while True:
        temperature_sensor.measure_temperature()
        print("Ambient temperature in degrees Celsius: {0}".
            format(temperature_sensor.temperature_celsius))
        print("Ambient temperature in degrees Fahrenheit: {0}".
            format(temperature_sensor.temperature_fahrenheit))
        # Sleep 10 seconds (10000 milliseconds)
        time.sleep(10)
```

The first line creates an instance of the previously coded `TemperatureSensor` class with `0` as the values of the `analog_pin` argument. This way, the instance will read the analog values from the pin labeled **A0**. Then, the code runs a loop forever that calls the `measure_temperature` method to update the ambient temperature values and then prints them, expressed in degrees Celsius (°C) and degrees Fahrenheit (°F).

The following line will start the example:

```
python iot_python_chapter_07_04.py
```

After you run the example, turn on an air conditioner or a heating system to generate a change in the ambient temperature and you will see how the measured temperature changes after a few minutes. The following lines show some a sample output:

```
Ambient temperature in degrees Celsius: 13
Ambient temperature in degrees Fahrenheit: 55.4
Ambient temperature in degrees Celsius: 14
Ambient temperature in degrees Fahrenheit: 57.2
Ambient temperature in degrees Celsius: 15
Ambient temperature in degrees Fahrenheit: 59
Ambient temperature in degrees Celsius: 16
Ambient temperature in degrees Fahrenheit: 60.8
```

Wiring a digital temperature and humidity sensor to the I²C bus

Now, we will use a multifunctional digital sensor that will provide us with temperature and relative humidity information. We will use a breakout board that uses the I²C bus to allow the Intel Galileo Gen 2 board to communicate with the sensor. The sensor is useful when we don't need to measure temperature and humidity in extreme conditions. We cannot use this sensor at the top of Mount Etna, just in case we work in a research project related to volcanoes.

We will use the two pins labeled **SDA** and **SCL** to connect the data and clock lines of the I²C bus to the corresponding pins in the digital temperature and humidity breakout board. After we finish the necessary wirings, we will write a Python code to measure, display the ambient temperature, and the relative humidity. This way, we will read the result of sending commands to the sensor through the I²C bus, reading the responses, and decoding them into the ambient temperature and the relative humidity expressed in the appropriate units.

We need a SeeedStudio Grove temperature & humidity sensor (high-accuracy & mini) breakout to work with this example. The following URL provides detailed information about this breakout board: http://www.seeedstudio.com/depot/Grove-TemperatureHumidity-Sensor-HighAccuracy-Mini-p-1921.html. The breakout board incorporates the TH02 digital humidity and temperature sensor and provides support for both the I²C bus.

The following diagram shows the digital temperature, humidity breakout, the necessary wirings, and the wirings from the Intel Galileo Gen 2 board to the breadboard. The Fritzing file for the sample is `iot_fritzing_chapter_07_05.fzz` and the following picture is the breadboard view:

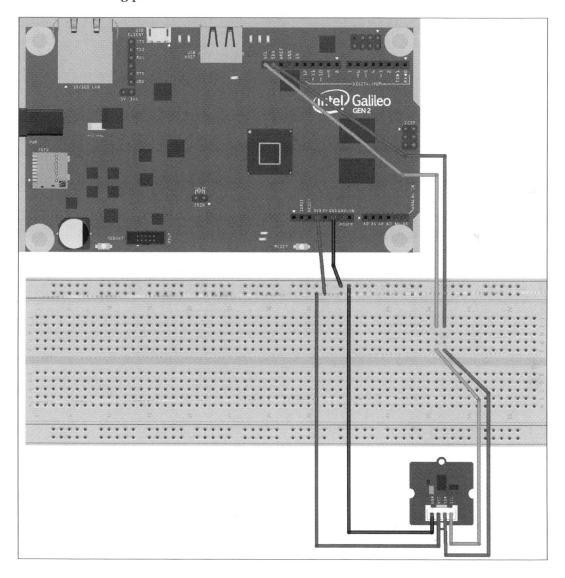

The following picture shows the schematic with the electronic components represented as symbols:

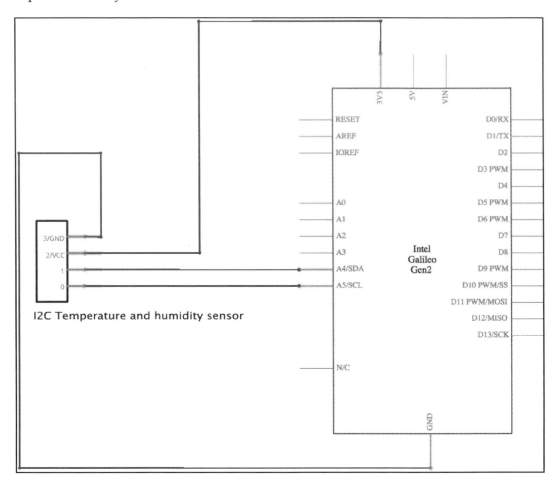

As seen in the previous schematic, we have the following connections:

- The **SDA** pin is connected to the breakout board pin labeled **SDA**. This way, we connect the digital temperature and humidity sensor to the serial data line for the I²C bus.

- The **SCL** pin is connected to the breakout board pin labeled **SCL**. This way, we connect the digital temperature and humidity sensor to the serial clock line for the I²C bus.

- The power pin labeled **3V3** is connected to the breakout board power pin labeled **VCC**.

- The ground pin labeled **GND** is connected to the breakout board ground pin labeled **GND**.

Now, it is time make all the necessary wirings. Don't forget to shutdown the Yocto Linux, wait for all the onboard LEDs to turn off, and unplug the power supply from the Intel Galileo Gen 2 board before adding or removing any wire from the board's pins.

Measuring temperature and humidity with a digital sensor

The upm library includes support for the digital temperature and humidity breakout board that uses the TH02 sensor in the pyupm_th02 module. The TH02 class declared in this module represents a digital temperature and humidity sensor that uses the TH02 sensor, connected to our board. The class makes it easy to initialize the sensor and retrieve the temperature and humidity values through the I²C bus. The class works with the mraa.I2c class under the hoods to talk with the sensor, that is, to write data to and read data from the TH02 sensor that acts as a slave device connected to the I²C bus.

We will create a new TemperatureAndHumiditySensor class to represent the temperature and humidity sensor and make it easier for us to retrieve the temperature and humidity values in the appropriate units working with an instance of the TH02 class. We will use the TH02 class to interact with the sensor. The following lines show the code for the new TemperatureSensor class that works with the upm library, specifically with the pyupm_th02 module. The code file for the sample is iot_python_chapter_07_05.py.

```
import pyupm_th02 as upmTh02
import time


class TemperatureAndHumiditySensor:
    def __init__(self, bus):
        self.th02_sensor = upmTh02.TH02(bus)
        self.temperature_celsius = 0.0
        self.temperature_fahrenheit = 0.0
        self.humidity = 0.0
```

```
def measure_temperature_and_humidity(self):
    # Retrieve the temperature expressed in Celsius degrees
    temperature_celsius = self.th02_sensor.getTemperature()
    self.temperature_celsius = temperature_celsius
    self.temperature_fahrenheit = \
        (temperature_celsius * 9.0 / 5.0) + 32.0
    # Retrieve the humidity
    self.humidity = self.th02_sensor.getHumidity()
```

We have to specify the I²C bus number to which the digital temperature and humidity sensor is wired when we create an instance of the TemperatureAndHumiditySensor class in the bus required argument. The constructor, that is, the __init__ method, creates a new upmTh02.TH02 instance with the received bus argument and saves its reference in the th02_sensor attribute.

> The datasheet for the TH02 sensor specifies a formula to convert the raw read temperature to degrees Celsius (°C), and therefore, by reading the datasheet we might think the upmTh02.TH02 instance will provide us a value in degrees Fahrenheit (°F). However, this is not what happens. The upmTh02.TH02 instance performs the conversion from degrees Fahrenheit (°F) to degrees Celsius (°C) and provides us a value in the latter unit of measure. Thus, if we want to display the value in degrees Fahrenheit (°F), we must perform the conversion from degrees Celsius (°C) to degrees Fahrenheit (°F). Unluckily, the only way of realizing about this situation is by looking at the C++ source code for the upm module because there is no documentation about the unit of measure that the code uses to return the temperature value.

We want to work with easy to understand attributes, and therefore, the constructor creates and initializes three attributes with 0.0: temperature_celsius, temperature_fahrenheit, and humidity. After the constructor is executed, we have an initialized digital temperature and humidity sensor ready to retrieve values.

The class defines a measure_temperature_and_humidity method that updates the ambient temperature and humidity values in the sensor, retrieves these values, and finally saves them in the following three attributes: temperature_celsius, temperature_fahrenheit, and humidity.

First, the code within the `measure_temperature_and_humidity` method calls the `getTemperature` method for `self.th02_sensor` to request the sensor to retrieve the temperature value. The method returns the read value converted to degrees Celsius (°C) and the code saves it in the `temperature_celsius` local variable. The code saves the value in the attribute with the same name and saves the value converted to degrees Fahrenheit (°F) in the `temperature_fahrenheit` attribute. Finally, the code calls the `getHumidity` method for `self.th02_sensor` to request the sensor to retrieve the humidity value and saves it in the `humidity` attribute.

Now, we will write a loop that will retrieve and display the temperature values expressed in degrees Celsius (°C) and degrees Fahrenheit, and the humidity value, every 10 seconds. The code file for the sample is `iot_python_chapter_07_05.py`.

```python
if __name__ == "__main__":
    temperature_and_humidity_sensor = \
        TemperatureAndHumiditySensor(0)

    while True:
        temperature_and_humidity_sensor.\
            measure_temperature_and_humidity()
        print("Ambient temperature in degrees Celsius: {0}".
            format(temperature_and_humidity_sensor.temperature_
celsius))
        print("Ambient temperature in degrees Fahrenheit: {0}".
            format(temperature_and_humidity_sensor.temperature_
fahrenheit))
        print("Ambient humidity: {0}%".
            format(temperature_and_humidity_sensor.humidity))
        # Sleep 10 seconds (10000 milliseconds)
        time.sleep(10)
```

The first line creates an instance of the previously coded `TemperatureAndHumiditySensor` class with 0 as the value of the `bus` argument. This way, the instance will establish a communication with the digital accelerometer through the I²C bus. As happened in our previous example with a sensor connected to the I²C bus, the Intel Galileo Gen 2 board is the master in the bus and the digital temperature and humidity sensor, acts as a slave.

Then, the code runs a loop forever that calls the `measure_temperature_and_humidity` method to update the temperature values expressed in two units and the humidity.

The following line will start the example:

```
python iot_python_chapter_07_05.py
```

After you run the example, turn on an air conditioner or a heating system, to generate a change in the ambient temperature and humidity.

```
Ambient temperature in degrees Celsius: 24
Ambient temperature in degrees Fahrenheit: 73.4
Ambient humidity: 48%
```

Test your knowledge

1. Which of the following sensors allows us to measure the magnitude and direction of proper acceleration?

    1. A temperature sensor.
    2. An accelerometer.
    3. A light sensor.

2. Which of the following acronym that defines a connection type for a module with a sensor is analog:

    1. AIO.
    2. I²C.
    3. UART.

3. How many wires do we need to connect a device to the I²C bus:

    1. 1.
    2. 2.
    3. 3.

4. How many wires do we need to connect a device to the SPI bus:

    1. 1.
    2. 2.
    3. 3.

5. Which of the following is not a connection of the I²C bus:

    1. MISO.
    2. SDA.
    3. SCL.

Summary

In this chapter, we learned about sensors and their connection types. We understood that it is necessary to consider many important things when choosing sensors and that they make it easy for us to measure different variables from the real world. We learned the importance of considering the units of measure because sensors always provide values measured in a specific unit that we must consider.

We wrote code that took advantage of the modules and classes included in the upm library that made it easier for us to start working with analog and digital sensors. In addition, we wrote code that interacted with a digital accelerometer through the I²C bus because we wanted to be able to take advantage of additional features provided by the sensor but not included in the upm library module.

We measured the magnitude and direction of proper acceleration or g-force, ambient temperature and humidity. As in the previous chapters, we continued taking advantage of Python's object-oriented features and we created classes to encapsulate sensors and the necessary configurations with the upm and mraa libraries. Our code is easy to read and understand and we can easily hide the low-level details.

Now that we are able to retrieve data from the real world with sensors, we will make our IoT device perform actions with different actuators and shields, which is the topic of the next chapter.

8

Displaying Information and Performing Actions

In this chapter, we will work with a variety of breakout boards and an actuator to display data and perform actions by writing a Python code. We shall:

- Understand LCD displays and their connection types
- Learn the most important things we must consider when choosing LCD displays
- Take advantage of the upm library with LCD displays and actuators
- Use an LCD display with an RGB backlight that works with the I²C bus
- Display and update text in a 16x2 LCD screen
- Use an OLED display that works with the I²C bus
- Display and update text on a 96-by-96 dot matrix OLED display
- Wire a standard servo motor to be controlled with PWM
- Display a value with a servo motor and a shaft

Understanding LCD displays and their connection types

Sometimes, our IoT device has to provide information to the user with any device connected to an Intel Galileo Gen 2 board. We can use different kinds of electronic components, shields, or breakout boards to achieve this goal.

For example, we can use simple LEDs to provide information that we can represent with colors. For example, a red LED that turns on can indicate that our temperature sensor connected to the board has detected that the ambient temperature is higher than 80 degrees Fahrenheit (°F) or 26.66 degrees Celsius (°C). A blue LED that turns on can indicate that our temperature sensor had detected that the ambient temperature is lower than 40 degrees Fahrenheit (°F) or 4.44 degrees Celsius (°C). A red LED turned on can indicate that the temperature is between these two values. These three LEDs allow us to provide valuable information to the user.

We can also achieve the same goal using a single RGB LED and work with **pulse width modulation** (**PWM**) to change its color based on the measured ambient temperature value, as we learned in *Chapter 4, Working with a RESTful API and Pulse Width Modulation*.

However, sometimes colors aren't enough to provide a detailed and accurate information to the user. For example, sometimes we want to display the humidity level with a percentage value and a few LEDs aren't enough to represent numbers from 0 to 100%. If we want to be able to display a 1% step, we would require 100 LEDs. We don't have 100 GPIO pins, and therefore, we would require a shield or breakout board with 100 LEDs and a digital interface such as an I²C bus to allow us to send commands indicating the number of LEDs that we want to be turned on.

In these cases, an LCD screen that allows us to print a specific number of characters might be an appropriate solution. For example, on an LCD screen that allows us to display 16 characters per line, with 2 lines of 16 characters, known as a 16x2 LCD module, we can display the temperature in the first line and the humidity level in the second line. The following table shows an example of each line with the text and the values considering that we have 16 columns and 2 rows for the characters.

T	e	m	p	.					4	0	.	2	F		
H	u	m	i	d	i	t	y				8	0	%		

The 16x2 LCD module provides a clear description for each value, a floating point value and a unit of measure. Thus, we will use a 16x2 LCD module for our example. The following picture shows an example of the location of each character in a 16x2 LCD screen:

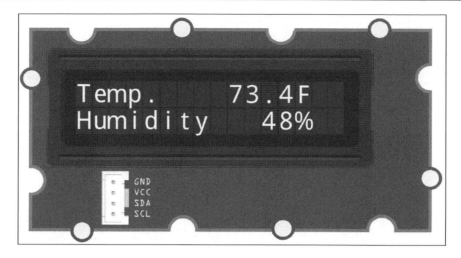

There are LCD modules with different features and we must consider a lot of the things we learned when we analyzed sensors in *Chapter 7, Retrieving Data from the Real World with Sensors*. The following list enumerates the most important things that we must consider when we select an LCD module and their description. As we analyzed many of these things when we learned about sensors, we won't repeat the descriptions for the common items.

- **Compatibility with Intel Galileo Gen 2 board and the voltage supply that we are using (5V or 3.3V).**
- **Power consumption.**
- **Connection type**: Some LCD displays consume too many pins, and therefore, it is very important to check all the pins that they require. The most common connection types for LCD displays are the I²C bus, the SPI bus, and the UART port. However, some LCD displays require a bus or port combined with additional GPIO pins.
- **Operating range and special environment requirements.**
- **Dimensions**: LCD displays come with different dimensions. Sometimes only specific dimensions are suitable for our project.
- **Number of columns and rows**: Based on the text we have to display, we will select the LCD display with the appropriate number of columns and rows that can display the characters.

- **Response time**: It is very important to determine how much we can wait for the LCD display to show the new content that replaces the text that is being displayed or to clear the display.

- **Protocol, support in the upm library and Python bindings**.

- **Supported character set and built-in fonts**: Some LCD displays support user-defined characters, and therefore, they allow us to configure and display custom characters. It is also important to check whether the LCD display supports characters for the languages in which we have to display the text.

- **Backlight color, text color and contrast level**: Some LCD displays allow us to change the backlight color while others have a fixed backlight color. An RGB backlight makes it possible to combine red, green, and blue components to determine the desired backlight color. In addition, it is always important to take into account whether the contrast level is appropriate for the light conditions in which you will need to display information.

- **Cost**.

Wiring an LCD RGB backlight to the I²C bus

In our last example in *Chapter 7, Retrieving Data from the Real World with Sensors*, we worked with a multifunctional digital sensor that provided us with the temperature and relative humidity information. We worked with a breakout board that uses the I²C bus to allow the Intel Galileo Gen 2 board to communicate with the sensor. Now, we will add a breakout board with a 16x2 LCD RGB backlight to allow us to display the measured temperature and humidity values with text and numbers.

The LCD RGB backlight breakout board will also be connected to the same I²C bus to which the temperature and humidity digital sensor is connected. We can connect many slaves to the I²C bus in the Intel Galileo Gen 2 board as long as their have different I²C addresses. In fact, the LCD RGB backlight breakout board has two I²C addresses: one for the LCD display and the other for the backlight.

We need the following parts to work with this example:

- A SeeedStudio Grove temperature and humidity sensor (high-accuracy and mini) breakout. The following URL provides detailed information about this breakout board: `http://www.seeedstudio.com/depot/Grove-TemperatureHumidity-Sensor-HighAccuracy-Mini-p-1921.html`.

- A SeeedStudio Grove LCD RGB backlight breakout. The following URL provides detailed information about this breakout board: http://www. seeedstudio.com/depot/Grove-LCD-RGB-Backlight-p-1643.html.

The following diagram shows the digital temperature and humidity breakout, the LCD RGB backlight breakout, the necessary wirings, and the wirings from the Intel Galileo Gen 2 board to the breadboard. The Fritzing file for the sample is iot_ fritzing_chapter_08_01.fzz and the following image is the breadboard view:

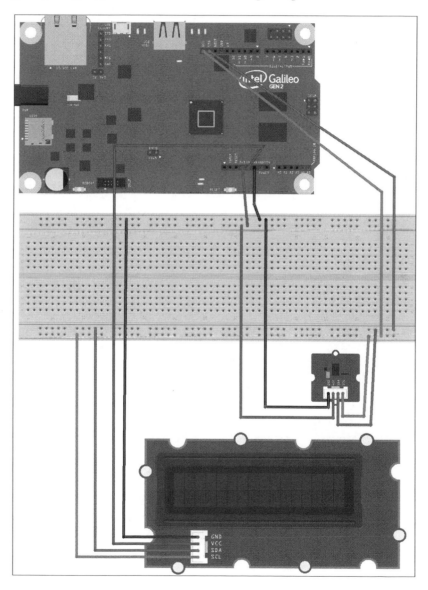

The following image shows the schematic with the electronic components represented as symbols:

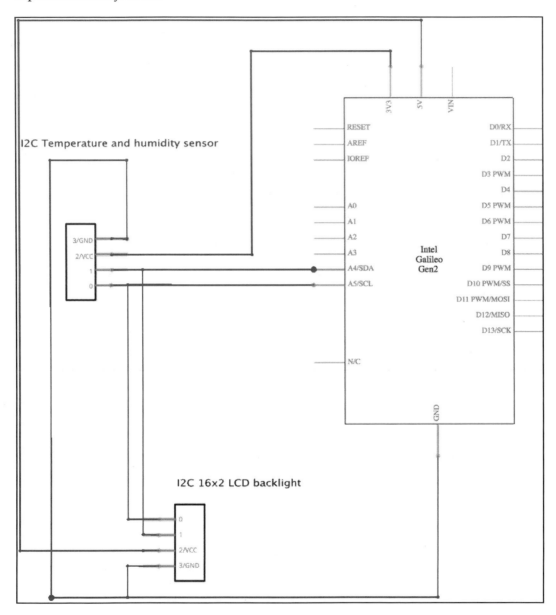

As seen in the previous schematic, we have the following connections:

- The **SDA** pin is connected to both the breakout board pins labeled **SDA**. This way, we connect both the digital temperature and humidity sensor and the LCD backlight to the serial data line for the I²C bus.

- The **SCL** pin is connected to both the breakout board pins labeled **SCL**. This way, we can connect both the digital temperature and humidity sensor and the LCD backlight to the serial clock line for the I²C bus.

- The power pin labeled **3V3** is connected to the digital temperature and humidity sensor breakout board power pin labeled **VCC**.

- The power pin labeled **5V** is connected to the LCD backlight breakout board power pin labeled **VCC**.

- The ground pin labeled **GND** is connected to both the breakout board pins labeled **GND**.

Now, it is time make all the necessary wirings. Don't forget to shut down the Yocto Linux, wait for all the onboard LEDs to turn off and unplug the power supply from the Intel Galileo Gen 2 board before adding or removing any wire from the board's pins.

Displaying text on an LCD display

The upm library includes support for the 16x2 LCD RGB backlight breakout board in the pyupm_i2clcd module. The Jhd1313m1 class declared in this module represents a 16x2 LCD display and its RGB backlight, connected to our board. The class makes it easy to set the color components for the RGB backlight, clear the LCD display, specify the cursor location, and write text through the I²C bus. The class works with the mraa.I2c class under the hoods to talk with the RGB backlight and the LCD display. These two devices act as slave devices connected to the I²C bus, and therefore, each of them have a specific address in this bus.

We will take the code we wrote in the previous chapter when we read temperature and humidity values from the sensor and we will use this code as a baseline to add the new features. The code file for the sample was iot_python_chapter_07_05.py.

We will create an `Lcd` class to represent the 16x2 LCD RGB backlight and make it easier for us to set the background color and write the text in two lines without worrying about the specific methods when working with an instance of the `Jhd1313m1` class. We will use the `Jhd1313m1` class to interact with the LCD and its RGB backlight. The following lines show the code for the new `Lcd` class that works with the `upm` library, specifically with the `pyupm_i2clcd` module. The code file for the sample is `iot_python_chapter_08_01.py`.

```python
import pyupm_th02 as upmTh02
import pyupm_i2clcd as upmLcd
import time


class Lcd:
    # The I2C address for the LCD display
    lcd_i2c_address = 0x3E
    # The I2C address for the RBG backlight
    rgb_i2c_address = 0x62

    def __init__(self, bus, red, green, blue):
        self.lcd = upmLcd.Jhd1313m1(
            bus,
            self.__class__.lcd_i2c_address,
            self.__class__.rgb_i2c_address)
        self.lcd.clear()
        self.set_background_color(red, green, blue)

    def set_background_color(self, red, green, blue):
        self.lcd.setColor(red, green, blue)

    def print_line_1(self, message):
        self.lcd.setCursor(0, 0)
        self.lcd.write(message)

    def print_line_2(self, message):
        self.lcd.setCursor(1, 0)
        self.lcd.write(message)
```

The Lcd class declares two class attributes: lcd_i2c_address and rgb_i2c_address. The first class attribute defines the I²C address for the LCD display, that is, the address that will process the commands that locate the cursor and write text once the cursor is located in a specific row and column. The address is 3E in hexadecimal (0x3E). If we just see a 0x3E within the code, we don't understand that it is an I²C bus address for the LCD display. The second class attribute defines the I²C address for the RGB backlight, that is, the address that will process the commands that set the red, green, and blue components for the backlight color. The address is 62 in hexadecimal (0x62). If we just see a 0x62 within the code, we don't understand that it is an I²C bus address for the RGB backlight. These class attributes make it easier to read the code.

We have to specify the I²C bus number to which the both the 16x2 LCD and the RGB backlight are wired when we create an instance of the Lcd class in the bus required argument. In addition, it is necessary to specify the values for the red, green and blue color components to configure the background color for the RGB backlight. The constructor, that is, the __init__ method, creates a new upmLcd.Jhd1313m1 instance with the received bus argument followed by the lcd_i2c_address and rgb_i2c_address class attributes and saves the reference for the new instance in the lcd attribute. Then, the code calls the clear method for the new instance to clear the LCD screen. Finally, the code calls the set_background_color method with the red, green, and blue values received as arguments to configure the background color for the RGB backlight.

The class declares the set_background_color method that calls the lcd.setColor method with the red, green and blue values received as arguments. Under the hoods, the upmLcd.Jhd1313m1 instance will write data to the slave device whose address is equal to the rgb_i2c_address class attribute through the I²C bus to specify the desired value for each color component. We just create a specific method to follow Python naming conventions and make our final code that uses our class easier to read.

The class defines the following two additional methods to make it easy to print text on the first and the second row of the LCD display:

- print_line_1
- print_line_2

The print_line_1 method calls the setCursor method for the upmLcd.Jhd1313m1 instance (self.lcd), with 0 as the value for both the row and the column argument, to locate the cursor in the first row and the first column. Then, a call to the write method for the the upmLcd.Jhd1313m1 instance (self.lcd) with the message reviewed as a parameter as an argument prints the received string in the LCD display. Under the hoods, the upmLcd.Jhd1313m1 instance will write the data to the slave device whose address is equal to the lcd_i2c_address class attribute through the I²C bus to specify the desired location for the cursor and then to write the specified text starting in the position in which we have located the cursor. The first row is identified with 0, but we named the method print_line_1 because it makes it easier for us to understand that we are writing a message in the first line of the LCD screen.

The print_line_2 method has the same two lines of code than the print_line_1 method with just one difference: the call to the setCursor method specifies 1 as the value for the row argument. This way, the method prints a message in the second line of the LCD screen.

Now, we will create a subclass of the previously coded Lcd class named TemperatureAndHumidityLcd. The subclass will specialize the Lcd class to allow us to easily print a temperature value expressed in degrees Fahrenheit in the first line of the LCD screen and print a humidity value expressed in percentage in the second line of the LCD screen. The following lines show the code for the new TemperatureAndHumidityLcd class. The code file for the sample is iot_python_chapter_08_01.py.

```
class TemperatureAndHumidityLcd(Lcd):
    def print_temperature(self, temperature_fahrenheit):
        self.print_line_1("Temp.    {:5.2f}F".format(temperature_
fahrenheit))

    def print_humidity(self, humidity):
        self.print_line_2("Humidity   {0}%".format(humidity))
```

The new class (TemperatureAndHumidityLcd) adds the following two methods to its superclass (Lcd):

- print_temperature: Calls the print_line_1 method with the formatted text that displays the temperature value expressed in degrees Fahrenheit (°F) received in the temperature_fahrenheit argument.

- print_humidity: Calls the print_line_2 method with the formatted text that displays the humidity level expressed in percentage received in the humidity argument.

Now, we will write a loop that will display the ambient temperature expressed in degrees Fahrenheit (°F) and the humidity value in the LCD screen, every 10 seconds. The code file for the sample is `iot_python_chapter_08_01.py`.

```python
if __name__ == "__main__":
    temperature_and_humidity_sensor = \
        TemperatureAndHumiditySensor(0)
    lcd = TemperatureAndHumidityLcd(0, 0, 0, 128)

    while True:
        temperature_and_humidity_sensor.\
            measure_temperature_and_humidity()
        lcd.print_temperature(
            temperature_and_humidity_sensor.temperature_fahrenheit)
        lcd.print_humidity(
            temperature_and_humidity_sensor.humidity)
        print("Ambient temperature in degrees Celsius: {0}".
            format(temperature_and_humidity_sensor.temperature_
celsius))
        print("Ambient temperature in degrees Fahrenheit: {0}".
            format(temperature_and_humidity_sensor.temperature_
fahrenheit))
        print("Ambient humidity. {0}".
            format(temperature_and_humidity_sensor.humidity))
        # Sleep 10 seconds (10000 milliseconds)
        time.sleep(10)
```

The highlighted lines show the changes made to the `__main__` method compared with the previous version. The first highlighted line creates an instance of the previously coded `TemperatureAndHumidityLcd` class with `0` as the value of the `bus` argument, `0` for `red` and `green`, and `128` for `blue` to set the background color to light blue. The code saves the reference to this instance in the `lcd` local variable. This way, the instance will establish a communication with the LCD screen and the RGB backlight through the I²C bus. The RGB backlight will display a light blue background.

Then, the code runs a loop forever and the highlighted line calls the `lcd.print_temperature` method with `temperature_and_humidity_sensor.temperature_fahrenheit`, that is, the measured temperature expressed in degrees Fahrenheit (°F), as an argument. This way, the code displays this temperature value in the first line of the LCD screen.

The next hightlighted line calls the `lcd.print_humidity` method with `temperature_and_humidity_sensor.humidity`, that is, the measured humidity expressed in percentage, as an argument. This way, the code displays this humidity value in the second line of the LCD screen.

The following line will start the example:

```
python iot_python_chapter_08_01.py
```

After you run the example, turn on an air conditioner or heating system, to generate a change in the ambient temperature and humidity. The LCD screen will display the temperature and humidity and refresh it every 10 seconds.

Wiring an OLED dot matrix to the I²C bus

LCD displays are not the only option when we have to display content on an external screen through the I²C or SPI buses. There are also OLED dot matrixes that allow us to control a specific number of dots. In OLED dot matrices we have control over each dot, instead of controlling each character space. Some of them are grayscale and others RGB.

The key advantage of OLED dot matrixes is that we can display any kind of graphics and not just text. In fact, we can mix any kind of graphics and images with text. The Grove OLED Display 0.96" is an example of a 16 grayscale 96-by-96 dot matrix OLED display module that works with the I²C bus. The following URL provides detailed information about this breakout board: `http://www.seeedstudio.com/depot/Grove-OLED-Display-096-p-824.html`. The Xadow RGB OLED 96x24 is an example of an RGB color 96-by-64 dot matrix OLED display module that works with the SPI bus. The following URL provides detailed information about this breakout board: `http://www.seeedstudio.com/depot/Xadow-RGB-OLED-96x64-p-2125.html`.

 Another option is to work with TFT LCD dot matrices or displays. Some of them include support for touch detection.

Now, we will replace the breakout board with a 16x2 LCD RGB backlight with a 16 grayscale 96-by-96 dot matrix OLED display module that also works with the I²C bus, and we will use this new screen to display similar values with a different configuration. The wirings are compatible with the previous breakout board.

As it happened in our previous example, the dot matrix OLED will also be connected to the same I²C bus to which the temperature and humidity digital sensor is connected. As the dot matrix OLED has an I²C address that is different than the one used by the temperature and humidity digital sensor, we don't have problems to wire the two devices to the same I²C bus.

We need the following additional part to work with this example: A SeeedStudio Grove OLED Display 0.96", 16 grayscale 96-by-96 dot matrix OLED display module. The 96-by-96 dot matrix OLED display provides us the chance to control 9,216 dots, known as pixels. However, in this case, we just want to use the OLED display to display a similar text than the one we displayed in our previous example, but with a different layout.

If we use the default 8-by-8 character box, we have 12 columns (96/8) and 12 rows (96/8) for characters. The following table shows an example of each line with the text and the values.

T	e	m	p	e	r	a	t	u	r	e	
F	a	h	r	e	n	h	e	i	t		
4	0	.	2								
C	e	l	s	i	u	s					
4	.	5	5								
H	u	m	i	d	i	t	y				
L	e	v	e	l							
8	0	%									

The possibility to work with 12 columns and 12 rows of characters allows us to provide a very clear description for each value. In addition, we are able to display the temperature values expressed in both degrees Fahrenheit and degrees Celsius. The following picture shows an example of the location of each character in the 96-by-96 dot matrix OLED display module with an 8-by-8 character box.

After we replace the LCD screen breakout board with the OLED module, we will have the following connections:

- The **SDA** pin is connected to both breakout board pins labeled **SDA**. This way, we connect both the digital temperature and humidity sensor and the OLED module to the serial data line for the I²C bus.

- The **SCL** pin is connected to both the breakout board pins labeled **SCL**. This way, we connect both the digital temperature and humidity sensor and the OLED module to the serial clock line for the I²C bus.

- The power pin labeled **3V3** is connected to the digital temperature and humidity sensor breakout board power pin labeled **VCC**.

- The power pin labeled **5V** is connected to the OLED module power pin labeled **VCC**.

- The ground pin labeled **GND** is connected to both the breakout board pins labeled **GND**.

Now, it is time make all the necessary wirings. Don't forget to shutdown the Yocto Linux, wait for all the onboard LEDs to turn off, and unplug the power supply from the Intel Galileo Gen 2 board before adding or removing any wire from the board's pins.

Displaying text on an OLED display

The upm library includes support for the SeeedStudio Grove OLED display 0.96",
16 grayscale 96-by-96 dot matrix OLED display breakout board the in the pyupm_
i2clcd module. As this OLED display uses SSD1327 driver integrated circuit, the
SSD1327 class declared in this module represents a 96-by-96 dot matrix OLED
display, connected to our board. The class makes it easy to clear the OLED screen,
draw bitmap images, specify the cursor location, and write text through the I²C
bus. The class works with the mraa.I2c class under the hoods to talk with the
OLED display.

We will create a new Oled class that will represent the 96-by-96 dot matrix OLED
and will use its default 8-by-8 character box to display text. We will use the SSD1327
class to interact with the OLED display. The following lines show the code for
the new Oled class that works with the upm library, specifically with the pyupm_
i2clcd module and its SSD1327 class. The code file for the sample is iot_python_
chapter_08_02.py:

```python
class Oled:
    # The I2C address for the OLED display
    oled_i2c_address = 0x3C

    def __init__(self, bus, red, green, blue):
        self.oled = upmLcd.SSD1327(
            bus,
            self.__class__.oled_i2c_address)
        self.oled.clear()

    def print_line(self, row, message):
        self.oled.setCursor(row, 0)
        self.oled.setGrayLevel(12)
        self.oled.write(message)
```

The Oled class declares the oled_i2c_address class attribute that defines the I²C
address for the OLED display, that is, the address that will process the commands
that locate the cursor and write text once the cursor is located in a specific row and
column. The address is 3C in hexadecimal (0x3C).

We have to specify the I²C bus number to which the OLED display is wired when we
create an instance of the Oled class in the bus required argument. The constructor,
that is, the __init__ method, creates a new upmLcd.SSD1327 instance with the
received bus argument followed by the oled_i2c_address class attribute, and saves
the reference for the new instance in the oled attribute. Finally, the code calls the
clear method for the new instance to clear the OLED screen.

The class declared the `print_line` method to make it easy to print text on a specific row. The code calls the `setCursor` method for the `upmLcd.SSD1327` instance (`self.oled`), with the received `row` value as the value for the `row` argument and 0 for the `column` argument, to locate the cursor in the specified row and the first column. Then, a call to the `setGrayLevel` and the `write` method for the the `upmLcd.SSD1327` instance (`self.oled`) with the `message` reveiced as a parameter as an argument prints the received string in the OLED display with the default 8-by-8 character box with the gray level set to 12. Under the hoods, the `upmLcd.SSD1327` instance will write data to the slave device whose address is equal to the `oled_i2c_address` class attribute through the I²C bus to specify the desired location for the cursor and then to write the specified text starting in the position in which we have located the cursor.

Now, we will create a subclass of the previously coded `Oled` class named `TemperatureAndHumidityOled`. The subclass will specialize the `Oled` class to allow us to easily print a temperature value expressed in degrees Fahrenheit, the temperature value expressed in degrees Celsius and a humidity value expressed in percentage. We will use the previously explained layout for the text. The following lines show the code for the new `TemperatureAndHumidityOled` class. The code file for the sample is `iot_python_chapter_08_02.py`.

```
class TemperatureAndHumidityOled(Oled):
    def print_temperature(self, temperature_fahrenheit, temperature_
celsius):
        self.oled.clear()
        self.print_line(0, "Temperature")
        self.print_line(2, "Fahrenheit")
        self.print_line(3, "{:5.2f}".format(temperature_fahrenheit))
        self.print_line(5, "Celsius")
        self.print_line(6, "{:5.2f}".format(temperature_celsius))

    def print_humidity(self, humidity):
        self.print_line(8, "Humidity")
        self.print_line(9, "Level")
        self.print_line(10, "{0}%".format(humidity))
```

The new class (`TemperatureAndHumidityOled`) adds the following two methods to its superclass (`Oled`):

- `print_temperature`: Calls the `print_line` method many times to display the temperature in both degrees Fahrenheit (°F) and Celsius (°C) received as arguments

- `print_humidity`: Calls the `print_line` method many times to display the humidity value received as an argument

In this case, we refresh many lines to change just a few values. As we will run a loop every 10 seconds, it won't be a problem. However, in other cases in which we want to update values in a shorter amount of time, we can write optimized code that just clears a single line and updates the specific value in this line.

Now, we will write a loop that will display the ambient temperature expressed in Fahrenheit (°F) and Celsius (°C) and the humidity value in the OLED screen, every 10 seconds. The code file for the sample is iot_python_chapter_08_02.py.

```python
if __name__ == "__main__":
    temperature_and_humidity_sensor = \
        TemperatureAndHumiditySensor(0)
    oled = TemperatureAndHumidityOled(0)

    while True:
        temperature_and_humidity_sensor.\
            measure_temperature_and_humidity()
        oled.print_temperature(
            temperature_and_humidity_sensor.temperature_fahrenheit,
            temperature_and_humidity_sensor.temperature_celsius)
        oled.print_humidity(
            temperature_and_humidity_sensor.humidity)
        print("Ambient temperature in degrees Celsius: {0}".
            format(temperature_and_humidity_sensor.temperature_
celsius))
        print("Ambient temperature in degrees Fahrenheit: {0}".
            format(temperature_and_humidity_sensor.temperature_
fahrenheit))
        print("Ambient humidity: {0}".
            format(temperature_and_humidity_sensor.humidity))
        # Sleep 10 seconds (10000 milliseconds)
        time.sleep(10)
```

The highlighted lines show the changes made in the __main__ method compared with the previous version. The first highlighted line creates an instance of the previously coded TemperatureAndHumidityOled class with 0 as the value of the bus argument. The code saves the reference to this instance in the oled local variable. This way, the instance will establish a communication with the OLED screen through the I²C bus.

Then, the code runs a loop forever and the highlighted line calls the `oled.print_temperature` method with `temperature_and_humidity_sensor.temperature_fahrenheit` and `temperature_and_humidity_sensor.temperature_celsius` as arguments. This way, the code displays both temperature values in the first lines of the OLED screen.

The next hightlighted line calls the `oled.print_humidity` method with `temperature_and_humidity_sensor.humidity`. This way, the code uses many lines to display this humidity value at the bottom of the OLED screen.

The following line will start the example:

```
python iot_python_chapter_08_02.py
```

After you run the example, turn on an air conditioner or a heating system to generate a change in the ambient temperature and humidity. The OLED screen will display the temperature and humidity and refresh it every 10 seconds.

Wiring a servo motor

So far, we have been using sensors to retrieve data from the real world and we displayed information in LCD and OLED displays. However, IoT devices are not limited to sensing and displaying data, they can also move things. We can connect different components, shields, or breakout boards to our Intel Galileo Gen 2 board and write Python code to move things connected to the board.

Standard servo motors are extremely useful to precisely control a shaft and position it at various angles, usually between 0 and 180 degrees. In *Chapter 4, Working with a RESTful API and Pulse Width Modulation*, we worked with pulse width modulation, known as PWM, to control the brightness of an LED and a RGB LED. We can also use PWM to control a standard analog servo motor and position its shaft at a specific angle.

Standard servo motors are DC motors that includes gears and feedback control loop circuitry that provides precision positioning. They are ideal for pinion steering, robot arms and legs, among other usages that require a precise positioning. Standard servo motors don't require motor drivers.

Obviously, not all servor motors have the same features and we must take into account many of them when we select a specific servo motor for our project. It depends on what we need to position, the accuracy, the required torque, the optimal servo rotational velocity, among other factors. In this case, we will focus on the usage of PWM to position a standard servo motor. However, you cannot use the same servo to rotate a lighter plastic piece than the one you will need to rotate a heavy robotic arm. It is necessary to research about the appropriate servo for each task.

Now, we will wire a standard high sensitive mini servo motor to our existing project and we will rotate the shaft to display the measured temperature expressed in degrees Fahrenheit with the shaft. The shaft will allow us to display the measured temperature in a half circle protractor that measures angles in degrees and will display the number for the angle from 0 to 180 degrees. The combination of the servo with the shaft and the protractor will allow us to display the temperature with moving parts. Then, we can create our own protractor with a scale that can add colors, specific thresholds and many other visual artifacts to make temperature measurement funnier. Specifically, we can create a gauge chart, speedometer or semicircle donut, that is, a combination of a doughnut chart and a pie chart in a single chart with the different temperature values. The following picture shows and example of a half circle protractor that we can use in combination with the servo with the shaft.

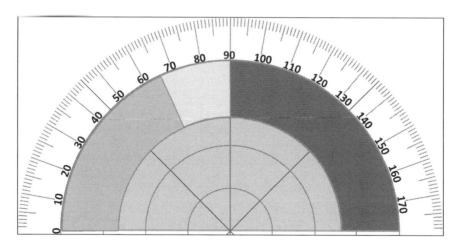

We need the following additional part to work with this example: A SeeedStudio Grove Servo or a EMAX 9g ES08A High Sensitive Mini Servo. The following URLs provide detailed information about these servos: `http://www.seeedstudio.com/depot/Grove-Servo-p-1241.html` and `http://www.seeedstudio.com/depot/EMAX-9g-ES08A-High-Sensitive-Mini-Servo-p-760.html`.

The following diagram shows the digital temperature and humidity breakout, the LCD RGB backlight breakout, the mini servo, the necessary wirings and the wirings from the Intel Galileo Gen 2 board to the breadboard. The Fritzing file for the sample is `iot_fritzing_chapter_08_03.fzz` and the following picture is the breadboard view:

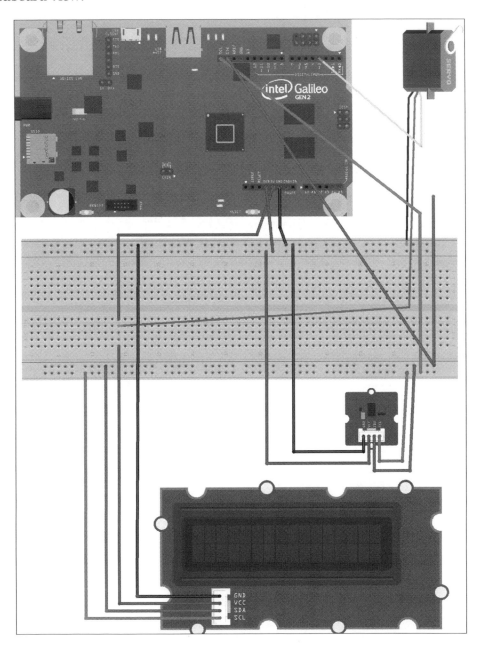

The following picture shows the schematic with the electronic components represented as symbols:

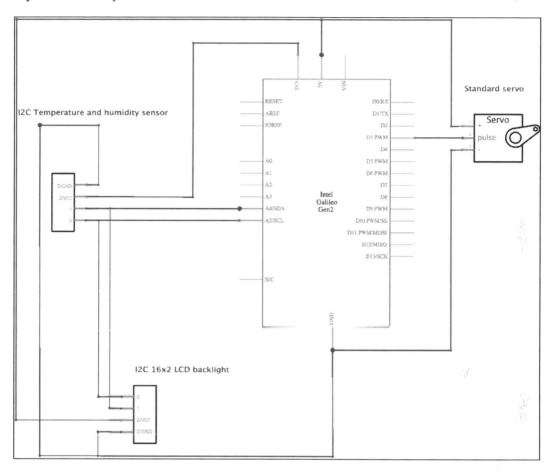

As seen in the previous schematic, we added the following additional connections to our existing project:

- The power pin labeled **5V** in the board's symbol is connected to the servo's pin labeled **+**. Servos usually use a red wire for this connection.

- The PWM capable GPIO pin labeled **D3 PWM** in the board's symbol is connected to the servo's pin labeled **PULSE**. Servos usually use a yellow wire for this connection.

- The ground pin labeled **GND** in the board's symbol is connected to the servo's pin labeled **-**. Servos usually use a black wire for this connection.

Now, it is time make all the necessary wirings. Don't forget to shut down the Yocto Linux, wait for all the onboard LEDs to turn off, and unplug the power supply from the Intel Galileo Gen 2 board before adding or removing any wire from the board's pins.

Positioning a shaft to indicate a value with a servo motor

We can use the `mraa.Pwm` class to control PWM on the PWM capable GPIO pin labeled **~3**, as we learned in *Chapter 4, Working with a RESTful API and Pulse Width Modulation*. However, this would require us to read the detailed specs for the servo. The upm library includes support for both the SeeedStudio Grove Servo or the EMAX 9g ES08A High Sensitive Mini Servo in the `pyupm_servo` module. The ES08A class declared in this module represents any of the two mentioned servors connected to our board.

The class makes it easy to set the desired angle for the servo shaft and work with angles instead of duty cycles and other PWM details. The class works with the `mraa.Pwm` class under the hoods to configure PWM and control the duty cycle based on the desired angle for the shaft.

We will take the code we wrote in the previous example and we will use this code as a baseline to add the new features. The code file for the sample was `iot_python_chapter_08_02.py`.

We will create a `TemperatureServo` class to represent the servo and make it easier for us to position the shaft in a valid angle (from 0 to 180 degrees) based on the temperature expressed in degrees Fahrenheit. We will use the ES08A class to interact with the servo. The following lines show the code for the new `TemperatureServo` class that works with the upm library, specifically with the `pyupm_servo` module. The code file for the sample is `iot_python_chapter_08_03.py`.

```python
import pyupm_th02 as upmTh02
import pyupm_i2clcd as upmLcd
import pyupm_servo as upmServo
import time


class TemperatureServo:
    def __init__(self, pin):
        self.servo = upmServo.ES08A(pin)
        self.servo.setAngle(0)
```

```
def print_temperature(self, temperature_fahrenheit):
    angle = temperature_fahrenheit
    if angle < 0:
        angle = 0
    elif angle > 180:
        angle = 180
    self.servo.setAngle(angle)
```

We have to specify the pin number to which the servo is connected when we create an instance of the `TemperatureServo` class in the `pin` required argument. The constructor, that is, the `__init__` method, creates a new `upmServo.ES08A` instance with the received `pin` as its `pin` argument, saves its reference in the `servo` attribute and calls its `setAngle` with `0` as the value for the `angle` required argument. This way, the underlying code will configure the output duty cycle for the PWM enabled GPIO pin based on the received value in the `angle` argument to position the shaft at the desired angle. In this case, we want the shaft to be positioned at 0 degrees.

The class defines a `print_temperature` method that receives a temperature value expressed in degrees Fahrenheit (°F) in the `temperature_fahrenheit` argument. The code defines an `angle` local variable that makes sure that the desired angle for the shaft is in a valid range: from 0 to 180 (inclusive). If the value received in the `temperature_fahrenheit` argument is lower than `0`, the `angle` value will be `0`. If the value received in the `temperature_fahrenheit` argument is greater than `180`, the `angle` value will be `180`. Then, the code calls the `setAngle` method for the `upmServo.ES08A` instance (`self.servo`) with `angle` as an argument. Under the hoods, the `upmServo.ES08A` instance will configure the output duty cycle for the PWM enabled GPIO pin based on the received value in the `angle` argument to position the shaft at the desired angle. This way, the shaft will position at an angle that will be the same than the received temperature in degrees Fahrenheit (°F), as long as the temperature value is between 0 and 180 degrees Fahrenheit (°F).

In case it is too cold, (less than 0 degrees Fahrenheit) the shaft will stay at a 0 degrees angle. In case the temperature is higher than 180 degrees Fahrenheit, the shaft will stay at a 180 degrees angle.

Now, we will make changes to our main loop to display the ambient temperature expressed in Fahrenheit (°F) with the shaft, every 10 seconds. The code file for the sample is `iot_python_chapter_08_03.py`.

```
if __name__ == "__main__":
    temperature_and_humidity_sensor = \
        TemperatureAndHumiditySensor(0)
    oled = TemperatureAndHumidityOled(0)
    temperature_servo = TemperatureServo(3)
    while True:
```

```
        temperature_and_humidity_sensor.\
            measure_temperature_and_humidity()
        oled.print_temperature(
            temperature_and_humidity_sensor.temperature_fahrenheit,
            temperature_and_humidity_sensor.temperature_celsius)
        oled.print_humidity(
            temperature_and_humidity_sensor.humidity)
        temperature_servo.print_temperature(
            temperature_and_humidity_sensor.temperature_fahrenheit)
        print("Ambient temperature in degrees Celsius: {0}".
            format(temperature_and_humidity_sensor.temperature_
celsius))
        print("Ambient temperature in degrees Fahrenheit: {0}".
            format(temperature_and_humidity_sensor.temperature_
fahrenheit))
        print("Ambient humidity: {0}".
            format(temperature_and_humidity_sensor.humidity))
        # Sleep 10 seconds (10000 milliseconds)
        time.sleep(10)
```

The highlighted lines show the changes made to the __main__ method compared with the previous version. The first highlighted line creates an instance of the previously coded TemperatureServo class with 3 as the value of the pin argument. The code saves the reference to this instance in the temperature_servo local variable. This way, the instance will configure PWM for pin number 3 and position the shaft at 0 degrees.

Then, the code runs a loop forever and the highlighted line calls the temperature_servo.print_temperature method with temperature_and_humidity_sensor.temperature_fahrenheit as an argument. This way, the code makes the shaft point to the temperature value in the protractor.

The following line will start the example.

```
python iot_python_chapter_08_03.py
```

After you run the example, turn on an air conditioner or a heating system and generate a change in the ambient temperature. You will notice how the shaft starts moving to reflect the changes in the temperature every 10 seconds.

Test your knowledge

1. The Intel Galileo Gen 2 board works as an I²C bus master and allows us to:

   1. Connect many slaves to the I²C bus as long as their have different I²C addresses.

   2. Connect many slaves to the I²C bus as long as their have the same I²C addresses.

   3. Connect a maximum of two slaves to the I²C bus as long as their have different I²C addresses.

2. A 16x2 LCD module allows us to display:

   1. Two lines of text with 16 characters each.

   2. Sixteen lines of text with 2 characters each.

   3. Sixteen lines of text with 3 characters each.

3. A 16 grayscale 96-by-96 dot matrix OLED display module allows us to control:

   1. 96 lines of text with 96 characters each.

   2. A single line with 96 dots or 96 characters, based on how we configure the OLED display.

   3. 9,216 dots (96*96).

4. A 16 grayscale 96-by-96 dot matrix OLED display with an 8-by-8 character box allows us to display:

   1. 96 lines of text with 96 characters each: 96 columns and 96 rows.

   2. 16 lines of text with 16 characters each: 16 columns and 16 rows.

   3. 12 lines of text with 12 characters each: 12 columns and 12 rows.

5. Standard servos allow us to:

   1. Display text on an OLED display.

   2. Position the shaft at various specific angles.

   3. Move the shaft to a specific location by specifying the desired latitude and longitude.

Summary

In this chapter, we learned about different displays the we could connect to our board through the I²C bus. We worked with an LCD display, an RGB backlight, and then replaced it with an OLED dot matrix.

We wrote the code that took advantage of the modules and classes included in the upm library that made it easier for us to work with LCD and OLED display and show text on them. In addition, we wrote the code that interacted with an analog servo. Instead of writing our own code to set the output duty cycle based on the desired position for the shaft, we took advantage of a specific module and a class in the upm library. We could control the shaft to allow us to create a gauge chart to display the temperature value retrieved with a sensor. Our Python code could make things move.

Now that we are able to show data next to the board and work with servos, we will connect our IoT device to the entire world and work with cloud services, which is the topic of the next chapter.

Working with the Cloud

In this chapter, we will take advantage of many cloud services to publish and visualize data collected for sensors and to establish bi-directional communications between Internet-connected things. We will cover the following topics:

- Publishing data to the cloud with dweepy and `dweet.io`
- Building a web-based dashboard with freeboard.io
- Sending and receiving data in real time through Internet with PubNub
- Publishing messages with commands through the PubNub cloud
- Working with bi-directional communications between IoT devices and other devices
- Publishing messages to the cloud with a Python PubNub client
- Using the MQTT protocol with Mosquitto and Eclipse Paho
- Publishing messages to a Mosquitto broker with a Python client

Publishing data to the cloud with dweepy

In *Chapter 8, Displaying Information and Performing Actions*, we worked with a digital temperature and humidity sensor combined with displays and a servo. Now, we want to take advantage of two cloud services to build a real time and interactive web-based dashboard that allows us to watch gauges with the following information in a web browser:

- Ambient temperature measured in degrees Fahrenheit (°F)
- Ambient temperature measured in degrees Celsius (°C)
- Ambient humidity level expressed in percentage (%)

First, we will take advantage of dweet.io to publish the data retrieved from the sensors and make it available to different computers and devices all over the world. The dweet.io data sharing utility allows us to easily publish data or messages and alerts from IoT devices and then use other devices to subscribe to this data. The dweet.io data sharing utility defines itself as something similar to Twitter for social machines. You can read more about dweet.io in its Webpage: http://dweet.io.

 In our example, we will take advantage of the free services offered by dweet.io and we won't use some advanced features that provide privacy for our data but also require a paid subscription. Our data will be available to anyone that can access the dweet.io web page because we are not working with locked dweets.

The dweet.io data sharing utility provides a Web api that we can send data from our IoT device, known as *thing* in dweet.io documentation. First, we have to chose a unique name for our thing. It is convenient to combine a string with a **GUID** (short for **Global Unique Identifier**). Another option is to click on the **Try It Now** button on the main dweet.io web page and grab the name that the web page chooses for our thing. This way, we are sure that the name is unique and nobody else is using this name for another thing to publish data with dweet.io.

Once we have chosen a unique name for our thing, we can start publishing data, a process known as dweeting. We just need to compose a POST HTTP verb with the desired JSON data in the body and with the following request URL: https://dweet.io/dweet/for/my-thing-name. We must replace my-thing-name with the name we have chosen for our thing. In our examples, we will use iot_python_chapter_09_01_gaston_hillar to name our IoT device that will publish temperature and humidity values, that is, the thing that will dweet. Thus, we have to compose a POST HTTP verb with the desired JSON data in the body and with the following request URL: https://dweet.io/dweet/for/iot_python_chapter_09_01_gaston_hillar. Make sure you replace the name with the name you have chosen for your thing.

Dweepy is a simple Python client for dweet.io that allows us to easily publish data to dweet.io with Python. Instead of manually building and sending an HTTP request to a specific URL with Python, we can use the methods provided by this useful module. The following is the Web page for the Dweepy module: https://pypi.python.org/pypi/dweepy/0.2.0. Under the hoods, Dweepy uses the popular features provided by the popular requests module to build and send the HTTP requests.

One of the nice things of working with Python as our main programming language for IoT is that there is always a package that makes things easy for us in Python.

In *Chapter 2, Working with Python on Intel Galileo Gen 2*, we installed `pip` installer to easily install additional Python 2.7.3 packages in the Yocto Linux that we are running on the board. Now, we will use `pip` installer to install Dweepy 0.2.0. We just need to run the following command in the SSH terminal to install the package:

```
pip install dweepy
```

The last lines for the output will indicate that the `dweepy` package has been successfully installed. Don't worry about the error messages related to building wheel and the insecure platform warning:

```
Collecting dweepy
Downloading dweepy-0.2.0.tar.gz
Requirement already satisfied (use --upgrade to upgrade):
requests<3,>=2 in /usr/lib/python2.7/site-packages (from dweepy)
Installing collected packages: dweepy
  Running setup.py install for dweepy
Successfully installed dweepy-0.2.0
```

We will take the code we wrote in the previous chapter when we read temperature and humidity values from the sensor and we will use this code as a baseline to add the new features. The code file for the sample was `iot_python_chapter_08_03.py`.

We will use the recently installed `dweepy` module to publish data to `dweet.io` and make it available as a data source for another cloud service that will allow us to build a web-based dashboard. We will add the necessary lines to our loop and it will publish the measured values every 10 seconds. The code file for the sample is `iot_python_chapter_09_01.py`.

```python
import pyupm_th02 as upmTh02
import pyupm_i2clcd as upmLcd
import pyupm_servo as upmServo
import dweepy
import time

if __name__ == "__main__":
    temperature_and_humidity_sensor = \
        TemperatureAndHumiditySensor(0)
    oled = TemperatureAndHumidityOled(0)
    temperature_servo = TemperatureServo(3)
    # Don't forget to replace the thing_name value
```

```
    # with your own thing name
    thing_name = "iot_python_chapter_09_01_gaston_hillar"
    while True:
        temperature_and_humidity_sensor.\
            measure_temperature_and_humidity()
        oled.print_temperature(
            temperature_and_humidity_sensor.temperature_fahrenheit,
            temperature_and_humidity_sensor.temperature_celsius)
        oled.print_humidity(
            temperature_and_humidity_sensor.humidity)
        temperature_servo.print_temperature(
            temperature_and_humidity_sensor.temperature_fahrenheit)
        # Push data to dweet.io
        dweet = {"temperature_celsius": "{:5.2f}".format(temperature_
and_humidity_sensor.temperature_celsius),
                "temperature_fahrenheit": "{:5.2f}".
format(temperature_and_humidity_sensor.temperature_fahrenheit),
                "humidity_level_percentage": "{:5.2f}".
format(temperature_and_humidity_sensor.humidity)}
        dweepy.dweet_for(thing_name, dweet)
        print("Ambient temperature in degrees Celsius: {0}".
            format(temperature_and_humidity_sensor.temperature_
celsius))
        print("Ambient temperature in degrees Fahrenheit: {0}".
            format(temperature_and_humidity_sensor.temperature_
fahrenheit))
        print("Ambient humidity: {0}".
            format(temperature_and_humidity_sensor.humidity))
        # Sleep 10 seconds (10000 milliseconds)
        time.sleep(10)
```

The highlighted lines show the changes made to the __main__ method compared with the previous version. The first highlighted line creates a local variable named thing_name that saves a string with the name we have chosen for our thing to use with dweet.io. Remember that you have to replace the string with the name you have chosen for your thing before running the sample code.

Then, the code runs a loop forever and the first highlighted line creates a dictionary and saves it in the `dweet` local variable. The dictionary defines the key-value pairs that we want to send as JSON data to `dweet.io` for our thing. The following are the keys the code will send:

- `temperature_celsius`
- `temperature_fahrenheit`
- `humidity_level_percentage`

The values for the previously enumerated keys are the values retrieved by the sensor converted to strings. Once the dictionary with the desired JSON data is built, the code calls the `dweepy.dweet_for` method with `thing_name` and `dweet` as arguments, that is, the thing name and the JSON data we want to publish for the specified thing name. Under the hoods, the `dweepy.dweet_for` method uses the `requests` module to compose a POST HTTP verb with the `dweet` dictionary as the desired JSON data in the body and with the following request URL: `https://dweet.io/dweet/for/` followed by the thing name specified in the `thing_name` local variable. This way, the code dweets the temperature and humidity values retrieved from the sensor in different units.

The following line will start the example.

```
python iot_python_chapter_09_01.py
```

After you run the example, turn on an air conditioner or a heating system, to generate a change in the ambient temperature and humidity. This way, we will notice changes in the data that is being published every 10 seconds.

Wait around 20 seconds and open the following URL in any Web browser: `http://dweet.io/follow/iot_python_chapter_09_01_gaston_hillar`. Don't forget to replace `iot_python_chapter_09_01_gaston_hillar` with the name you have chosen for your thing. In this case, we can enter the URL in any device connected to the Internet. We don't need the device to be in the same LAN than the board because the values are published with `dweet.io` and they are available everywhere.

The **Visual** view will display a line graph with the humidity level and the temperature values as they were changing over time. The right-hand side will display the latest value that was published. The view will be refreshed automatically when the Python code dweets new values. The following picture shows a screenshot with the **Visual** view:

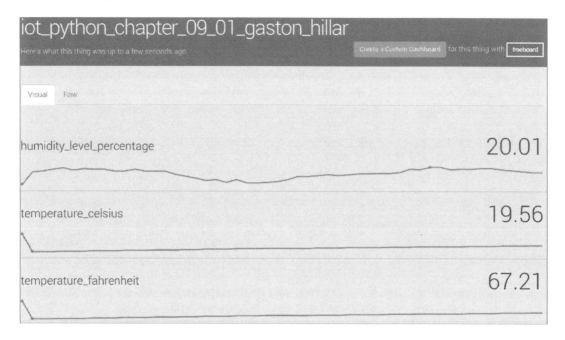

Click on the **Raw** view and the page will display the latest JSON data that the Python code running on the board has published and received by dweet.io for our thing. The following lines show an example of the latest JSON data that was received and that was shown in the previous picture:

```
{
    "humidity_level_percentage": 20.01,
    "temperature_celsius": 19.56,
    "temperature_fahrenheit": 67.21
}
```

In *Chapter 4, Working with a RESTful API and Pulse Width Modulation,* we installed HTTPie, a command-line HTTP client written in Python that makes is easy to send HTTP requests and uses a syntax that is easier than curl (also known as cURL). We can run the following HTTPie command in any computer or device to retrieve the latest dweet made for our thing.

```
http -b https://dweet.io:443/get/latest/dweet/for/iot_python_
chapter_09_01_gaston_hillar
```

The previous command will compose and send the following HTTP request: GET
https://dweet.io:443/get/latest/dweet/for/iot_python_chapter_09_01_
gaston_hillar. The dweet.io API will return the latest dweet for the specified
thing. The following lines show a sample response from dweet.io. The JSON data is
included in the value for the content key.

```
{
    "by": "getting",
    "the": "dweets",
    "this": "succeeded",
    "with": [
        {
            "content": {
                "humidity_level_percentage": 19.92,
                "temperature_celsius": 20.06,
                "temperature_fahrenheit": 68.11
            },
            "created": "2016-03-27T00:11:12.598Z",
            "thing": "iot_python_chapter_09_01_gaston_hillar"
        }
    ]
}
```

We can run the following HTTPie command in any computer or device to retrieve all
of the saved dweets for our thing.

```
http -b https://dweet.io:443/get/ dweets/for/iot_python_chapter_09_01_
gaston_hillar
```

The previous command will compose and send the following HTTP request: GET
https://dweet.io:443/get/ dweets/for/iot_python_chapter_09_01_gaston_
hillar. The dweet.io API will return the saved dweets from its long term storage
for the specified thing. The following lines show a sample response from dweet.
io. Notice that there are limitations in the number of dweets stored in the long term
storage and in the returned values.

```
{
    "by": "getting",
    "the": "dweets",
    "this": "succeeded",
    "with": [
        {
            "content": {
                "humidity_level_percentage": 19.94,
                "temperature_celsius": 20.01,
                "temperature_fahrenheit": 68.02
```

```
        },
        "created": "2016-03-27T00:11:00.554Z",
        "thing": "iot_python_chapter_09_01_gaston_hillar"
    },
    {

        "content": {
            "humidity_level_percentage": 19.92,
            "temperature_celsius": 19.98,
            "temperature_fahrenheit": 67.96
        },
        "created": "2016-03-27T00:10:49.823Z",
        "thing": "iot_python_chapter_09_01_gaston_hillar"
    },
    {

        "content": {
            "humidity_level_percentage": 19.92,
            "temperature_celsius": 19.95,
            "temperature_fahrenheit": 67.91
        },
        "created": "2016-03-27T00:10:39.123Z",
        "thing": "iot_python_chapter_09_01_gaston_hillar"
    },
    {

        "content": {
            "humidity_level_percentage": 19.91,
            "temperature_celsius": 19.9,
            "temperature_fahrenheit": 67.82
        },
        "created": "2016-03-27T00:10:28.394Z",
        "thing": "iot_python_chapter_09_01_gaston_hillar"
    }
    ]
}
```

Building a web-based dashboard with Freeboard

The dweet.io data sharing utility allowed us to easily publish data to the cloud with just a few lines of code. Now, we are ready to use dweet.io and our thing name as a data source to build a real-time web-based dashboard. We will take advantage of freeboard.io to visualize the data collected with the sensor and published to dweet.io in many gauges and make the dashboard available to different computers and devices all over the world. Freeboard.io allows us to build a dashboard by selecting data sources and dragging and dropping customizable widgets. Freeboard.io defines itself as a cloud-based service that allows us to visualize the Internet of Things. You can read more about freeboard.io in its Webpage: http://freeboard.io.

 In our example, we will take advantage of the free services offered by freeboard.io and we won't use some advanced features that provide privacy for our dashboards but also require a paid subscription. Our dashboard will be available to anyone that has the unique URL for it because we are not working with private dashboards.

Freeboard requires us to sign up and create an account with a valid e-mail and a password before we can build a web-based dashboard. We aren't required to enter any credit card or payment information. If you already have an account at freeboard.io, you can skip the next step.

Go to http://freeboard.io in your Web browser and click **Start Now**. You can achieve the same goal by visiting https://freeboard.io/signup. Enter your desired user name in **Pick a Username**, your e-mail in **Enter Your Email** and the desired password in **Create a Password**. Once you have filled up all the fields, click **Create My Account**.

Once you created your account, you can go to http://freeboard.io in your Web browser and click **Login**. You can achieve the same goal by visiting https://freeboard.io/login. Then, enter your user name or e-mail and password, and click **Sign In**. Freeboard will display your freeboards, also known as dashboards.

Enter `Ambient temperature and humidity` in the **enter a name** textbox at the left hand side of the **Create New** button and then click on this button. Freeboard.io will display an empty dashboard with many buttons that allow us to add panes and data sources, among other things. The following picture shows a screenshot with the empty dashboard.

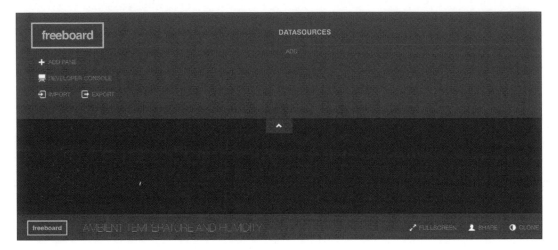

Click on **Add** below **Datasources** and the Website will open the **Datasource** dialog box. Select **Dweet.io** in the **Type** dropdown and the dialog box will display the fields required to define a `dweet.io` datasource.

Enter `Ambient temperature and humidity` in **Name** and the thing name we have been using for `dweet.io` in **Thing Name**. Remember that we were using `iot_python_chapter_09_01_gaston_hillar` to name our IoT device but you had replaced it with a different name. If the name you enter doesn't match the name you used when working with `dweet.io`, the datasource won't have the appropriate data. The following picture shows a screenshot with the configuration for the `dweet.io` datasource that uses the sample thing name.

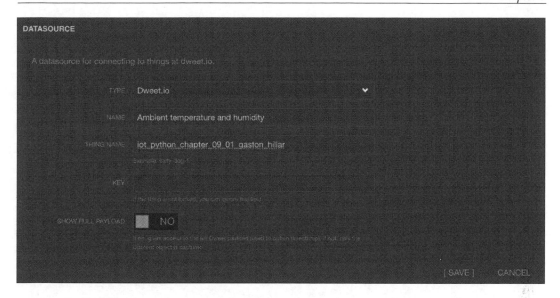

Click **Save** and the datasource will appear listed below **Datasources**. As the board is
running the Python code that is dweeting, the time shown below **Last Updated** will
change every 10 seconds. If the time doesn't change every 10 seconds, it means that
the datasource has a wrong configuration or that the board is not running the Python
code that is dweeting anymore.

Click on **Add pane** to add a new empty pane to the dashboard. Then, click on the
plus sign (**+**) at the upper right corner of the new empty pane and Freeboard will
display the **Widget** dialog box.

Select **Gauge** in the **Type** dropdown and the dialog box will display the fields
required to add a gauge widget to the pane within the dashboard. Enter
`Temperature in degrees Fahrenheit` in **Title**.

Click **+ Datasource** at the right-hand side of the **Value** textbox, select **Ambient
Temperature and humidity** and then select **temperature_fahrenheit**. After you
make the selections the following text will appear in the **Value** textbox: `datasources`
`["Ambient temperature and humidity"] ["temperature_fahrenheit"]`.

Enter °F in **Units**, -30 in **Minimum** and 130 in **Maximum**. Then, click **Save** and Freeboard will close the dialog box and add the new gauge to the previously created pane within the dashboard. The gauge will display the latest value that the code running in the board dweeted for the ambient temperature in degrees Fahrenheit, that is, the value for the temperature_fahrenheit key in the JSON data that the code has published for the last time to dweet.io. The following picture shows the **Ambient temperature and humidity** datasource displaying the last updated time and the gauge showing the latest value for the ambient temperature measured in degrees Fahrenheit.

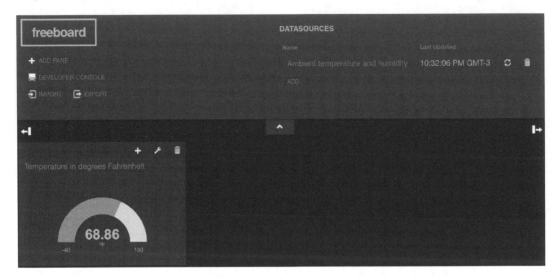

Click on **Add pane** to add another new empty pane to the dashboard. Then, click on the plus sign (**+**) at the upper right corner of the new empty pane and Freeboard will display the **Widget** dialog box.

Select **Gauge** in the **Type** dropdown and the dialog box will display the fields required to add a gauge widget to the pane within the dashboard. Enter Humidity level in percentage in **Title**.

Click **+ Datasource** at the right-hand side of the **Value** textbox, select **Ambient Temperature and humidity** and then select **humidity_level_percentage**. After you make the selections the following text will appear in the **Value** textbox: datasources ["Ambient temperature and humidity"] ["humidity_level_percentage"].

Enter % in **Units**, 0 in **Minimum** and 100 in **Maximum**. Then, click **Save** and Freeboard will close the dialog box and add the new gauge to the previously created pane within the dashboard. The gauge will display the latest value that the code running in the board dweeted for the ambient humidity level in percentage, that is, the value for the `humidity_level_percentage` key in the JSON data that the code has published for the last time to `dweet.io`.

Now, click on the plus sign (**+**) at the upper right corner of the pane that is displaying the temperature in degrees Fahrenheit and Freeboard will display the **Widget** dialog box.

Select **Gauge** in the **Type** dropdown and the dialog box will display the fields required to add a gauge widget to the pane within the dashboard. Enter `Temperature in degrees Celsius` in **Title**.

Click **+ Datasource** at the right-hand side of the **Value** textbox, select **Ambient Temperature and humidity** and then select **temperature_celsius**. After you make the selections the following text will appear in the **Value** textbox: `datasources ["Ambient temperature and humidity"] ["temperature_celsius"]`.

Enter °C in **Units**, -40 in **Minimum** and 55 in **Maximum**. Then, click **Save** and Freeboard will close the dialog box and add the new gauge to the previously existing pane within the dashboard. This way, the pane will display two gauges, with the temperature expressed in two different units. The new gauge will display the latest value that the code running in the board dweeted for the ambient temperature in degrees Celsius, that is, the value for the `temperature_celsius` key in the JSON data that the code has published for the last time to `dweet.io`.

Now, click on the configuration icon at the right-hand side of the **+** button of the pane that displays both temperatures. Freeboard will display the **Pane** dialog box. Enter `Temperature` in **Title** and click **Save**.

Click on the configuration icon at the right-hand side of the **+** button of the pane that displays the humidity level. Freeboard will display the **Pane** dialog box. Enter `Humidity` in **Title** and click **Save**.

Drag and drop the panes to locate the **Humidity** pane at the left-hand side of the **Temperature** pane. The following picture shows the dashboard we built, with two panes and three gauges that refresh the data automatically when the code running on the Intel Galileo Gen 2 board dweets new data.

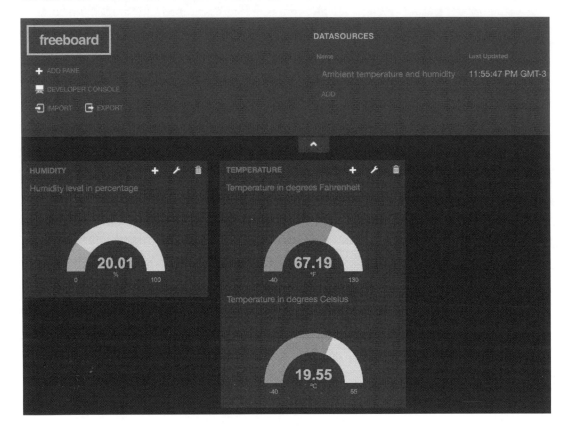

We can access the recently built dashboard in any device by entering the URL that our Web browser is displaying at the time we are working with the dashboard. The URL is composed of the `https://freeboard.io/board/` prefix followed by letters and numbers. For example, in case the URL is `https://freeboard.io/board/EXAMPLE`, we just need to enter it in any Web browser running on any device or computer connected to the Internet and we can watch the gauges and they will be refreshed as new data is being publishes from our Intel Galileo Gen 2 board to `dweet.io`.

The combination of dweet.io as our datasource and freeboard.io as our web-based dashboard made it easy for us to monitor the data retrieved from the sensor wired to our Intel Galileo Gen 2 board with any device that provides a Web browser. The combination of these two cloud-based services for IoT is just one example of how we can easily combine different services. There is an increase in the number of IoT cloud-based services, which can be used in our solutions.

Sending and receiving data in real-time through Internet with PubNub

In *Chapter 4, Working with a RESTful API and Pulse Width Modulation*, we developed and consumed a RETful API that allows us to control electronic components connected to our Intel Galileo Gen 2 board through HTTP requests. Now, we want to send and receive data in real-time through the Internet and a RESTful API is not the most appropriate option to do this. Instead, we will work with a publish/subscribe model based on a protocol that is lighter than the HTTP protocol. Specifically, we will use a service based on the **MQTT** (short for **MQ Telemetry Transport**) protocol.

The MQTT protocol is a **machine-to-machine** (short for **M2M**) and Internet of Things connectivity protocol. MQTT is a lightweight messaging protocol that runs on top of the TCP/IP protocol and works with a publish-subscribe mechanism. It is possible for any device to subscribe to a specific channel (also known as topic) and it will receive all the messages published to this channel. In addition, the device can publish message to this or other channel. The protocol is becoming very popular in IoT and M2M projects. You can read more about the MQTT protocol in the following Webpage: http://mqtt.org.

PubNub provides many cloud-based services and one of them allows us to easily stream data and signal any device in real-time, working with the MQTT protocol under the hoods. We will take advantage of this PubNub service to send and receive data in real-time through Internet and make it easy to control our Intel Galileo Gen 2 board through the Internet. As PubNub provides a Python API with high quality documentation and examples, it is extremely easy to use the service in Python. PubNub defines itself as the global data stream network for IoT, Mobile and Web applications. You can read more about PubNub in its Webpage: http://www.pubnub.com.

In our example, we will take advantage of the free services offered by PubNub and we won't use some advanced features and additional services that might empower our IoT project connectivity requirements but also require a paid subscription.

PubNub requires us to sign up and create an account with a valid e-mail and a password before we can create an application within PubNub that allows us to start using their free services. We aren't required to enter any credit card or payment information. If you already have an account at PubNub, you can skip the next step.

Once you created your account PubNub will redirect you to the **Admin Portal** that lists your PubNub applications. It is necessary to generate your PubNub publish and subscribe keys in order to send and receive messages in the network. A new pane will represent the application in the Admin portal. The following screenshot shows the Temperature Control application pane in the PubNub Admin portal:

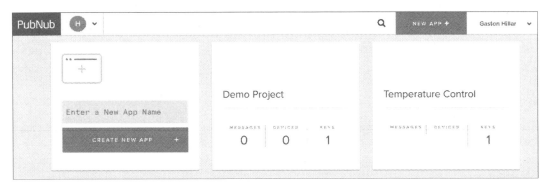

Click on the **Temperature Control** pane and PubNub will display the **Demo Keyset** pane that has been automatically generated for the application. Click on this pane and PubNub will display the publish, subscribe, and secret keys. We must copy and paste each of these keys to use them in our code that will publish messages and subscribe to them. The following screenshot shows the prefixes for the keys and the remaining characters have been erased in the image:

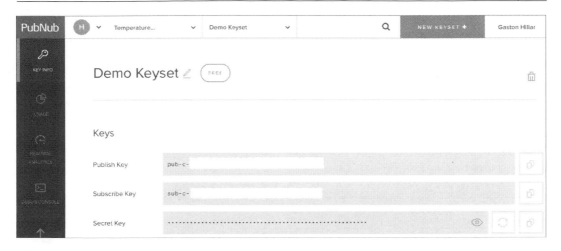

In order to copy the secret key, you must click on the eye icon at the right-hand side of the key and PubNub will make all the characters visible.

In *Chapter 2, Working with Python on Intel Galileo Gen 2*, we installed `pip` installer to easily install additional Python 2.7.3 packages in the Yocto Linux that we are running on the board. Now, we will use `pip` installer to install PubNub Python SDK 3.7.6. We just need to run the following command in the SSH terminal to install the package. Notice that it can take a few minutes to complete the installation.

```
pip install pubnub
```

The last lines for the output will indicate that the `pubnub` package has been successfully installed. Don't worry about the error messages related to building wheel and the insecure platform warning.

```
    Downloading pubnub-3.7.6.tar.gz
Collecting pycrypto>=2.6.1 (from pubnub)
    Downloading pycrypto-2.6.1.tar.gz (446kB)
      100% |##############################| 446kB 25kB/s
Requirement already satisfied (use --upgrade to upgrade):
requests>=2.4.0 in /usr/lib/python2.7/site-packages (from pubnub)
Installing collected packages: pycrypto, pubnub
    Running setup.py install for pycrypto
Installing collected packages: pycrypto, pubnub
    Running setup.py install for pycrypto
Running setup.py install for pubnub
Successfully installed pubnub-3.7.6 pycrypto-2.6.1
```

We will take the code we wrote in the previous chapter when we read temperature and humidity values from the sensor, we printed the values in an OLED matrix and rotated a servo's shaft to display the measured temperature expressed in degrees Fahrenheit with the shaft. The code file for the sample was `iot_python_chapter_08_03.py`. We will use this code as a baseline to add new features that will allow us to perform the following actions with PubNub messages sent to a specific channel from any device that has a Web browser:

- Rotate the servo's shaft to display a temperature value in degrees Fahrenheit received as part of the message.
- Display a line of text received as part of the message at the bottom of the OLED matrix.

We will use the recently installed `pubnub` module to subscribe to a specific channel and run code when we receive messages in the channel. We will create a `MessageChannel` class to represent the communications channel, configure the PubNub subscription and declare the code for the callbacks that are going to be executed when certain events are fired. The code file for the sample is `iot_python_chapter_09_02.py`. Remember that we use the code file `iot_python_chapter_08_03.py` as a baseline, and therefore, we will add the class to the existing code in this file and we will create a new Python file. Don't forget to replace the strings assigned to the `publish_key` and `subscribe_key` local variables in the `__init__` method with the values you have retrieved from the previously explained PubNub key generation process.

```python
import time
from pubnub import Pubnub


class MessageChannel:
    command_key = "command"

    def __init__(self, channel, temperature_servo, oled):
        self.temperature_servo = temperature_servo
        self.oled = oled
        self.channel = channel
        # Publish key is the one that usually starts with the "pub-c-"
prefix
        # Do not forget to replace the string with your publish key
        publish_key = "pub-c-xxxxxxxx-xxxx-xxxx-xxxx-xxxxxxxxxxxx"
        # Subscribe key is the one that usually starts with the
"sub-c" prefix
        # Do not forget to replace the string with your subscribe key
```

```
        subscribe_key = "sub-c-xxxxxxxx-xxxx-xxxx-xxxx-xxxxxxxxxxxx"
        self.pubnub = Pubnub(publish_key=publish_key, subscribe_
key=subscribe_key)
        self.pubnub.subscribe(channels=self.channel,
                              callback=self.callback,
                              error=self.callback,
                              connect=self.connect,
                              reconnect=self.reconnect,
                              disconnect=self.disconnect)

    def callback(self, message, channel):
        if channel == self.channel:
            if self.__class__.command_key in message:
                if message[self.__class__.command_key] == "print_
temperature_fahrenheit":
                    self.temperature_servo.print_temperature(message["
temperature_fahrenheit"])
                elif message[self.__class__.command_key] == "print_
information_message":
                    self.oled.print_line(11, message["text"])
            print("I've received the following message: {0}".
format(message))

    def error(self, message):
        print("Error: " + str(message))

    def connect(self, message):
        print("Connected to the {0} channel".
            format(self.channel))
        print(self.pubnub.publish(
            channel=self.channel,
            message="Listening to messages in the Intel Galileo Gen 2
board"))

    def reconnect(self, message):
        print("Reconnected to the {0} channel".
            format(self.channel))

    def disconnect(self, message):
        print("Disconnected from the {0} channel".
            Format(self.channel))
```

The MessageChannel class declares the command_key class attribute that defines the key string that defines what the code will understand as the command. Whenever we receive a message that includes the specified key string, we know that the value associated to this key in the dictionary will indicate the command that the message wants the code running in the board to be processed. Each command requires additional key-value pairs that provide the necessary information to execute the command.

We have to specify the PubNub channel name, the TemperatureServo instance the Oled instance in the channel, temperature_servo, and oled required arguments. The constructor, that is, the __init__ method, saves the received arguments in three attributes with the same names. The channel argument specifies the PubNub channel to which we are going to subscribe to listen to the messages that other devices send to this channel. We will also publish messages to this channel, and therefore, we will be both a subscriber and a publisher for this channel.

In this case, we will only subscribe to one channel. However, it is very important to know that we are not limited to subscribe to a single channel, we might subscribe to many channels.

Then, the constructor declares two local variables: publish_key and subscribe_key. These local variables save the publish and subscribe keys that we had generated with the PubNub Admin portal. Then, the code creates a new Pubnub instance with publish_key and subscribe_key as the arguments, and saves the reference for the new instance in the pubnub attribute. Finally, the code calls the subscribe method for the new instance to subscribe to data on the channel saved in the channel attribute. Under the hoods, the subscribe method makes the client create an open TCP socket to the PubNub network that includes an MQTT broker and starts listening to messages on the specified channel. The call to this method specifies many methods declared in the MessageChannel class for the following named arguments:

- callback: Specifies the function that will be called when there is a new message received from the channel
- error: Specifies the function that will be called on an error event
- connect: Specifies the function that will be called when a successful connection is established with the PubNub cloud
- reconnect: Specifies the function that will be called when a successful re-connection is completed with the PubNub cloud
- disconnect: Specifies the function that will be called when the client disconnects from the PubNub cloud

This way, whenever one of the previously enumerated events occur, the specified method will be executed. The `callback` method receives two arguments: `message` and `channel`. First, the method checks whether the received `channel` matches the value in the `channel` attribute. In this case, whenever the `callback` method is executed, the value in the `channel` argument will always match the value in the `channel` attribute because we just subscribed to one channel. However, in case we subscribe to more than one channel, is is always necessary to check which is the channel in which the message was sent and in which we are receiving the message.

Then, the code checks whether the `command_key` class attribute is included in the `message` dictionary. If the expression evaluates to `True`, it means that the message includes a command that we have to process. However, before we can process the command, we have to check which is the command, and therefore, it is necessary to retrieve the value associated with the key equivalent to the `command_key` class attribute. The code is capable of running code when the value is any of the following two commands:

- `print_temperature_fahrenheit`: The command must specify the temperature value expressed in degrees Fahrenheit in the value of the `temperature_fahrenheit` key. The code calls the `self.temperature_servo.print_temperature` method with the temperature value retrieved from the dictionary as an argument. This way, the code moves the servo's shaft based on the specified temperature value in the message that includes the command.

- `print_information_message`: The command must specify the line of text that has to be displayed at the bottom of the OLED matrix in the value of the `print_information_message` key. The code calls the `self.oled.print_line` method with `11` and the text value retrieved from the dictionary as arguments. This way, the code displays the text received in the message that includes the command at the bottom of the OLED matrix.

No matter whether the message included a valid command or not, the method prints the raw message that it received in the console output.

The `connect` method prints a message indicating that a connection has been established with the channel. Then, the method prints the results of calling the `self.pubnub.publish` method that publishes a message in the channel name saved in `self.channel` with the following message: `"Listening to messages in the Intel Galileo Gen 2 board"`. In this case, the call to this method runs with a synchronous execution. We will work with asynchronous execution for this method in our next example.

At this time, we are already subscribed to this channel, and therefore, we will receive the previously published message and the callback method will be executed with this message as an argument. However, as the message doesn't include the key that identifies a command, the code in the callback method will just display the received message and it won't process any of the previously analyzed commands.

The other methods declared in the `MessageChannel` class just display information to the console output about the event that has occurred.

Now, we will use the previously coded `MessageChannel` class to create a new version of the `__main__` method that uses the PubNub cloud to receive and process commands. The new version doesn't rotate the servo's shaft when the ambient temperature changes, instead, it will do this when it receives the appropriate command from any device connected to PubNub cloud. The following lines show the new version of the `__main__` method. The code file for the sample is `iot_python_chapter_09_02.py`.

```python
if __name__ == "__main__":
    temperature_and_humidity_sensor = \
        TemperatureAndHumiditySensor(0)
    oled = TemperatureAndHumidityOled(0)
    temperature_servo = TemperatureServo(3)
    message_channel = MessageChannel("temperature", temperature_servo,
oled)
    while True:
        temperature_and_humidity_sensor.\
            measure_temperature_and_humidity()
        oled.print_temperature(
            temperature_and_humidity_sensor.temperature_fahrenheit,
            temperature_and_humidity_sensor.temperature_celsius)
        oled.print_humidity(
            temperature_and_humidity_sensor.humidity)
        print("Ambient temperature in degrees Celsius: {0}".
                format(temperature_and_humidity_sensor.temperature_
celsius))
        print("Ambient temperature in degrees Fahrenheit: {0}".
                format(temperature_and_humidity_sensor.temperature_
fahrenheit))
```

```
print("Ambient humidity: {0}".
      format(temperature_and_humidity_sensor.humidity))
# Sleep 10 seconds (10000 milliseconds)
time.sleep(10)
```

The highlighted line creates an instance of the previously coded `MessageChannel` class with `"temperature"`, `temperature_servo`, and `oled` as the arguments. The constructor will subscribe to the `temperature` channel in the PubNub cloud, and therefore, we must send the messages to this channel in order to send the commands that the code will process with an asynchronous execution. The loop will read the values from the sensor and print the values to the console as in the previous version of the code, and therefore, we will have code running in the loop and we will also have code listening to the messages in the `temperature` channel in the PubNub cloud. We will start the example later because we want to subscribe to the channel in the PubNub debug console before we run the code in the board.

Publishing messages with commands through the PubNub cloud

Now, we will take advantage of the PubNub console to send messages with commands to the `temperature` channel and make the Python code running on the board process these commands. In case you have logged out of PubNub, login again and click on the **Temperature Control** pane in the **Admin Portal**. PubNub will display the **Demo Keyset** pane.

Click on the **Demo Keyset** pane and PubNub will display the publish, subscribe, and secret keys. This way, we select the keyset that we want to use for our PubNub application.

Click on **Debug Console** on the sidebar located the left-hand side of the screen. PubNub will create a client for a default channel and subscribe to this channel using the secret keys we have selected in the previous step. We want to subscribe to the temperature channel, and therefore, enter temperature in the **Default Channel** textbox within a pane that includes the **Add client** button at the bottom. Then, click on **Add client** and PubNub will add a new pane with a random client name as a title and the channel name, temperature, in the second line. PubNub makes the client subscribe to this channel and we will be able to receive messages published to this channel and send messages to this channel. The following picture shows the pane for the generated client named **Client-ot7pi**, subscribed to the temperature channel. Notice that the client name will be different when you follow the explained steps.

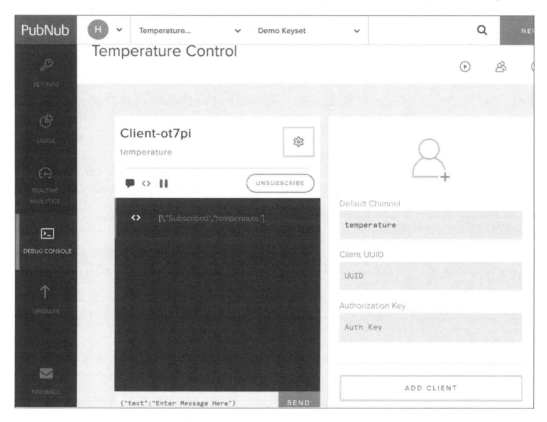

The client pane displays the output generated when PubNub subscribed the client to the channel. PubNub returns a formatted response for each command. In this case, it indicates that the status is equal to Subscribed and the channel name is temperature.

```
[1,"Subscribed","temperature"]
```

Now, it is time to start running the example in the Intel Galileo Gen 2 board. The following line will start the example in the SSH console:

```
python iot_python_chapter_09_02.py
```

After you run the example, go to the Web browser in which you are working with the PubNub debug console. You will see the following message listed in the previously created client:

```
"Listening to messages in the Intel Galileo Gen 2 board"
```

The Python code running in the board published this message, specifically, the `connect` method in the `MessageChannel` class sent this message after the application established a connection with the PubNub cloud. The following picture shows the message listed in the previously created client. Notice that the icon at the left-hand side of the text indicates it is a message. The other message was a debug message with the results of subscribing to the channel.

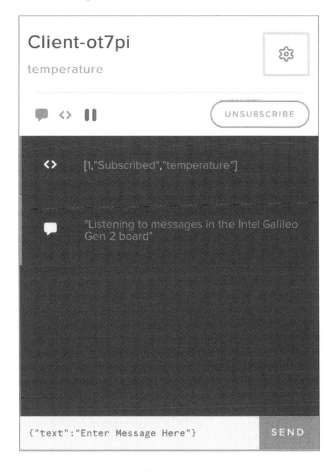

At the bottom of the client pane, you will see the following text and the **Send** button at the right-hand side:

```
{"text":"Enter Message Here"}
```

Now, we will replace the previously shown text with a message. Enter the following JSON code and click **Send**:

```
{"command":"print_temperature_fahrenheit", "temperature_fahrenheit":
50 }
```

> The text editor where you enter the message has some issues in certain browsers. Thus, it is convenient to use your favorite text editor to enter the JSON code, copy it and then past it to replace the text that is included by default in the text for the message to be sent.

After you click **Send**, the following lines will appear in the client log. The first line is a debug message with the results of publishing the message and indicates that the message has been sent. The formatted response includes a number (1 message), the status (Sent) and a time token. The second line is the message that arrives to the channel because we are subscribed to the temperature channel, that is, we also receive the message we sent.

```
[1,"Sent","14594756860875537"]
{
  "command": "print_temperature_fahrenheit",
  "temperature_fahrenheit": 50
}
```

The following picture shows the messages and debug messages log for the PubNub client after we clicked the **Send** button:

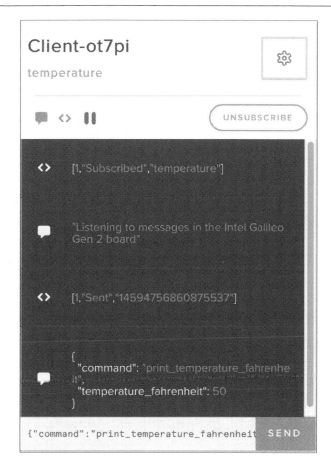

After you publish the previous message, you will see the following output in the SSH console for the Intel Galileo Gen 2 board. You will notice the servo's shaft rotates to 50 degrees.

```
I've received the following message: {u'command': u'print_temperature_
fahrenheit', u'temperature_fahrenheit': 50}
```

Now, enter the following JSON code and click **Send**:

```
{"command":"print_information_message", "text": "Client ready"}
```

After you click **Send**, the following lines will appear in the client log. The first line is a debug message with the previously explained formatted response with the results of publishing the message and indicates that the message has been sent. The second line is the message that arrives to the channel because we are subscribed to the temperature channel, that is, we also receive the message we sent.

```
[1,"Sent","14594794434885921"]
{
  "command": "print_information_message",
  "text": "Client ready"
}
```

The following picture shows the messages and debug messages log for the PubNub client after we clicked the **Send** button.

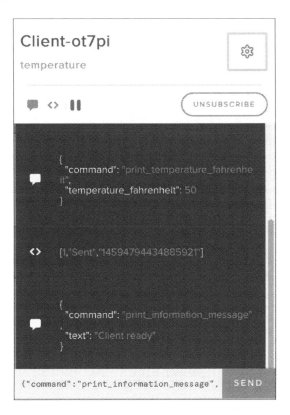

After you publish the previous message, you will see the following output in the SSH console for the Intel Galileo Gen 2 board. You will see the following text displayed at the bottom of the OLED matrix: Client ready.

```
I've received the following message: {u'text': u'Client ready',
u'command': u'print_information_message'}
```

When we published the two messages with the commands, we have definitely noticed a problem. We don't know whether the command was processed or not in the code that is running on the IoT device, that is, in the Intel Galileo Gen 2 board. We know that the board started listening messages in the temperature channel, but we don't receive any kind of response from the IoT device after the command has been processed.

Working with bi-directional communications

We can easily add a few lines of code to publish a message to the same channel in which we are receiving messages to indicate that the command has been successfully processed. We will use our previous example as a baseline and we will create a new version of the MessageChannel class. The code file was iot_python_chapter_09_02.py. Don't forget to replace the strings assigned to the publish_key and subscribe_key local variables in the __init__ method with the values you have retrieved from the previously explained PubNub key generation process. The following lines show the new version of the MessageChannel class that publishes a message after a command has been successfully processed. The code file for the sample is iot_python_chapter_09_03.py.

```
import time
from pubnub import Pubnub

class MessageChannel:
    command_key = "command"
    successfully_processed_command_key = "successfully_processed_command"

    def __init__(self, channel, temperature_servo, oled):
        self.temperature_servo = temperature_servo
        self.oled = oled
        self.channel = channel
        # Do not forget to replace the string with your publish key
        publish_key = "pub-c-xxxxxxxx-xxxx-xxxx-xxxx-xxxxxxxxxxxx"
        # Subscribe key is the one that usually starts with the
"sub-c" prefix
        # Do not forget to replace the string with your subscribe key
        subscribe_key = "sub-c-xxxxxxxx-xxxx-xxxx-xxxx-xxxxxxxxxxxx"
        self.pubnub = Pubnub(publish_key=publish_key, subscribe_key=subscribe_key)
        self.pubnub.subscribe(channels=self.channel,
                              callback=self.callback,
```

```
                            error=self.callback,
                            connect=self.connect,
                            reconnect=self.reconnect,
                            disconnect=self.disconnect)


    def callback_response_message(self, message):
        print("I've received the following response from PubNub cloud:
{0}".format(message))


    def error_response_message(self, message):
        print("There was an error when working with the PubNub cloud:
{0}".format(message))


    def publish_response_message(self, message):
        response_message = {
            self.__class__.successfully_processed_command_key:
                message[self.__class__.command_key]}
        self.pubnub.publish(
            channel=self.channel,
            message=response_message,
            callback=self.callback_response_message,
            error=self.error_response_message)


    def callback(self, message, channel):
        if channel == self.channel:
            print("I've received the following message: {0}".
format(message))
            if self.__class__.command_key in message:
                if message[self.__class__.command_key] == "print_
temperature_fahrenheit":
                    self.temperature_servo.print_temperature(message["
temperature_fahrenheit"])
                    self.publish_response_message(message)
                elif message[self.__class__.command_key] == "print_
information_message":
                    self.oled.print_line(11, message["text"])
                    self.publish_response_message(message)


    def error(self, message):
        print("Error: " + str(message))
```

```
def connect(self, message):
    print("Connected to the {0} channel".
        format(self.channel))
    print(self.pubnub.publish(
        channel=self.channel,
        message="Listening to messages in the Intel Galileo Gen 2
board"))

def reconnect(self, message):
    print("Reconnected to the {0} channel".
        format(self.channel))

def disconnect(self, message):
    print("Disconnected from the {0} channel".
        format(self.channel))
```

The highlighted lines in the previous code for the new version of the
`MessageChannel` class show the changes we made in the code. First, the code
declares the `successfully_processed_command_key` class attribute that defines
the key string that defines what the code will use as a successfully processed
command key in a response message published to the channel. Whenever we
publish a message that includes the specified key string, we know that the value
associated to this key in the dictionary will indicate the command that the board
has successfully processed.

The code declares the following three new methods:

- `callback_response_message`: This method will be used as the callback that
  will be executed when a successfully processed command response message
  is published to the channel. The method just prints the formatted response
  that PubNub returns when a message has been successfully published in
  the channel. In this case, the `message` argument doesn't hold the original
  message that has been published, it holds the formatted response. We use
  `message` for the argument name to keep consistency with the PubNub API.

- `error_response_message`: This method will be used as the callback that
  will be executed when an error occurs when trying to publish a successfully
  processed command response message to the channel. The method just
  prints the error message that PubNub returns when a message hasn't been
  successfully published in the channel.

- `publish_response_message`: This method receives the message with the command that was successfully processed in the `message` argument. The code creates a `response_message` dictionary with the `successfully_processed_command_key` class attribute as the key and the value of the key specified in the `command_key` class attribute for the message dictionary as the value. Then, the code calls the `self.pubnub.publish` method to publish the `response_message` dictionary to the channel saved in the `channel` attribute. The call to this method specifies `self.callback_response_message` as the callback to be executed when the message is successfully published and `self.error_response_message` as the callback to be executed when an error occurred during the publishing process. When we specify a callback, the publish method works with an asynchronous execution, and therefore, the execution is non-blocking. The publication of the message and the callbacks that are specified will run in a different thread.

Now, the `callback` method defined in the `MessageChannel` class adds a call to the `publish_response_message` method with the message that included the command that has been successfully processed (`message`) as an argument. As previously explained, the `publish_response_message` method is non-blocking and will return immediately while the successfully processed message is published in another thread.

Now, it is time to start running the example in the Intel Galileo Gen 2 board. The following line will start the example in the SSH console:

```
python iot_python_chapter_09_03.py
```

After you run the example, go to the Web browser in which you are working with the PubNub debug console. You will see the following message listed in the previously created client:

```
"Listening to messages in the Intel Galileo Gen 2 board"
```

Enter the following JSON code and click **Send**:

```
{"command":"print_temperature_fahrenheit", "temperature_fahrenheit":
90 }
```

After you click **Send**, the following lines will appear in the client log. The last message has been published by the board to the channel and indicates that the `print_temperature_fahrenheit` command has been successfully processed.

```
[1,"Sent","14595406989121047"]
{
  "command": "print_temperature_fahrenheit",
  "temperature_fahrenheit": 90
}
{
  "successfully_processed_command": "print_temperature_fahrenheit"
}
```

The following picture shows the messages and debug messages log for the PubNub client after we clicked the **Send** button:

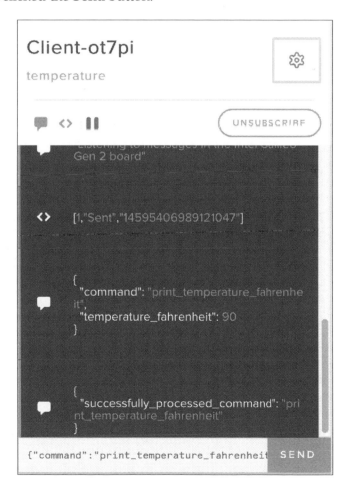

After you publish the previous message, you will see the following output in the SSH console for the Intel Galileo Gen 2 board. You will notice the servo's shaft rotates to 90 degrees. The board also receives the successfully processed command message because it is subscribed to the channel in which the message has been published.

```
I've received the following message: {u'command': u'print_temperature_
fahrenheit', u'temperature_fahrenheit': 90}
I've received the following response from PubNub cloud: [1, u'Sent',
u'14595422426124592']
I've received the following message: {u'successfully_processed_
command': u'print_temperature_fahrenheit'}
```

Now, enter the following JSON code and click **Send**:

```
{"command":"print_information_message", "text": "2nd message"}
```

After you click **Send**, the following lines will appear in the client log. The last message has been published by the board to the channel and indicates that the `print_information_message` command has been successfully processed.

```
[1,"Sent","14595434708640961"]
{
  "command": "print_information_message",
  "text": "2nd message"
}
{
  "successfully_processed_command": "print_information_message"
}
```

The following picture shows the messages and debug messages log for the PubNub client after we clicked the **Send** button.

After you publish the previous message, you will see the following output in the SSH console for the Intel Galileo Gen 2 board. You will see the following text displayed at the bottom of the OLED matrix: 2nd message. The board also receives the successfully processed command message because it is subscribed to the channel in which the message has been published.

```
I've received the following message: {u'text': u'2nd message',
u'command': u'print_information_message'}
2nd message
I've received the following response from PubNub cloud: [1, u'Sent',
u'14595434710438777']
I've received the following message: {u'successfully_processed_
command': u'print_information_message'}
```

We can work with the different SDKs provided by PubNub to subscribe and publish to a channel. We can also make different IoT devices talk to themselves by publishing messages to channels and processing them. In this case, we just created a few commands and we didn't add detailed information about the device that has to process the command or the device that has generated a specific message. A more complex API would require commands that include more information and security.

Publishing messages to the cloud with a Python PubNub client

So far, we have been using the PubNub debug console to publish messages to the `temperature` channel and make the Python code running in the Intel Galileo Gen 2 board process them. Now, we are going to code a Python client that will publish messages to the `temperature` channel. This way, we will be able to design applications that can talk to IoT devices with Python code in the publisher and in the subscriber devices.

We can run the Python client on another Intel Galileo Gen 2 board or in any device that has Python 2.7.x installed. In addition, the code will run with Python 3.x. For example, we can run the Python client in our computer. We just need to make sure that we install the `pubnub` module we have previously installed with pip in the Python version that is running in the Yocto Linux for the board.

We will create a `Client` class to represent a PubNub client, configure the PubNub subscription, make it easy to publish a message with a command and the required values for the command and declare the code for the callbacks that are going to be executed when certain events are fired. The code file for the sample is `iot_python_chapter_09_04.py`. Don't forget to replace the strings assigned to the `publish_key` and `subscribe_key` local variables in the `__init__` method with the values you have retrieved from the previously explained PubNub key generation process. The following lines show the code for the `Client` class:

```
import time
from pubnub import Pubnub


class Client:
    command_key = "command"

    def __init__(self, channel):
        self.channel = channel
        # Publish key is the one that usually starts with the "pub-c-"
prefix
```

```
        publish_key = "pub-c-xxxxxxxx-xxxx-xxxx-xxxx-xxxxxxxxxxxx"
        # Subscribe key is the one that usually starts with the
"sub-c" prefix
        # Do not forget to replace the string with your subscribe key
        subscribe_key = "sub-c-xxxxxxxx-xxxx-xxxx-xxxx-xxxxxxxxxxxx"
        self.pubnub = Pubnub(publish_key=publish_key, subscribe_
key=subscribe_key)
        self.pubnub.subscribe(channels=self.channel,
                              callback=self.callback,
                              error=self.callback,
                              connect=self.connect,
                              reconnect=self.reconnect,
                              disconnect=self.disconnect)

    def callback_command_message(self, message):
        print("I've received the following response from PubNub cloud:
{0}".format(message))

    def error_command_message(self, message):
        print("There was an error when working with the PubNub cloud:
{0}".format(message))

    def publish_command(self, command_name, key, value):
        command_message = {
            self.__class__.command_key: command_name,
            key: value}
        self.pubnub.publish(
            channel=self.channel,
            message=command_message,
            callback=self.callback_command_message,
            error=self.error_command_message)

    def callback(self, message, channel):
        if channel == self.channel:
            print("I've received the following message: {0}".
format(message))

    def error(self, message):
        print("Error: " + str(message))

    def connect(self, message):
        print("Connected to the {0} channel".
              format(self.channel))
        print(self.pubnub.publish(
            channel=self.channel,
```

```
                    message="Listening to messages in the PubNub Python
        Client"))

            def reconnect(self, message):
                print("Reconnected to the {0} channel".
                    format(self.channel))

            def disconnect(self, message):
                print("Disconnected from the {0} channel".
                    format(self.channel))
```

The `Client` class declares the `command_key` class attribute that defines the key string that defines what the code understands as a command in the messages. Our main goal is to build and publish command messages to a specified channel. We have to specify the PubNub channel name in the `channel` required argument. The constructor, that is, the `__init__` method, saves the received argument in an attribute with the same name. We will be both a subscriber and a publisher for this channel.

Then, the constructor declares two local variables: `publish_key` and `subscribe_key`. These local variables save the publish and subscribe keys we had generated with the PubNub Admin portal. Then, the code creates a new `Pubnub` instance with `publish_key` and `subscribe_key` as the arguments, and saves the reference for the new instance in the `pubnub` attribute. Finally, the code calls the `subscribe` method for the new instance to subscribe to data on the channel saved in the `channel` attribute. The call to this method specifies many methods declared in the `Client` class as we did for our previous examples.

The `publish_command` method receives a command name, the key and the value that provide the necessary information to execute the command in the `command_name`, `key` and `value` required arguments. In this case, we don't target the command to a specific IoT device and all the devices that subscribe to the channel and run the code in our previous example will process the commands that we publish. We can use the code as a baseline to work with more complex examples in which we have to generate commands that target specific IoT devices. Obviously, it is also necessary to improve the security.

The method creates a dictionary and saves it in the `command_message` local variable. The `command_key` class attribute is the first key for the dictionary and the `command_name` received as an argument, the value that composes the first key-value pair. Then, the code calls the `self.pubnub.publish` method to publish the `command_message` dictionary to the channel saved in the `channel` attribute. The call to this method specifies `self.callback_command_message` as the callback to be executed when the message is successfully published and `self.error_command_message` as the callback to be executed when an error occurred during the publishing process. As happened in our previous example, when we specify a callback, the `publish` method works with an asynchronous execution.

Now, we will use the previously coded `Client` class to write a `__main__` method that uses the PubNub cloud to publish two commands that our board will process. The following lines show the code for the `__main__` method. The code file for the sample is `iot_python_chapter_09_04.py`.

```
if __name__ == "__main__":
    client = Client("temperature")
    client.publish_command(
        "print_temperature_fahrenheit",
        "temperature_fahrenheit",
        45)
    client.publish_command(
        "print_information_message",
        "text",
        "Python IoT"
    )
    # Sleep 60 seconds (60000 milliseconds)
    time.sleep(60)
```

The code in the `__main__` method is very easy to understand. The code creates an instance of the `Client` class with `"temperature"` as an argument to become both a subscriber and a publisher for this channel in the PubNub cloud. The code saves the new instances in the `client` local variable.

The code calls the `publish_command` method with the necessary arguments to build and publish the `print_temperature_fahrenheit` command with a temperature value of 45. The method will publish the command with an asynchronous execution. Then, the code calls the `publish_command` method again with the necessary arguments to build and publish the `print_information_message` command with a text value of `"Python IoT"`. The method will publish the second command with an asynchronous execution.

Finally, the code sleeps for 1 minute (60 seconds) in order to make it possible for the asynchronous executions to successfully publish the commands. The different callbacks defined in the `Client` class will be executed as the different events fire. As we are also subscribed to the channel, we will also receive the messages we publish in the `temperature` channel.

Keep the Python code we have executed in our previous example running on the board. We want the board to process our commands. In addition, keep the Web browser in which you are working with the PubNub debug console opened because we also want to see all the messages in the log.

The following line will start the example for the Python client in any computer or device that you want to use as a client. It is possible to run the code in another SSH terminal in case you want to use the same board as a client.

```
python iot_python_chapter_09_04.py
```

After you run the example, you will see the following output in the Python console that runs the Python client, that is, the `iot_python_chapter_09_04.py` Python script.

```
Connected to the temperature channel
I've received the following response from PubNub cloud: [1, u'Sent',
u'14596508980494876']
I've received the following response from PubNub cloud: [1, u'Sent',
u'14596508980505581']
[1, u'Sent', u'14596508982165140']
I've received the following message: {u'text': u'Python IoT',
u'command': u'print_information_message'}
I've received the following message: {u'command': u'print_temperature_
fahrenheit', u'temperature_fahrenheit': 45}
I've received the following message: Listening to messages in the
PubNub Python Client
I've received the following message: {u'successfully_processed_
command': u'print_information_message'}
I've received the following message: {u'successfully_processed_
command': u'print_temperature_fahrenheit'}
```

The code used the PubNub Python SDK to build and publish the following two command messages in the `temperature` channel:

```
{"command":"print_temperature_fahrenheit", "temperature_fahrenheit":
"45"}
{"command":"print_information_message", "text": "Python IoT"}
```

As we are also subscribed to the temperature channel, we receive the messages we sent with an asynchronous execution. Then, we received the successfully processed command messages for the two command messages. The board has processed the commands and published the messages to the `temperature` channel.

After you run the example, go to the Web browser in which you are working with the PubNub debug console. You will see the following messages listed in the previously created client:

```
[1,"Subscribed","temperature"]
"Listening to messages in the Intel Galileo Gen 2 board"
{
  "text": "Python IoT",
  "command": "print_information_message"
}
{
  "command": "print_temperature_fahrenheit",
  "temperature_fahrenheit": 45
}
"Listening to messages in the PubNub Python Client"
{
  "successfully_processed_command": "print_information_message"
}
{
  "successfully_processed_command": "print_temperature_fahrenheit"
}
```

The following picture shows the last messages displayed in the log for the PubNub client after we run the previous example:

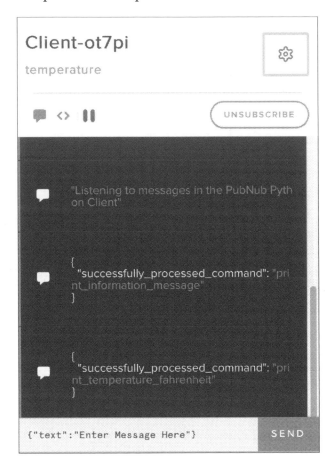

You will see the following text displayed at the bottom of the OLED matrix: `Python IoT`. In addition, the servo's shaft will rotate to 45 degrees.

We can use the PubNub SDKs available in different programming languages to create applications and apps that publish and receive messages in the PubNub cloud and interact with IoT devices. In this case, we worked with the Python SDK to create a client that publishes commands. It is possible to create mobile apps that publish commands and easily build an app that can interact with our IoT device.

Using MQTT with Mosquitto and Eclipse Paho

Mosquitto is an open source message broker that implements the versions 3.1 and 3.1.1 of the MQTT protocol, and therefore, allows us to work with messages using the publish/subscribe model. Mosquitto is an iot.eclipse.org project and is provided with the Eclipse Public Project (EPL)/EDL license. The following is the Web page for Mosquitto: `http://mosquitto.org`.

The Eclipse Paho project provides an open source client implementation of MQTT. The project includes a Python client, also known as the Paho Python Client or Eclipse Paho MQTT Python client library. This Python client has been contributed from the Mosquitto project and was originally the Mosquitto Python Client. The following is the Web page for the Eclipse Paho project: `http://www.eclipse.org/paho`. The following is the Web page for the Eclipse Paho MQTT Python client library, that is, the paho-mqtt module: `https://pypi.python.org/pypi/paho-mqtt/1.1.`

In *Chapter 2, Working with Python on Intel Galileo Gen 2*, we installed `pip` installer to easily install additional Python 2.7.3 packages in the Yocto Linux that we are running on the board. Now, we will use `pip` installer to install paho-mqtt 1.1. We just need to run the following command in the SSH terminal to install the package.

```
pip install paho-mqtt
```

The last lines for the output will indicate that the `paho-mqtt` package has been successfully installed. Don't worry about the error messages related to building wheel and the insecure platform warning.

```
Collecting paho-mqtt
  Downloading paho-mqtt-1.1.tar.gz (41kB)
    100% |###############################| 45kB 147kB/s
Installing collected packages: paho-mqtt
  Running setup.py install for paho-mqtt
Successfully installed paho-mqtt-1.1
```

> Eclipse allows us to use a publically accessible sandbox server for the Eclipse IoT projects at `iot.eclipse.org`, port 1883. In the following examples, we will use this sandbox server as our Mosquitto message broker. This way, we don't have to setup a Mosquitto message broker to test the examples and learn how to work with the Paho Python Client. However, in a real-life application, we should setup a Mosquitto message broker and use it for our project.

We will take the code we wrote in the previous chapter when we read temperature and humidity values from the sensor, we printed the values in an OLED matrix and rotated a servo's shaft to display the measured temperature expressed in degrees Fahrenheit with the shaft. The code file for the sample was `iot_python_chapter_08_03.py`. We will use this code as a baseline to add the same features that we added when we worked with the PubNub cloud. However, in this case, we will use the Paho Python Client and the publically accessible sandbox server that provides us with a Mosquitto message broker. We will be able to perform the following actions with MQTT messages sent to a specific topic from any device that can publish MQTT messages in the topic to which we are subscribed:

- Rotate the servo's shaft to display a temperature value in degrees Fahrenheit received as part of the message
- Display a line of text received as part of the message at the bottom of the OLED matrix

 The Paho Python Client uses the topic name instead of channel. You can think of a topic as a channel.

We will use the recently installed `paho-mqtt` module to subscribe to a specific topic and run code when we receive messages in the topic. We will create a `MessageTopic` class to represent the communications topic, configure the MQTT client, the subscription to the client and declare the code for the callbacks that are going to be executed when certain events are fired. The code file for the sample is `iot_python_chapter_09_05.py`. Remember that we use the code file `iot_python_chapter_08_03.py` as a baseline, and therefore, we will add the class to the existing code in this file and we will create a new Python file. Don't forget to replace the strings assigned to the `topic` class attribute with your unique topic name. As the Mosquitto broker we are using is public, you should use a unique topic to make sure you only receive the messages you publish.

```
import time
import paho.mqtt.client as mqtt
import json


class MessageTopic:
    command_key = "command"
    successfully_processed_command_key = "successfully_processed_
command"
    # Replace with your own topic name
    topic = "iot-python-gaston-hillar/temperature"
```

```
    active_instance = None

    def __init__(self, temperature_servo, oled):
        self.temperature_servo = temperature_servo
        self.oled = oled
        self.client = mqtt.Client()
        self.client.on_connect = MessageTopic.on_connect
        self.client.on_message = MessageTopic.on_message
        self.client.connect(host="iot.eclipse.org",
                             port=1883,
                             keepalive=60)
        MessageTopic.active_instance = self

    def loop(self):
        self.client.loop()

    @staticmethod
    def on_connect(client, userdata, flags, rc):
        print("Connected to the {0} topic".
              format(MessageTopic.topic))
        subscribe_result = client.subscribe(MessageTopic.topic)
        publish_result_1 = client.publish(
            topic=MessageTopic.topic,
            payload="Listening to messages in the Intel Galileo Gen 2
board")

    @staticmethod
    def on_message(client, userdata, msg):
        if msg.topic == MessageTopic.topic:
            print("I've received the following message: {0}".
format(str(msg.payload)))
            try:
                message_dictionary = json.loads(msg.payload)
                if MessageTopic.command_key in message_dictionary:
                    if message_dictionary[MessageTopic.command_key] ==
"print_temperature_fahrenheit":
                        MessageTopic.active_instance.temperature_
servo.print_temperature(
                            message_dictionary["temperature_
fahrenheit"])
                        MessageTopic.active_instance.publish_response_
message(
                            message_dictionary)
                    elif message_dictionary[MessageTopic.command_key]
== "print_information_message":
```

```
                              MessageTopic.active_instance.oled.print_line(
                                 11, message_dictionary["text"])
                              MessageTopic.active_instance.publish_response_
    message(message_dictionary)
            except ValueError:
                # msg is not a dictionary
                # No JSON object could be decoded
                pass

    def publish_response_message(self, message):
        response_message = json.dumps({
            self.__class__.successfully_processed_command_key:
                message[self.__class__.command_key]})
        result = self.client.publish(topic=self.__class__.topic,
                                payload=response_message)
        return result
```

The `MessageTopic` class declares the `command_key` class attribute that defines the key string that defines what the code will understand as the command. Whenever we receive a message that includes the specified key string, we know that the value associated to this key in the dictionary will indicate the command that the message wants the code running in the board to be processed. In this case, we don't receive messages as dictionaries, and therefore, it is necessary to convert them from strings to dictionaries when they are not just a string.

The code declares the `successfully_processed_command_key` class attribute that defines the key string that defines what the code will use as a successfully processed command key in a response message published to the topic. Whenever we publish a message that includes the specified key string, we know that the value associated to this key in the dictionary will indicate the command that the board has successfully processed.

We have to specify the `TemperatureServo` instance and the `Oled` instance in the `temperature_servo` and `oled` required arguments. The constructor, that is, the `__init__` method, saves the received arguments in two attributes with the same names. The `topic` class attribute argument specifies the Mosquitto topic to which we are going to subscribe to listen to the messages that other devices send to this topic. We will also publish messages to this topic, and therefore, we will be both a subscriber and a publisher for this channel.

Then, the constructor creates an instance of the `mqtt.Client` class that represents an MQTT client and we will use to communicate with an MQTT broker. As we create the instance with the default parameters, we will create an instance of `paho.mqtt.client.MQTTv31` and we will work with MQTT version 3.1.

The code also saves a reference to this instance in the `active_instance` class attribute because we have to access the instance in static methods that we will be specified as callbacks for the different events that the MQTT client fires.

Then, the code assigns the `self.client.on_connect` attribute to the `on_connect` static method and the `self.client.on_message` attribute to the `on_message` static method. Static methods do not receive either `self` of `cls` as the first argument, and therefore, we can use them as callbacks with the required number of arguments.

Finally, the constructor calls the `self.client.connect` method and specifies the publically accessible sandbox server for the Eclipse IoT projects at iot.eclipse.org, port 1883, in the arguments. This way, the code asks the MQTT client to establish a connection to the specified MQTT broker. In case you decide to use your own Mosquitto broker, you just need to change the values for the `host` and `port` arguments, according to the configuration for the Mosquitto broker. The `connect` method runs with an asynchronous execution, and therefore, it is a non-blocking call.

After a connection has been successfully established with the MQTT broker, the specified callback in the `self.client.on_connect` attribute will be executed, that is, the `on_connect` static method (marked with the `@staticmethod` decorator). This static method receives the `mqtt.Client` instance that established the connection with the MQTT broker in the `client` argument. The code calls the `client.subscribe` method with `MessageTopic.topic` as an argument to subscribe to the topic specified in the `topic` class attribute.

In this case, we will only subscribe to one topic. However, it is very important to know that we are not limited to subscribe to a single topic, we might subscribe to many topics with a single call to the `subscribe` method.

Finally, the code calls the `client.publish` method with `MessageTopic.topic` as the `topic` argument and a message string in the `payload` argument. This way, we publish a string message that says `"Listening to messages in the Intel Galileo Gen 2 board"` to the topic specified in the `topic` class attribute.

Whenever there is a new message received in the topic to which we have subscribed, the specified callback in the `self.client.on_messsage` attribute will be executed, that is, the `on_message` static method (marked with the `@staticmethod` decorator). This static method receives the `mqtt.Client` instance that established the connection with the MQTT broker in the `client` argument and an `mqtt.MQTTMessage` instance in the `msg` argument. The `mqtt.MQTTMessage` class describes an incoming message. First, the static method checks whether the `msg.topic` attribute, that indicates the topic in which the message has been received, matches the value in the `topic` class attribute. In this case, whenever the `on_message` method is executed, the value in `msg.topic` will always match the value in the `topic` class attribute because we just subscribed to one topic. However, in case we subscribe to more than one topic, is is always necessary to check which is the topic in which the message was sent and in which we are receiving the message.

The code prints the message that has been received, that is, the `msg.payload` attribute. Then, the code assigns the result of the `json.loads` function to deserialize `msg.payload` to a Python object and assigns the results to the `message_dictionary` local variable. In case the contents of `msg.payload` are not JSON, a `ValueError` exception will be captured and no more code will be executed in the method. In case the contents of `msg.payload` are JSON, we will have a dictionary in the `message_dictionary` local variable.

Then, the code checks whether the `command_key` class attribute is included in the `message_dictionary` dictionary. If the expression evaluates to `True`, it means that the JSON message converted to a dictionary includes a command that we have to process. However, before we can process the command, we have to check which is the command, and therefore, it is necessary to retrieve the value associated with the key equivalent to the `command_key` class attribute. The code is capable of running specific code when the value is any of the two commands that we used in our previous example when we worked with the PubNub cloud.

The code uses the `active_instance` class attribute that has a reference to the active `MessageTopic` instance to call the necessary methods for either the `temperature_servo` or the `oled` attribute based on the command that has to be processed. We had to declare the callbacks as static methods, and therefore, we use this class attribute to access the active instance.

Once the command has been successfully processed, the code calls the `publish_response_message` for the `MessageTopic` instance saved in the `active_instance` class attribute. This method receives the message dictionary that has been received with the command in the `message` argument. The method calls the `json.dumps` function to serialize a dictionary to a JSON formatted string with the response message that indicates the command has been successfully processed. Finally, the code calls the `client.publish` method with the `topic` class attribute as the `topic` argument and the JSON formatted string (`response_message`) in the `payload` argument.

> In this case, we are not evaluating the response from the `publish` method. In addition, we are using the default value for the `qos` argument that specifies the desired quality of service. In more advanced scenarios, we should add code to check the results of the method and probably adding code on the `on_publish` callback that is fired when a message is successfully published.

Now, we will use the previously coded `MessageTopic` class to create a new version of the `__main__` method that uses the Mosquitto broker and the MQTT client to receive and process commands. The new version doesn't rotate the servo's shaft when the ambient temperature changes, instead, it will do this when it receives the appropriate command from any device connected to the Mosquitto broker. The following lines show the new version of the `__main__` method. The code file for the sample is `iot_python_chapter_09_05.py`.

```python
if __name__ == "__main__":
    temperature_and_humidity_sensor = \
        TemperatureAndHumiditySensor(0)
    oled = TemperatureAndHumidityOled(0)
    temperature_servo = TemperatureServo(3)
    message_topic = MessageTopic(temperature_servo, oled)
    while True:
        temperature_and_humidity_sensor.\
            measure_temperature_and_humidity()
        oled.print_temperature(
            temperature_and_humidity_sensor.temperature_fahrenheit,
            temperature_and_humidity_sensor.temperature_celsius)
        oled.print_humidity(
            temperature_and_humidity_sensor.humidity)
```

```
        print("Ambient temperature in degrees Celsius: {0}".
            format(temperature_and_humidity_sensor.temperature_
    celsius))
        print("Ambient temperature in degrees Fahrenheit: {0}".
            format(temperature_and_humidity_sensor.temperature_
    fahrenheit))
        print("Ambient humidity: {0}".
            format(temperature_and_humidity_sensor.humidity))
        # Sleep 10 seconds (10000 milliseconds) but process messages
    every 1 second
        for i in range(0, 10):
            message_channel.loop()
            time.sleep(1)
```

The highlighted line creates an instance of the previously coded `MessageTopic` class with `temperature_servo` and `oled` as the arguments. The constructor will subscribe to the `"iot-python-gaston-hillar/temperature"` topic in the Mosquitto broker, and therefore, we must publish messages to this topic in order to send the commands that the code will process. The loop will read the values from the sensor and print the values to the console as in the previous version of the code, and therefore, we will have code running in the loop and we will also have code listening to the messages in the `"iot-python-gaston-hillar/temperature"` topic in the Mosquitto broker. The last lines of the loop call the `message_channel.loop` method 10 times and sleep 1 second each time between the calls. The `loop` method calls the loop method for the MQTT client to and ensures communication with the broker is carried out. Think about the call to the loop method as synchronizing your mailbox. Any pending messages to the published in the outgoing box will be sent and any incoming messages will arrive to the inbox and the events that we have previously analyzed will be fired.

> There is also a threaded interface that we can run by calling the `loop_start` method for the MQTT client. This way, we can avoid multiple calls to the `loop` method.

The following line will start the example.

```
python iot_python_chapter_09_05.py
```

Keep the code running in the board. We will start receiving messages later because we have to write the code that will publish messages to this topic and send the commands to be processed.

Publishing messages to a Mosquitto broker with a Python client

We have the code that is going to be running in the Intel Galileo Gen 2 board to process the command messages received from the Mosquitto message broker. Now, we are going to code a Python client that will publish messages to the `"iot-python-gaston-hillar/temperature"` channel. This way, we will be able to design applications that can talk to IoT devices with MQTT messages. Specifically, the applications will be able to communicate through a Mosquitto message broker with Python code in the publisher and in the subscriber devices.

We can run the Python client on another Intel Galileo Gen 2 board or in any device that has Python 2.7.x installed. In addition, the code will run with Python 3.x. For example, we can run the Python client in our computer. We just need to make sure that we install the `pubnub` module we have previously installed with pip in the Python version that is running in the Yocto Linux for the board.

We will create many functions that we will assign as the callbacks to the events in the MQTT client. In addition, we will declare variables and a helper function to make it easy to publish a message with a command and the required values for the command. The code file for the sample is `iot_python_chapter_09_06.py`. Don't forget to replace the string assigned to the `topic` variable with the topic name you have specified in the previous code. The following lines show the code that defines the variables and the functions:

```python
command_key = "command"
topic = "iot-python-gaston-hillar/temperature"


def on_connect(client, userdata, flags, rc):
    print("Connected to the {0} topic".
        format(topic))
    subscribe_result = client.subscribe(topic)
    publish_result_1 = client.publish(
        topic=topic,
        payload="Listening to messages in the Paho Python Client")
    publish_result_2 = publish_command(
        client,
        topic,
        "print_temperature_fahrenheit",
        "temperature_fahrenheit",
        45)
```

```
        publish_result_3 = publish_command(
            client,
            topic,
            "print_information_message",
            "text",
            "Python IoT")


    def on_message(client, userdata, msg):
        if msg.topic == topic:
            print("I've received the following message: {0}".
format(str(msg.payload)))


    def publish_command(client, topic, command_name, key, value):
        command_message = json.dumps({
            command_key: command_name,
            key: value})
        result = client.publish(topic=topic,
                                payload=command_message)
        return result
```

The code declares the command_key variable that defines the key string that indicates what the code understands as a command in the messages. Our main goal is to build and publish command messages to the topic specified in the topic variable. We will be both a subscriber and a publisher for this topic.

The on_connect function is the callback that will be executed once a successful connection has been established with the Mosquitto MQTT broker. The code calls the subscribe method for the MQTT client received in the client argument and then calls the publish method to send the following string message to the topic: "Listening to messages in the Paho Python Client"

The code calls the publish_command function with the necessary arguments to build and publish the print_temperature_fahrenheit command with a temperature value of 45. Finally, the code calls the publish_command function again with the necessary arguments to build and publish the print_information_message command with a text value of "Python IoT".

The `publish_command` function receives the MQTT client, the topic, the command name, the key and the value that provide the necessary information to execute the command in the `client`, `topic`, `command_name`, `key` and `value` required arguments. In this case, we don't target the command to a specific IoT device and all the devices that subscribe to the topic and run the code in our previous example will process the commands that we publish. We can use the code as a baseline to work with more complex examples in which we have to generate commands that target specific IoT devices. As happened in our previous examples, it is also necessary to improve the security.

The function creates a dictionary and saves the results of serializing the dictionary to a JSON formatted string in the `command_message` local variable. The `command_key` variable is the first key for the dictionary and the `command_name` received as an argument, the value that composes the first key-value pair. Then, the code calls the `client.publish` method to publish the `command_message` JSON formatted string to the topic received as an argument.

The `on_message` function will be executed each time a new message arrives to the topic to which we have subscribed. The function just prints the raw string with the payload of the received message.

Now, we will use the previously coded `functions` to write a `__main__` method that publishes the two commands included in MQTT messages that our board will process. The following lines show the code for the `__main__` method. The code file for the sample is `iot_python_chapter_09_06.py`.

```
if __name__ == "__main__":
    client = mqtt.Client()
    client.on_connect = on_connect
    client.on_message = on_message
    client.connect(host="iot.eclipse.org",
                   port=1883,
                   keepalive=60)
    client.loop_forever()
```

The code in the `__main__` method is very easy to understand. The code creates an instance of the `mqtt.Client` class that represents an MQTT client and we will use it to communicate with an MQTT broker. As we create the instance with the default parameters, we will create an instance of `paho.mqtt.client.MQTTv31` and we will work with MQTT version 3.1.

Then, the code assigns the `client.on_connect` attribute to the previously coded `on_connect` function and the `client.on_message` attribute to the `on_message` function. The code calls the `client.connect` method and specifies the publically accessible sandbox server for the Eclipse IoT projects at iot.eclipse.org, port 1883, in the arguments. This way, the code asks the MQTT client to establish a connection to the specified MQTT broker. In case you decide to use your own Mosquitto broker, you just need to change the values for the `host` and `port` arguments, according to the configuration for the Mosquitto broker. Remember that the `connect` method runs with an asynchronous execution, and therefore, it is a non-blocking call.

After a connection has been successfully established with the MQTT broker, the specified callback in the `client.on_connect` attribute will be executed, that is, the `on_connect` function. The function receives the `mqtt.Client` instance that established the connection with the MQTT broker in the `client` argument. As previously explained, the function subscribes to a topic and schedules the publication of three messages to it.

Finally, the code calls the `client.loop_forever` method that calls the loop method for us in an infinite blocking loop. At this point, we only want to run the MQTT client loop in our program. The scheduled messages will be published and we will receive the messages with the successfully executed command details after the board processes the commands.

Keep the Python code we have executed in our previous example running on the board. We want the board to process our commands. The following line will start the example for the Python client in any computer or device that you want to use as a client. It is possible to run the code in another SSH terminal in case you want to use the same board as a client.

```
python iot_python_chapter_09_06.py
```

After you run the example, you will see the following output in the Python console that runs the Python client, that is, the `iot_python_chapter_09_06.py` Python script.

```
Connected to the iot-python-gaston-hillar/temperature topic
I've received the following message: Listening to messages in the Paho
Python Client
I've received the following message: {"command": "print_temperature_
fahrenheit", "temperature_fahrenheit": 45}
I've received the following message: {"text": "Python IoT", "command":
"print_information_message"}
```

```
I've received the following message: {"successfully_processed_
command": "print_temperature_fahrenheit"}
I've received the following message: {"successfully_processed_
command": "print_information_message"}
```

The code used the Eclipse Paho MQTT Python client library to build and publish the following two command messages in the `"iot-python-gaston-hillar/temperature"` topic in the Mosquitto broker:

```
{"command":"print_temperature_fahrenheit", "temperature_fahrenheit":
"45"}
{"command":"print_information_message", "text": "Python IoT"}
```

As we are also subscribed to the `"iot-python-gaston-hillar/temperature"` topic, we receive the messages we sent. Then, we received the successfully processed command messages for the two command messages. The board has processed the commands and published the messages to the `"iot-python-gaston-hillar/temperature"` topic.

You will see the following messages in the output for the SSH terminal that is running the code for the board that processes the commands, that is, the iot_python_chapter_09_05.py Python script:

```
I've received the following message: Listening to messages in the
Intel Galileo Gen 2 board
I've received the following message: Listening to messages in the Paho
Python Client
I've received the following message: {"command": "print_temperature_
fahrenheit", "temperature_fahrenheit": 45}
I've received the following message: {"text": "Python IoT", "command":
"print_information_message"}
I've received the following message: {"successfully_processed_
command": "print_temperature_fahrenheit"}
I've received the following message: {"successfully_processed_
command": "print_information_message"}
```

You will see the following text displayed at the bottom of the OLED matrix: Python IoT. In addition, the servo's shaft will rotate to 45 degrees.

Test your knowledge

1. MQTT is:

    1. A heavyweight messaging protocol that runs on top of the TCP/IP protocol and works with a publish-subscribe mechanism.

    2. A lightweight messaging protocol that runs on top of the TCP/IP protocol and works with a publish-subscribe mechanism.

    3. An equivalent to HTTP.

2. Mosquitto is:

    1. An open source message broker that implements the versions 3.1 and 3.1.1 of the MQTT protocol.

    2. A closed source message broker that implements the versions 3.1 and 3.1.1 of the MQTT protocol.

    3. An open source message broker that implements a RESTful API.

3. The Eclipse Paho project provides:

    1. An open source client implementation of HTTP.

    2. An open source client implementation of `dweet.io`.

    3. An open source client implementation of MQTT.

4. Which of the following Python modules is the Paho Python Client?

    1. paho-client-pip.

    2. paho-mqtt.

    3. paho-http.

5. Dweepy is:

    1. A simple Python client for `dweet.io` that allows us to easily publish data to `dweet.io` with Python.

    2. A simple Python client for Mosquitto that allows us to easily publish messages to a Mosquitto message broker.

    3. A simple Python client for PubNub cloud that allows us to easily publish messages to the PubNub cloud.

Summary

In this chapter, we combined many cloud-based services that allowed us to easily publish data collected from sensors and visualize it in a web-based dashboard. We realized that there is always a Python API, and therefore, it is easy to write Python code that interacts with popular cloud-based services.

We worked with the MQTT protocol and its publish/subscribe model to process commands in our board and indicate when the commands were successfully processed through messages. First, we worked with the PubNub cloud that works with the MQTT protocol under the hoods. Then, we developed the same example with Mosquitto and Eclipse Paho. Now, we know how we can write applications that can establish bi-directional communications with our IoT devices. In addition, we know how we can make IoT devices communicate with other IoT devices.

Now that we are able to take advantage of many cloud services and we worked with the MQTT protocol, we will learn how to analyze huge amounts of data, which is the topic of the next chapter.

10

Analyzing Huge Amounts of Data with Cloud-based IoT Analytics

In this chapter, we will work with Intel IoT Analytics to analyze huge amounts of data with this powerful cloud-based service. We will:

- Understand the relationship between Internet of Things and Big Data
- Learn the Intel IoT Analytics structure
- Set up devices in Intel IoT Analytics
- Configure components in Intel IoT Analytics
- Collect sensor data with Intel IoT Analytics
- Analyze sensor data with Intel IoT Analytics
- Trigger alerts with rules in Intel IoT Analytics

Understanding the relationship between Internet of Things and Big Data

Big Data is watching us. We are generating valuable data each time we perform an action without even knowing that. Every time we tap, click, tweet, stop on a red light signal, hop on a bus, or perform an action caught by the millions of real-time sensors in any city around the world, we are generating valuable data. We interact with IoT devices that have sensors, collect data, and publish it to the Cloud. In order to analyze and process Big Data, managers, architects, developers, and system administrators require many skills that were not necessary for applications that worked with smaller data sets.

We have been working with examples that collected data from the real world through sensors and published it to the Cloud. We also published messages that include data from sensors and commands that have to be processed by code running on an IoT device. Sometimes, we are retrieving data from the sensors every second. Thus, it is very easy to realize that we generate huge amounts of data, and therefore, it is very important to learn many things related to Big Data. Internet of Things comprises Big Data.

Imagine we write Python code that runs on an Intel Galileo Gen 2 board and performs the following actions every second:

- Read the measured ambient temperature from a temperature and humidity sensor
- Read the measured ambient humidity level from a temperature and humidity sensor
- Read the measured volumetric water content in soil from ten soil moisture sensor that measure the values in different locations
- Publish a message with the ambient temperature, ambient humidity, and the ten volumetric water contents

The first things that might come to our mind are the number of sensors we have to connect to our board. Let's consider that all the sensors are digital sensors and we have to connect them to the I²C bus. We can connect the digital temperature and humidity sensor plus then ten soil-moisture sensors to the I²C bus as long as all the sensors have different I²C bus addresses. We just need to make sure that we can configure the I²C bus address for the soil moisture sensors and we can assign a different I²C address to each of these sensors.

Catnip Electronics designed a digital soil moisture sensor that provides an I²C interface and one of its features is that it allows an I²C address change. The default I²C address for this sensor is 0x20 (hexadecimal 20) but we can easily change it. We just need to connect each sensor to the I²C bus, write the new address to register one and the new address will take effect after we reset the sensor. We just need to write a 6 to the sensor's I²C address to reset the sensor. We can follow the same procedure for all the sensors and assign different I²C addresses to them. You can read more about the digital soil moisture sensor in the following webpage: `http://www.tindie.com/products/miceuz/i2c-soil-moisture-sensor.`

We want to analyze hourly, daily, monthly, quarterly, and yearly data. However, we do need to measure every second and not every single day because it is very important to analyze how data changes per second. We are going to collect the following:

- 60 measurements for all the variables per minute
- 3,600 (60 * 60) measurements per hour
- 86,400 (3,600 x 24) measurements per day
- 31,536,000 (86,400 * 365) measurements per year (considering that we aren't talking about a leap year)

We won't have just one IoT device collecting data and publishing it. We will have 3,000 IoT devices running the same code and they will generate 94,608,000,000 (31,356,300 * 3,000), that is, ninety-four billion six hundred eight million, measurements per year. In addition, we have other data sources that we have to analyze: all the tweets about weather related issues in the locations in which the sensors are capturing data. Thus, we have huge volumes of both structured and unstructured data that we want to analyze computationally, to reveal patterns and associations. We are definitely talking about Big Data practices.

The sample numbers are useful to understand the relationship between Big Data and IoT. We won't deploy 3,000 boards for our next example and we won't cover all the topics related to IoT analytics and Big Data because it would be out of the scope of this book. However, we will work with the cloud-based analytics system that works with a component included in the Intel IoT Development Kit image that we have been using to boot the board with the Yocto Linux meta distribution in *Chapter 2, Working with Python on Intel Galileo Gen 2*.

Understanding the Intel IoT Analytics structure

Imagine that we have to collect and analyze sensor data for 3,000 IoT devices, that is, 3,000 Intel Galileo Gen 2 boards running the Python code that interacts with sensors. We would need to invest in the storage and processing capacity to perform IoT analytics with such a huge amount of data. Whenever we have a similar requirement, we can take advantage of a cloud-based solution. Intel IoT Analytics is one of them and it works very well with the Intel Galileo Gen 2 board and Python.

Intel IoT Analytics requires us to sign up, create an account with a valid e-mail and a password, and click on the activation link of a confirmation e-mail before we can publish the sensor data using their free services. We aren't required to enter any credit card or payment information. If you already have an account at Intel IoT Analytics, you can skip this step. You can also use your existing Facebook, Google+, or GitHub account to log in. The following is the main web page for the Intel IoT Analytics site: `https://dashboard.us.enableiot.com`. Make sure to review the terms and conditions before you use this cloud-based service with sensitive data.

Once you create your account and log in for the first time to Intel IoT Analytics, the site will display the **Create new Account** page. Enter the desired name to identity the account, that is, your analytics project in **Account Name**. Enter `Temperature and humidity` for our example and leave the default option for **Sensor health report**. Then, click **Create** and the site will display the **My Dashboard** page for the recently created account. Each account represents a separate workspace with its own set of sensors and related data. The site allows us to create more than one account and easily switch between them. The following screenshot shows the initial view for the **My Dashboard** page after we created a new account:

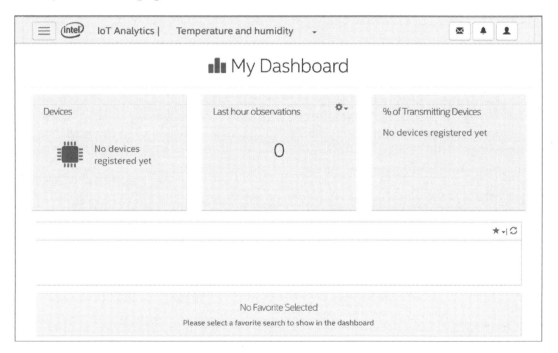

The **My Dashboard** page indicates that we still don't have registered devices, and therefore, we don't have either transmitting devices or observations. Each time we publish data from a registered device to Intel IoT Analytics, we create an observation for the device. Thus, the **My Dashboard** page provides the number of last observations in a specific period. By default, the page displays the sum of the last hour observations for all the registered devices. Keep the web site opened in your web browser because we will continue working with it later.

As a user, we can work with many accounts. Each account can contain many devices, has a name and an identifier known as `accountId`. Each device has a globally unique identifier known as `deviceId`. So, each Intel Galileo Gen 2 board that includes sensors will become one device for the account we have created. In our case, we will just work with a single Intel Galileo Gen 2 board. However, remember that our goal is to demonstrate how we can work with 3,000 IoT devices handled by a single account.

We can think of each device as an endpoint that contains one or more components that can provide one of the following in Intel IoT Analytics:

- **Actuator**: A setting that can be modified on a device. For example, rotate the angle of a servo's shaft or turn on an LED.
- **Time series**: A series of values captured from a sensor, that is, a collection of observations. For example, a collection of observations with ambient temperature values retrieved with a temperature and humidity sensor, expressed in degrees Fahrenheit and including timestamps.

In our case, we need a device to use the following components that will retrieve the values from the digital temperature and humidity sensor connected to our board:

- A time series with ambient temperature observations expressed in degrees Fahrenheit (°F)

- A time series with ambient temperature observations expressed in degrees Celsius (°C)

- A time series with ambient humidity level observations expressed in percentage

First, we will work with the UI provided by the Intel IoT Analytics web site in combination with the `iotkit-admin` utility to set up the device, activate it and register the three components included in the previous list. This way, we will learn to work with the structure required by Intel IoT Analytics. Then, we will write Python code that uses the REST API to create observations for the defined components that belong to an activated device included in our recently created account.

We can also the REST API to perform the previously explained setup tasks by writing a Python code. In case we have to work with more than a dozen devices, we won't want to perform the setup tasks by working with the UI provided by the Intel IoT Analytics web site, we would definitely want to write code that automates the setup tasks.

Setting up devices in Intel IoT Analytics

The image that we have been using to boot our Intel Galileo Gen 2 board includes a local agent for Intel IoT Analytics preinstalled. Unless we have made specific changes to the Yocto Linux meta distribution to disable specific components, we will have the agent running as a daemon on the device. The agent includes the `iotkit-admin` command-line utility that allows us to perform specific interactions with Intel IoT Analytics. We will use this command-line utility to perform the following tasks:

- Test the proper communication with Intel IoT Analytics
- Obtain the device id
- Activate a device
- Register three time series components for the device.
- Send test observations

First, we will check whether the `iotkit-admin` command-line utility can establish proper communication with Intel IoT Analytics. We just need to run the following command in the SSH terminal:

```
iotkit-admin test
```

If the connection is successful, we will see lines similar to the following ones. The last line provides information about the build, that is, the version.

```
2016-04-05T02:17:49.573Z - info: Trying to connect to host ...
2016-04-05T02:17:56.780Z - info: Connected to dashboard.us.enableiot.
com
2016-04-05T02:17:56.799Z - info: Environment: prod
2016-04-05T02:17:56.807Z - info: Build: 0.14.5
```

Now, run the following command in the SSH terminal to obtain the device ID, also known as `deviceId`:

```
iotkit-admin device-id
```

The previous command will generate an output line such as the following one with the device ID. By default, the device ID is equal to the MAC address of the network interface card.

```
2016-04-05T02:23:23.170Z - info: Device ID: 98-4F-EE-01-75-72
```

You can use the following command to change the device ID to a different one: `iotkit-admin set-device-id new-device-id`. You just need to replace `new-device-id` with the new device id you want to set up for your device. However, bear in mind the new device ID must be a globally unique identifier.

In this case, we will use `kansas-temperature-humidity-01` as our device ID for all our samples. You must replace it in all the commands, then include this name with the device name you retrieved or the new device ID you assign to the device.

The following command in the SSH terminal will rename the device:

```
iotkit-admin set-device-id kansas-temperature-humidity-01
```

The following lines show the output for the previous command:

```
2016-04-08T17:56:15.355Z - info: Device ID set to: kansas-temperature-
humidity
```

Go to the web browser in which you are working with the Intel IoT Analytics dashboard, click on the menu icon (a button with three horizontal lines located at the upper-left corner). Select **Account** and the site will display the **My Account** page with detailed information about the account we previously created.

The initial view will display the **Details** tab. In case the **Activation Code** includes the **(Code Expired)** text, it means that the activation code is not valid anymore and it is necessary to click on the refresh icon located on the right-hand side of the **Activation Code** textbox (the second icon with the two arrows). We have to make sure that the activation code hasn't expired in order to activate the device successfully. The following screenshot gives the initial view for the **My Account** page for the **Temperature and humidity** account with the activation code expired:

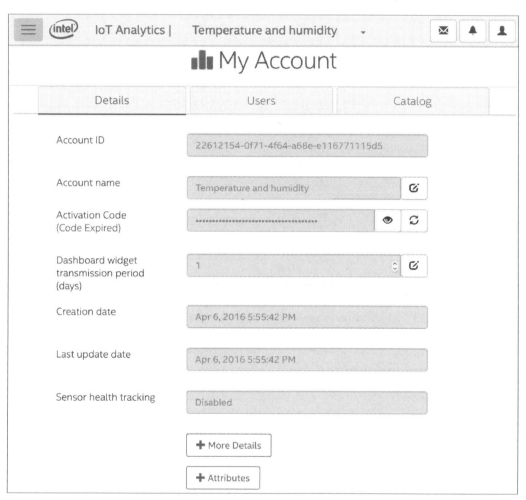

Once you refresh the activation code by clicking on the refresh button, a countdown stopwatch will indicate the time left for the activation code until it expires. You will have one hour after you click on the refresh button. Click on the eye icon to view the hidden activation code and copy it. We will use `01aCti0e` as our sample activation code and you will have to replace it with your activation code.

Now, run the following command in the SSH terminal to activate the device with the previously generated activation code. Replace `01aCti0e` with your activation code.

```
iotkit-admin activate 01aCti0e
```

The previous command will generate an output similar to the following lines:

```
2016-04-05T02:24:46.449Z - info: Activating ...
2016-04-05T02:24:49.817Z - info: Saving device token...
2016-04-05T02:24:50.646Z - info: Updating metadata...
2016-04-05T02:24:50.691Z - info: Metadata updated.
```

Our Intel Galileo Gen 2 board, that is, the device, is now associated with the **Temperature and humidity** account that provided us with the activation code and the command generated the necessary security credentials, that is, the device token.

Go to the web browser in which you are working with the Intel IoT Analytics dashboard, click on the menu icon (a button with three horizontal lines located at the upper-left corner). Select **Devices** and the site will display the **My Devices** page with the list of all the devices that we have activated for the current account. The previously activated `kansas-temperature-humidity-01` device will appear in the list with **Kansas-temperature-humidity-01-NAME** in its **Name** column and **active** in the **Status** column. The following screenshot shows the device listed in the **My Devices** page:

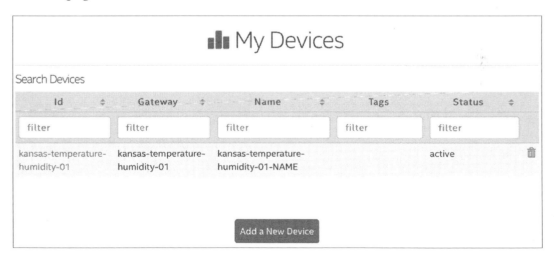

Click on the device **Id** in the previous list (**kansas-temperature-humidity-01**) to see and edit the device details. You can add tags and attributes to make it easier to filter the devices in the previous list. These possibilities are extremely useful when we have to work with more than a dozen devices as they make it easy for us to filter the devices in the list.

Setting up components in Intel IoT Analytics

Go to the web browser in which you are working with the Intel IoT Analytics dashboard, click on the menu icon, select **Account** and the site will display the **My Account** page. Then, click on the **Catalog** tab and the site will display the components registered in the catalog grouped in the following three categories:

- Humidity
- Powerswitch
- Temperature

Make sure that the **Humidity** components panel is expanded and click on **humidity. v1.0**. The site will display the **Component definition** dialog box for the **humidity. v1.0** component, that is, the component named **humidity** whose version is `1.0`. The following screenshot shows the values for the different fields in the component definition:

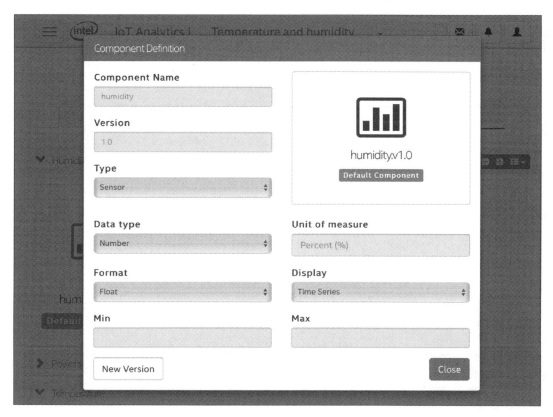

The `humidity` component version 1.0 represents a time series with ambient humidity level expressed in percentage. The **Data type** is **Number**, the **Unit of measure** is **Percent (%)**, the **Format** is **Float** and the **Display** is **Time Series**. We can use this component for our ambient humidity level observations.

Click on **Close**, make sure that the **Temperature** components panel is expanded and click on **temperature.v1.0**. The site will display the **Component definition** dialog box for the **temperature.v1.0** component, that is, the component named **temperature** whose version is 1.0. The following screenshot shows the values for the different fields in the component definition:

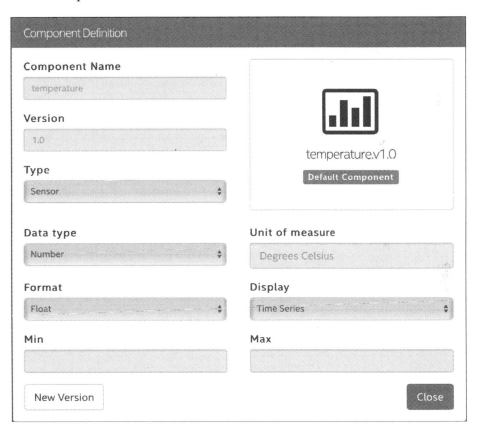

The `temperature` component version **1.0** represents a time series with temperature expressed in degrees Celsius. The **Data type** is **Number**, the **Unit of measure** is **Degrees Celsius**, the **Format** is **Float** and the **Display** is **Time Series**. We can use this component for our ambient temperature observations expressed in degrees Celsius.

Click on **Close** and make sure that the **Temperature** components panel is expanded. There is no other temperature component, and therefore, we will have to create a new component for our ambient temperature observations expressed in degrees Fahrenheit.

Click on **Add new Catalog Item** at the bottom of the page and the site will display the **Component definition** dialog box with all the fields empty except from the version that will have a fixed `1.0` value. We are creating the first version of a new catalog item. Enter and select the following values:

- Enter **temperaturef** in **Component Name**
- Select **Sensor** in **Type**
- Select **Number** in **Data type**
- Enter **Degrees Fahrenheit** in **Unit of measure**
- Select **Float** in **Format**
- Select **Time Series** in **Display**

Finally, click on **Save** and the site will add the new component definition at the bottom of the list with the `temperaturef.v.1.0` name.

Now that we are sure that we have all the required component definitions in the catalog, we have to register the components that our device will use to create observations. We must give a name or alias of each component we register, and we must specify the component type and version from the previous catalog. The following table summarizes the components that we will register for our device:

Component name or alias	Component type	Description
temperaturec	temperature.v1.0	A time series with ambient temperature observations expressed in degrees Celsius (°C)
temperaturef	temperaturef.v1.0	A time series with ambient temperature observations expressed in degrees Fahrenheit (°F)
humidity	humidity.v1.0	A time series with ambient humidity level observations expressed in percentage

We can use the following command to register each component: `iotkit-admin register component-name component-type`. We just need to replace `component-name` with the name that will identify the component and component-type with the name that identifies the component type in the catalog, including the version number.

The following command in the SSH terminal will register the `temperaturec` component from the previous table:

```
iotkit-admin register temperaturec temperature.v1.0
```

The following lines show the output for the previous command.

```
2016-04-08T22:40:04.581Z - info: Starting registration ...
2016-04-08T22:40:04.711Z - info: Device has already been activated.
Updating ...
2016-04-08T22:40:04.739Z - info: Updating metadata...
2016-04-08T22:40:04.920Z - info: Metadata updated.
Attributes sent
2016-04-08T22:40:10.167Z - info: Component registered
name=temperaturec, type=temperature.v1.0, cid=c37cb57d-002c-4a66-866e-
ce66bc3b2340, d_id=kansas-temperature-humidity-01
```

The last line provides us with the component id, that is, the value after `cid=` and before the next comma (,). In the previous output, the component id is `c37cb57d-002c-4a66-866e-ce66bc3b2340`. We have to save each component id because we will need it later to write code that creates observations using the REST API.

The following command in the SSH terminal will register the `temperaturef` component from the previous table:

```
iotkit-admin register temperaturef temperaturef.v1.0
```

The following lines show the output for the previous command:

```
2016-04-08T22:40:20.510Z - info: Starting registration ...
2016-04-08T22:40:20.641Z - info: Device has already been activated.
Updating ...
2016-04-08T22:40:20.669Z - info: Updating metadata...
2016-04-08T22:40:20.849Z - info: Metadata updated.
Attributes sent
2016-04-08T22:40:26.156Z - info: Component registered
name=temperaturef, type=temperaturef.v1.0, cid=0f3b3aae-ce40-4fb4-
a939-e7c705915f0c, d_id=kansas-temperature-humidity-01
```

As happened with the other command, the last line provides us with the component id, that is, the value after `cid=` and before the next comma (`,`). In the previous output, the component id is `0f3b3aae-ce40-4fb4-a939-e7c705915f0c`. We have to save this one for its later usage in our code.

The following command in the SSH terminal will register the `humidity` component from the previous table:

```
iotkit-admin register humidity humidity.v1.0
```

The following lines show the output for the previous command and the last line includes the component id.

```
2016-04-08T22:40:36.512Z - info: Starting registration ...
2016-04-08T22:40:36.643Z - info: Device has already been activated.
Updating ...
2016-04-08T22:40:36.670Z - info: Updating metadata...
2016-04-08T22:40:36.849Z - info: Metadata updated.
Attributes sent
2016-04-08T22:40:43.003Z - info: Component registered name=humidity,
type=humidity.v1.0, cid=71aba984-c485-4ced-bf19-c0f32649bcee, d_
id=kansas-temperature-humidity-01
```

> The component ids will be different from the values indicated in the previous outputs and you will have to take note of each of the component ids that have been generated with the previous commands.

Go to the web browser in which you are working with the Intel IoT Analytics dashboard, click on the menu icon. Select **Devices** and the site will display the **My Devices** page. Click on the device **Id** in the previous list (**kansas-temperature-humidity-01**) to see and edit the device details. Click on **+Components** to expand the components registered for the device and you will see a list with the following three components:

- **temperaturec**
- **temperaturef**
- **humidity**

The following screenshot shows the three components registered for the selected device:

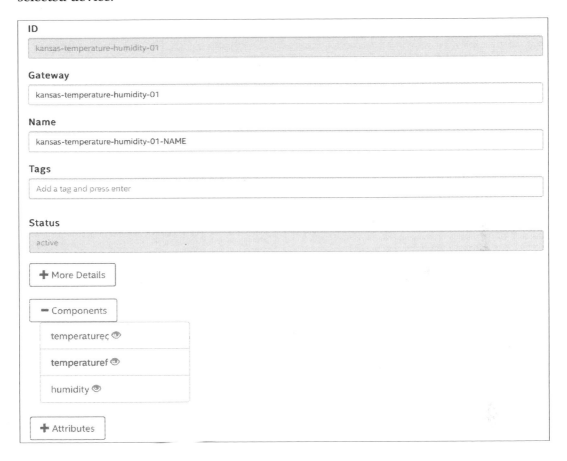

We can click on any of the three components and check the details for the registered component. In case we lose the component id, we can retrieve it by clicking on the component and the **Component Definition** dialog box will display the component id just below the component type description. The following screenshot shows the component definition for the `temperaturef` component. The component id **0f3b3aae-ce40-4fb4-a939-e7c705915f0c** appears below the **Custom Component** label on the right-hand side.

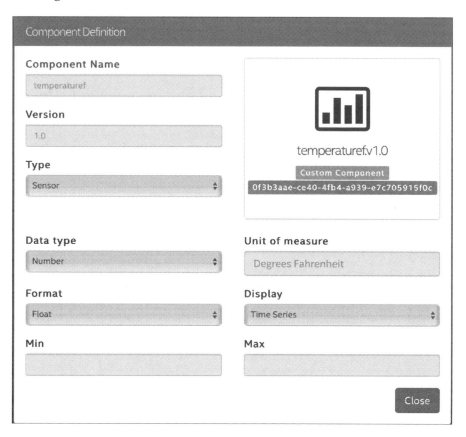

Unluckily, there is no way to retrieve the device token that was generated when we activated the device with the features included in the site. We need the device token to create observations for the registered components. The agent for Intel IoT Analytics saves the device token with other configuration values for the device in the `device.json` file and its default path is `/usr/lib/node_modules/iotkit-agent/data/device.json`. As the file name suggests, the file contains JSON code. We just need to run the following command in the SSH terminal to display the text content from the previous file and allow us to retrieve the device token:

```
cat /usr/lib/node_modules/iotkit-agent/data/device.json
```

The following lines show the output for the previous command that includes all the configurations we have made so far for our device. The line that defines the value for the device token is highlighted.

```
{
    "activation_retries": 10,
    "activation_code": null,
    "device_id": "kansas-temperature-humidity-01",
    "device_name": false,
    "device_loc": [
        88.34,
        64.22047,
        0
    ],
    "gateway_id": false,
    "device_token": "eyJ0eXAiOiJKV1QiLCJhbGciOiJSUzI1NiJ9.eyJqdGkiOi
JjOTNmMTJhMy05MWZlLTQ3MWYtODM4OS02OGM1NDYxNDIxMDUiLCJpc3
MiOiJodHRwOi8vZW5hYmxlaW90LmNvbSIsInN1YiI6ImthbnNhcy10ZW1wZXJhdHVyZ
S1odW1pZGl0eS0wMSIsImV4cCI6IjIwMjYtMDQtMDZUMTk6MjA6MTkuNzA0WiJ9.PH5y
Qas2FiQvUSR9V2pa3n3kIYZvmSe_xXY7QkFjlXUVUcyy9Sk_eVF4AL6qpZlBC9vjtdOL-
VMZiULC9YXxAV19s5Cl8ZqpQs36Elssv_1H9CBFXKiiPArplzaWXVzvIRBVVzwfQrGr
MoD_14DcHlH2zgn5UGxhZ3RMPUvqgeneG3P-hSbPScPQL1pW85VT2IHT3seWyW1c637I_
MDpHbJJCbkytPVpJpwKBxrCiKlGhvsh5pl4eLUXYUPlQAzB9QzC_ohujG23b-ApfHZug
YD7zJa-05u0lkt93EEnuCk39o5SmPmIiuBup-k_mLn_VMde5fUvbxDt_SMI0XY3_Q",
    "account_id": "22612154-0f71-4f64-a68e-e116771115d5",
    "sensor_list": [
        {
            "name": "temperaturec",
            "type": "temperature.v1.0",
            "cid": "c37cb57d-002c-4a66-866e-ce66bc3b2340",
            "d_id": "kansas-temperature-humidity-01"
        },
        {
            "name": "temperaturef",
            "type": "temperaturef.v1.0",
            "cid": "0f3b3aae-ce40-4fb4-a939-e7c705915f0c",
            "d_id": "kansas-temperature-humidity-01"
        },
        {
            "name": "humidity",
            "type": "humidity.v1.0",
            "cid": "71aba984-c485-4ced-bf19-c0f32649bcee",
            "d_id": "kansas-temperature-humidity-01"
        }
    ]
}
```

The previous lines also show the component id for each of the components that we have registered. Thus, we have all the necessary configuration values that we will have to use in our code in just one place. In this case, the device token is the following, that is, the string value for the `"device_token"` key. However, the value that you will retrieve will be different.

```
"eyJ0eXAiOiJKV1QiLCJhbGciOiJSUzI1NiJ9.eyJqdGkiOiJjOTNmMTJhMy05MWZlLT
Q3MWYtODM4OS02OGM1NDYxNDIxMDUiLCJpc3MiOiJodHRwOi8vZW5hYmxlaW90LmNvb
SIsInN1YiI6ImthbNhcy10ZW1wZXJhdHVyZS1odW1pZGl0eS0wMSIsImV4cCI6IjIw
MjYtMDQtMDZUMTk6MDA6MTkuNzA0WiJ9.PH5yQas2FiQvUSR9V2pa3n3kIYZvmSe_xXY
7QkFjlXUVUcyy9Sk_eVF4AL6qpZlBC9vjtd0L-VMZiULC9YXxAVl9s5Cl8ZqpQs36
E1ssv_1H9CBFXKiiPArplzaWXVzvIRBVVzwfQrGrMoD_l4DcHlH2zgn5UGxhZ3RMP
UvqgeneG3P-hSbPScPQL1pW85VT2IHT3seWyW1c637I_MDpHbJJCbkytPVpJpwKBxr
CiKlGhvsh5pl4eLUXYUPlQAzB9QzC_ohujG23b-ApfHZugYD7zJa-05u0lkt93EEnu
Ck39o5SmPmIiuBup-k_mLn_VMde5fUvbxDt_SMI0XY3_Q"
```

Collecting sensor data with Intel IoT Analytics

We will take the code we wrote in *Chapter 8, Displaying Information and Performing Actions*, when we read temperature and humidity values from the sensor, we printed the values in an OLED matrix and rotated a servo's shaft to display the measured temperature expressed in degrees Fahrenheit with the shaft. The code file for the sample was `iot_python_chapter_08_03.py`. We will use this code as a baseline to add new features that will allow us to create observations for the three components we registered for our activated device.

In *Chapter 2, Working with Python on Intel Galileo Gen 2*, we made sure that the `pip` installer was available to install additional Python 2.7.3 packages in the Yocto Linux that we are running on the board. Now, we will use `pip` installer to make sure that the `requests` package is installed. This package is a very popular HTTP library for Python that allows us to easily build and send HTTP requests with an extremely easy to understand syntax.

If you have worked with examples from the previous chapter, you will have this package already installed. However, in case you just jumped into this chapter, it might be necessary to install it. We just need to run the following command in the SSH terminal to install the package. Notice that it can take a few minutes to complete the installation.

```
pip install requests
```

In case you see the following output, it means that the requests package was already installed and you can move on to the next step.

```
Requirement already satisfied (use --upgrade to upgrade): requests in
/usr/lib/python2.7/site-packages
```

We will create an `IntelIotAnalytics` class to represent the interface to Intel IoT Analytics and make it easy for us to publish observations for the three components. However, before we code the class, we have to make sure that we can replace the content for many class attributes that define important values related to our account, the components, and the device. You will have to replace the strings specified for the following class attributes with the appropriate values:

- `account_name`: The value of the **Account name** field in the **My Account** page. In our example, we used `"Temperature and humidity"` for our account name.

- `account_id`: The value of the **Account ID** field in the **My Account** page. In our example, we use `" 22612154-0f71-4f64-a68e-e116771115d5"` for our account id. We can also retrieve the account id value by reading the string value specified for the `"account_id"` key in the `device.json` file.

- `device_id`: The value of the **ID** field in the **Add/Edit a Device** page that the site shows when we click on a device name in the list displayed in the **My Devices** page. In our example, we use `"kansas-temperature-humidity-01"` for our device id. We can also retrieve the device_id by running the following command in an SSH terminal: `iotkit-admin device-id` or by reading the string value specified for the `"device_id"` key in the `device.json` file.

- `device_token`: The value of the device token that was generated when we activated the device. As previously explained, we can retrieve the device token by reading the string value specified for the `"device_token"` key in the `device.json` file.

- `component_id_temperature_fahrenheit`: The value of the component id that was generated when we registered the `temperaturef` component. The component id is displayed below the component type in the **Component Definition** dialog box. In our example, we use `"0f3b3aae-ce40-4fb4-a939-e7c705915f0c"` for this value. We can also retrieve the component id value by reading the string value specified for the `"cid"` key in the same block that declares the `"name": "temperaturef"` key-value pair, in the `device.json` file.

- `component_id_temperature_celsius`: The value of the component id that was generated when we registered the `temperaturec` component. In our example, we use `"c37cb57d-002c-4a66-866e-ce66bc3b2340"` for this value.

- `component_id_humidity_level_percentage`: The value of the component id that was generated when we registered the `humidity` component. In our example, we use `"71aba984-c485-4ced-bf19-c0f32649bcee"` for this value.

The code file for the sample is `iot_python_chapter_10_01.py`. Remember that we use the code file `iot_python_chapter_08_03.py` as a baseline, and therefore, we will add the `IntelIotAnalytics` class to the existing code in this file and we will create a new Python file. The following lines show the code for the `IntelIotAnalytics` class that allows us to publish observations for the `temperaturef`, `temperaturec` and `humidity` components through the REST API.

```
import time
import json
import requests

class IntelIotAnalytics:
    base_url = "https://dashboard.us.enableiot.com/v1/api"
    # You can retrieve the following information from the My Account
page
    account_name = "Temperature and humidity"
    account_id = "22612154-0f71-4f64-a68e-e116771115d5"
    # You can retrieve the device token with the following command:
    # cat /usr/lib/node_modules/iotkit-agent/data/device.json
    device_token = "eyJ0eXAiOiJKV1QiLCJhbGciOiJSUzI1NiJ9.eyJqdGkiOi
JjOTNmMTJhMy05MWZlLTQ3MWYtODM4OS02OGM1NDYxNDIxMDUiLCJpc3MiOiJodHRwO
i8vZW5hYmxlaW90LmNvbSIsInN1YiI6ImthbnNhcy10ZW1wZXJhdHVyZS1odW1pZGl0e
S0wMSIsImV4cCI6IjIwMjYtMDQtMDZUMTk6MDA6MTkuNzA0WiJ9.PH5yQas2FiQvUSR
9V2pa3n3kIYZvmSe_xXY7QkFjlXUVUcyy9Sk_eVF4AL6qpZlBC9vjtd0L-VMZiULC9Y
XxAVl9s5Cl8ZqpQs36E1ssv_1H9CBFXKiiPArplzaWXVzvIRBVVzwfQrGrMoD_14DcHl
H2zgn5UGxhZ3RMPUvqgeneG3P-hSbPScPQL1pW85VT2IHT3seWyW1c637I_MDpHbJJC
bkytPVpJpwKBxrCiKlGhvsh5pl4eLUXYUPlQAzB9QzC_ohujG23b-ApfHZugYD7zJa-05
u0lkt93EEnuCk39o5SmPmIiuBup-k_mLn_VMde5fUvbxDt_SMI0XY3_Q"
    device_id = "kansas-temperature-humidity-01"
    component_id_temperature_fahrenheit = "0f3b3aae-ce40-4fb4-a939-
e7c705915f0c"
    component_id_temperature_celsius = "c37cb57d-002c-4a66-866e-
ce66bc3b2340"
    component_id_humidity_level_percentage = "71aba984-c485-4ced-bf19-
c0f32649bcee"
```

```
    def publish_observation(self,
                            temperature_fahrenheit,
                            temperature_celsius,
                            humidity_level):
        url = "{0}/data/{1}".\
            format(self.__class__.base_url, self.__class__.device_id)
        now = int(time.time()) * 1000
        body = {
            "on": now,
            "accountId": self.__class__.account_id,
            "data": []
        }
        temperature_celsius_data = {
            "componentId": self.__class__.component_id_temperature_
celsius,
            "on": now,
            "value": str(temperature_celsius)
        }
        temperature_fahrenheit_data = {
            "componentId": self.__class__.component_id_temperature_
fahrenheit,
            "on": now,
            "value": str(temperature_fahrenheit)
        }
        humidity_level_percentage_data = {
            "componentId": self.__class__.component_id_humidity_level_
percentage,
            "on": now,
            "value": str(humidity_level)
        }
        body["data"].append(temperature_celsius_data)
        body["data"].append(temperature_fahrenheit_data)
        body["data"].append(humidity_level_percentage_data)
        data = json.dumps(body)
        headers = {
            'Authorization': 'Bearer ' + self.__class__.device_token,
            'content-type': 'application/json'
        }
        response = requests.post(url, data=data, headers=headers,
proxies={}, verify=True)
        if response.status_code != 201:
            print "The request failed. Status code: {0}. Response
text: {1}.".\
                format(response.status_code, response.text)
```

The `IntelIotAnalytics` class declares many class attributes that we explained before and that you need to replace with your own string values: `account_name`, `account_id`, `device_token`, `device_id`, `component_id_temperature_fahrenheit`, `component_id_temperature_celsius` and `component_id_humidity_level_percentage`. The `base_url` class attribute defines the base URL to access the REST API: `https://dashboard.us.enableiot.com/v1/api`. We will use this value in combination with a `data` path and the `device_id` class attribute to build the URL to which we will send the HTTP request to publish an observation.

The class declares the `publish_observation` method that receives the temperature expressed in degrees Fahrenheit, the temperature expressed in degrees Celsius and the humidity level percentage in the `temperature_fahrenheit`, `temperature_celsius` and `humidity_level` arguments. The method builds the URL to which we will send the HTTP request to create an observation for the device and the three components. The URL is composed of the `base_url` class attribute, `/data/` and the `device_id` class attribute. As happens with many REST APIs, the `base_url` class attribute specifies the version number for the API. This way, we make sure that we are always working with a specific version and that our requests are compatible with this version. The code saves the value for the build URL in the `url` local variable.

Then, the code saves the board's current time in seconds multiplied by 1000 in the `now` local variable. The code creates a `body` dictionary that represents the request's body with the following key-value pairs:

- `"on"`: The value stored in the `now` local variable, that is, the board's current time. It is the time for the observations.

- `"accountId"`: The value stored in the `accountId` class attribute, that is, the Intel IoT Analytics account to which we will publish the observation.

- `"data"`: An empty array that we will fill later with one observation for each component.

Then, the code creates three dictionaries with the following key-value pairs that represent an observation for a specific component:

- `"componentId"`: The value stored in the class attribute that specifies the component id to which we will publish the observation.

- `"on"`: The value stored in the `now` local variable, that is, the board's current time. It is the time for the observation. We use the same variable for all the observations, and therefore, they are registered with the same time.

- `"value"`: The string representation of the value received as an argument in the method.

Then, the code calls the `append` method to add the three dictionaries to the `data` key in the `body` dictionary. This way, the `data` key will have an array with three dictionaries as its value. The code calls the `json.dumps` function to serialize the `body` dictionary to a JSON formatted string and saves it in the `data` local variable.

The next line creates a `headers` dictionary with the following key-value pairs that represent the headers for the HTTP request:

- `"Authorization"`: The authorization string composed of the concatenation of `"Bearer"` and the device token saved in the `device_token` class attribute
- `"content-type"`: Declares the content type as JSON: `"application/json"`

At this point, the code has built the headers and the body for the HTTP request that will publish the observations to Intel IoT Analytics. The next line calls the `requests.post` function to send an HTTP POST request to the URL specified by the `url` local variable, with the `data` dictionary as the JSON body data and the `headers` dictionary as the headers.

The `requests.post` method returns a response saved in the `response` local variable and the code evaluates whether the code attribute for response is not equal to `201`. In case the code is different than `201`, it means that the observations weren't successfully published, that is, something went wrong. In this case, the code prints the values for the `status_code` and `text` attributes for the response to the console output to allow us to understand what went wrong. In case we use a wrong device token or a wrong id for the account, the device or the components, we will receive errors.

Now, we will use the previously coded `IntelIoTAnalytics` class to create a new version of the `__main__` method that publishes observations to Intel IoT Analytics every 5 seconds. The following lines show the new version of the `__main__` method. The code file for the sample is `iot_python_chapter_10_01.py`.

```python
if __name__ == "__main__":
    temperature_and_humidity_sensor = \
        TemperatureAndHumiditySensor(0)
    oled = TemperatureAndHumidityOled(0)
    intel_iot_analytics = IntelIotAnalytics()
    while True:
        temperature_and_humidity_sensor.\
            measure_temperature_and_humidity()
        oled.print_temperature(
```

```
                temperature_and_humidity_sensor.temperature_fahrenheit,
                temperature_and_humidity_sensor.temperature_celsius)
            oled.print_humidity(
                temperature_and_humidity_sensor.humidity)
            print("Ambient temperature in degrees Celsius: {0}".
                format(temperature_and_humidity_sensor.temperature_
    celsius))
            print("Ambient temperature in degrees Fahrenheit: {0}".
                format(temperature_and_humidity_sensor.temperature_
    fahrenheit))
            print("Ambient humidity: {0}".
                format(temperature_and_humidity_sensor.humidity))
            intel_iot_analytics.publish_observation(
                temperature_and_humidity_sensor.temperature_fahrenheit,
                temperature_and_humidity_sensor.temperature_celsius,
                temperature_and_humidity_sensor.humidity
            )
            # Sleep 5 seconds (5000 milliseconds)
            time.sleep(5)
```

The highlighted lines show the code that creates an instance of the previously created `IntelIoTAnalytics` class and saves its reference in the `intel_iot_analytics` local variable. Then, the code within the loop that runs every 5 seconds calls the `publish_observation` method with the temperature and humidity values retrieved from the temperature and humidity sensor as arguments.

The following line will start the example:

```
python iot_python_chapter_10_01.py
```

After you run the example, turn on an air conditioner or a heating system, to generate a change in the ambient temperature and humidity. This way, we will notice changes in the data that is being published every 5 seconds. Keep the code running while we explore different features included in Intel IoT Analytics.

Go to the web browser in which you are working with the Intel IoT Analytics dashboard, click on the menu icon and select **Dashboard**. The site will display the **My Dashboard** page that will indicate you have one active device and it will update the number of observations published in the last hour as it receives observations from the board. The following pictures show the dashboard with the active device and the counter that includes 945 observations published in the last hour:

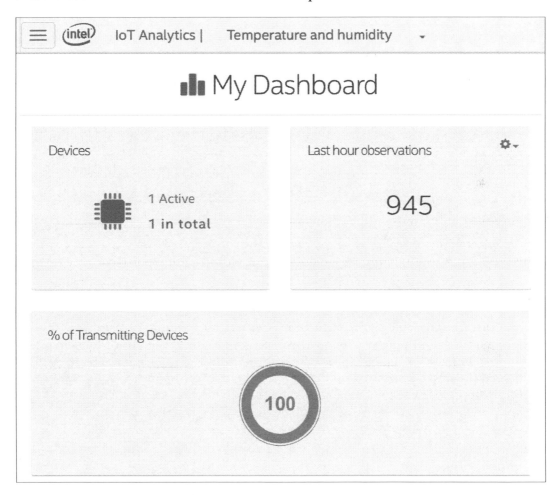

Keep the browser open with the dashboard view and you will notice that observations value increases in the last hour, as the code continues running on the board. You can click on the configuration icon located at the upper-right corner of the panel that displays the number of observations and a context-menu will allow you to configure the observations period you want to see in this panel. For example, you can change from **Last hour** to **Last week** to display the number of observations the device has registered during the last week.

Analyzing sensor data with Intel IoT Analytics

Intel IoT Analytics allows us to generate charts with the data generated for each component that has observations for a specific device. First, we have to select the device and then we have to choose one or more component to generate the chart with historic time series or the time series that are being generated with the code running on the board, that is, live data for the component.

Go to the web browser in which you are working with the Intel IoT Analytics dashboard, click on the menu icon and select **Charts**. The site will display the **My Charts** page that will allow you to search for devices using many search criteria, such as the device name, the associated tags, and its properties.

In this case, we just have one activated device, and therefore, we can select the device from the list of devices that the site shows us below the **Select Device** section. This section displays the first characters for the device name at the right-hand side of a checkbox and the number of components that have been registered for this device at the right-hand side of the text. The following picture shows the **Select Device** section with **kansas-temp...** representing the `kansas-temperature-humidity-01` device. If you hover the mouse over the checkbox or tap on the text, the site will display a popup with the complete name for the device and the types of the registered components. The following screenshot show the popup with this information displayed for the **kansas-temp...** checkbox.

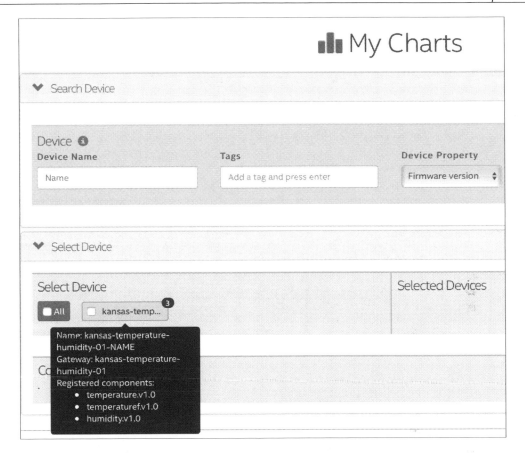

Check the **kansas-temp...** checkbox and the site will display the three registered components for the selected device. In this case, the site displays the component names (temperaturec, temperaturef, and humidity) while in the previously explained popup the site showed the component types (temperature.v1.0, temperaturef.v1.0, and humidity.v1.0).

Check the `temperaturef` checkbox and the site will display a chart with the ambient temperature measured in degrees Fahrenheit for the past hour. By default, the chart uses a line and generates a graph with the time series values registered in the past hour. By default, the refresh rate for the graph is set to 30 seconds, and therefore, the chart will be updated every 30 seconds and will display all the new observations that were published by the board through the REST API in this period.

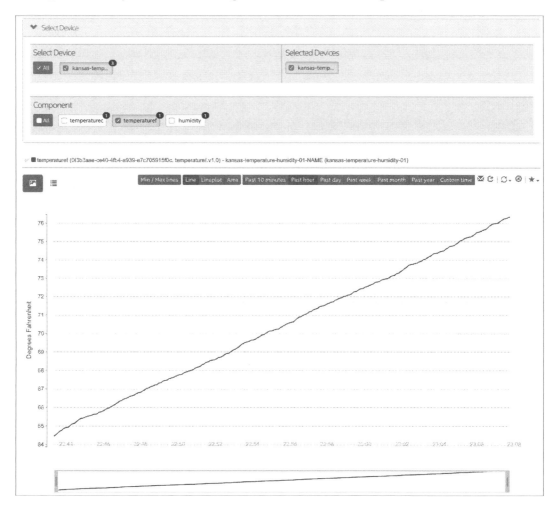

We can use the different buttons at the top of the chart to change the chart type and to select the time range we want to view displayed in the graph. We can also change the refresh rate to as low as five seconds or as high as 60 seconds. If we save the graph as favorite, the site will display it as part of the dashboard in **My Dashboard**.

Click on the **Raw data** button (A bullets icon) located at the right-hand side of the **Chart** button (A picture icon with mountains). The site will display a list with the raw data that has been sent to build the time series, that is, all the observations received for the selected component. The following screenshot shows an example of the first page of the raw data view for the `temperaturef` component in the past hour.

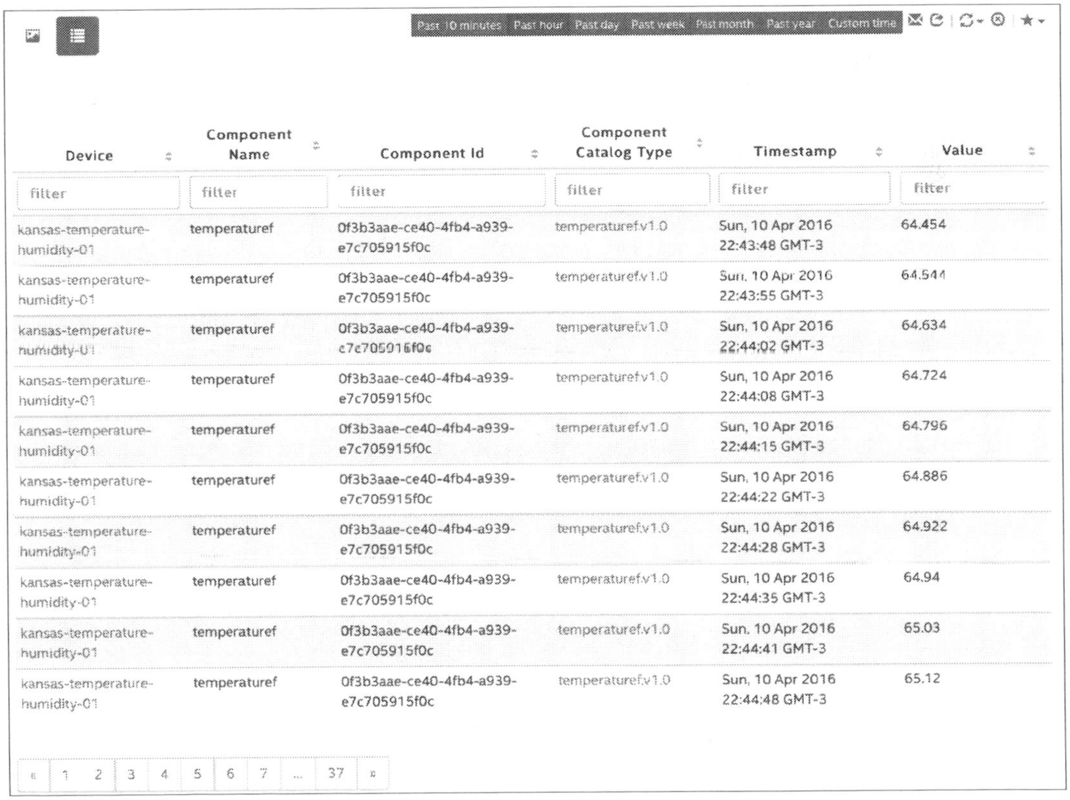

Device	Component Name	Component Id	Component Catalog Type	Timestamp	Value
filter	filter	filter	filter	filter	filter
kansas-temperature-humidity-01	temperaturef	0f3b3aae-ce40-4fb4-a939-e7c705915f0c	temperaturef.v1.0	Sun, 10 Apr 2016 22:43:48 GMT-3	64.454
kansas-temperature-humidity-01	temperaturef	0f3b3aae-ce40-4fb4-a939-e7c705915f0c	temperaturef.v1.0	Sun, 10 Apr 2016 22:43:55 GMT-3	64.544
kansas-temperature-humidity-01	temperaturef	0f3b3aae-ce40-4fb4-a939-c7c705915f0c	temperaturef.v1.0	Sun, 10 Apr 2016 22:44:02 GMT-3	64.634
kansas-temperature-humidity-01	temperaturef	0f3b3aae-ce40-4fb4-a939-e7c705915f0c	temperaturef.v1.0	Sun, 10 Apr 2016 22:44:08 GMT-3	64.724
kansas-temperature-humidity-01	temperaturef	0f3b3aae-ce40-4fb4-a939-e7c705915f0c	temperaturef.v1.0	Sun, 10 Apr 2016 22:44:15 GMT-3	64.796
kansas-temperature-humidity-01	temperaturef	0f3b3aae-ce40-4fb4-a939-e7c705915f0c	temperaturef.v1.0	Sun, 10 Apr 2016 22:44:22 GMT-3	64.886
kansas-temperature-humidity-01	temperaturef	0f3b3aae-ce40-4fb4-a939-e7c705915f0c	temperaturef.v1.0	Sun, 10 Apr 2016 22:44:28 GMT-3	64.922
kansas-temperature-humidity-01	temperaturef	0f3b3aae-ce40-4fb4-a939-e7c705915f0c	temperaturef.v1.0	Sun, 10 Apr 2016 22:44:35 GMT-3	64.94
kansas-temperature-humidity-01	temperaturef	0f3b3aae-ce40-4fb4-a939-e7c705915f0c	temperaturef.v1.0	Sun, 10 Apr 2016 22:44:41 GMT-3	65.03
kansas-temperature-humidity-01	temperaturef	0f3b3aae-ce40-4fb4-a939-e7c705915f0c	temperaturef.v1.0	Sun, 10 Apr 2016 22:44:48 GMT-3	65.12

« 1 2 3 4 5 6 7 ... 37 »

In this example, it is extremely useful to generate a chart with the temperature and the humidity level. Go back to the Chart view by clicking on the **Chart** button (A picture icon with mountains) and check the checkbox for humidity. This way, the site will generate a graph that combines the temperature expressed in degrees Fahrenheit and the humidity level expressed in percentage. The following screenshot shows the generated chart when **temperaturef** and **humidity** are both checked:

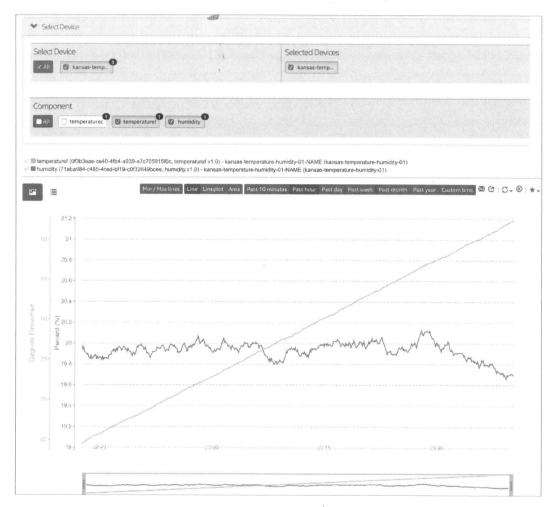

Triggering alerts with rules in Intel IoT Analytics

Intel IoT Analytics allows us to define the rules that can trigger any of the following notification types:

- Email
- HTTP Endpoint
- Actuation

Go to the web browser in which you are working with the Intel IoT Analytics dashboard, click on the menu icon and select **Rules**. The site will display the **My Rules** page that will allow you to define rules for the activated devices. In this case, we will define a rule that will send us an e-mail when the humidity level is lower than 10%.

Click on **Add a rule** and the site will display us a form that will allow us to enter the details for the new rule. Enter `Very low humidity level` in **Rule Name**, select `Low` in **Priority** and `Email` in **Notifications type**. Select the e-mail address to which you want to receive the notifications in the dropdown in the **Notifications To** panel.

Click **Next** and the site will ask us to select the devices to which the new rule has to be applied. In this case, we just have one activated device, and therefore, we can select the device from the list of devices that the site shows us below the **Select Device** section. As seen in previous device selection pages, this section displays the first characters for the device name at the right-hand side of a checkbox and the number of components that have been registered for this device at the right-hand side of the text. Check the **kansas-temp...** checkbox and the name will appear in the **Selected Devices** list.

Click **Next** and the site will ask us to specify the conditions for the new rule. Leave the **Enable Automatic Reset** checkbox unchecked because we want the rule to become inactive after every alert until it is acknowledged. This way, after we receive an alert, we will only receive additional alerts when we acknowledge the first alert that was generated.

Select humidity (Number) in **Monitored Measure** and Basic Condition in **Trigger When**. Then, select < in the additional dropdown that appears and enter 10 in the **Enter a value** textbox. This way, we are creating a rule that will trigger when the value in a humidity observation is lower than 10 (humidity < 10). The following screenshot shows the defined condition:

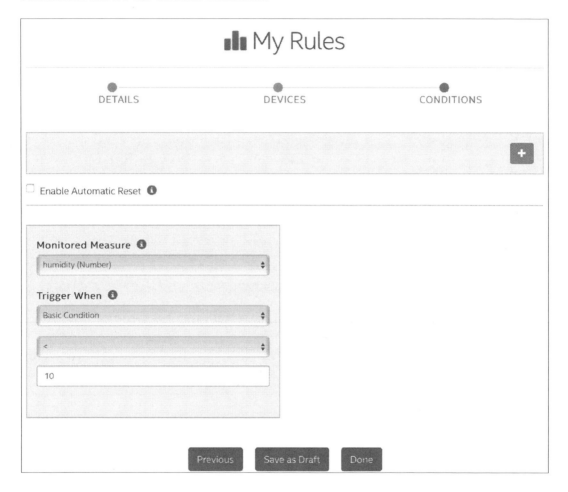

Click **Done** and the rule will be added to the list shown in **My Rules**. The following screenshot shows the rule definition included in this list after we define it:

After the humidity level is lower than 10%, an alert will be triggered and we will see a number 1 in the alerts icon (the bell). After we click on the icon, the site will display all the unread alerts we have. The following screenshot shows the My Dashboard page with one unread alert:

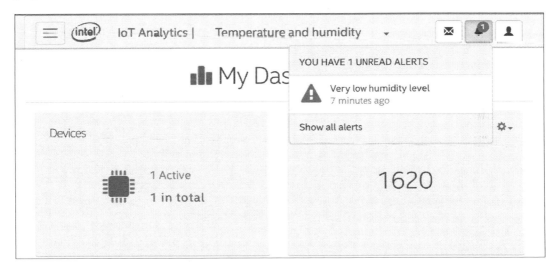

If we click on the alert, the site will display the details of the situation that triggered the alert. We can also go **Alerts** in the menu and see the list of the received alerts. The following screenshot show the alert included in the list of received alerts:

If we click on the **Alert** number, the site will display the details for the alert including the condition defined in the rule that triggered the alert and the measured value. In this case, the measured value was 7.99. It is possible to add comments to an alert. The following screenshot shows the details for the alert:

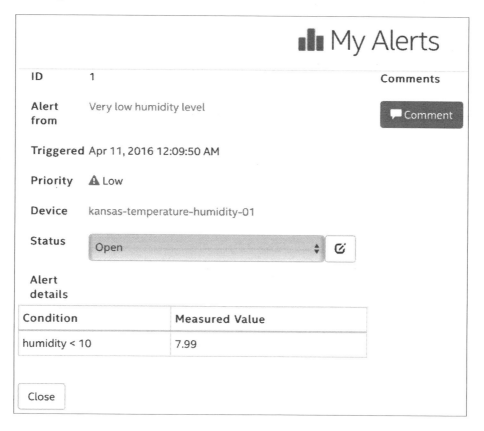

In addition, we receive an e-mail that includes the following text:

```
Alert Monitor has received an alert. Alert data:

- Alert Id: 1
- Device: kansas-temperature-humidity-01
- Reason: humidity < 10
- Priority: Low

Alert Data
Component Name    Values
humidity  7.99;



You can go here to check it on Dashboard
Regards
```

In this case, we defined a very simple condition in our rule. However, we can define a more complex condition that can include any of the following conditions:

- Time-based condition
- Statistics based condition
- Single-sensor change detection
- Multisensory change detection

We can play with the different options to trigger alerts for a large number of devices with multiple sensors and huge amounts of data. One of the most interesting features of Intel IoT Analytics is that we can easily work with huge amounts of data with the charts, the rules and the alerts.

Test your knowledge

1. The components for each device in Intel IoT Analytics can be either:

    1. Actuator or time series.

    2. Account, actuator or time series.

    3. Proxy, account, actuator or time series.

2. Each time we publish data from a registered device to Intel IoT Analytics, we create:

    1. An actuator.

    2. An account.

    3. An observation.

3. A time series is:

    1. A series of actions performed by an actuator, that is, a collection of actions.

    2. A series of values captured from a sensor, that is, a collection of observations.

    3. A series of triggered alarms, that is, a collection of alarms.

4. We can use the following command-line utility to activate our board as a device in an Intel IoT Analytics account:

    1. iotkit-admin

    2. iotkit-configure

    3. iotkit-setup

5. In order to send observations from a device with the REST API provided by Intel IoT Analytics, we need the following token:

    1. The sensor token.

    2. The observation token.

    3. The device token.

Summary

In this chapter, we understood the close relationship between Internet of Things and Big Data. We worked with a cloud-based service that allowed us to organize huge amounts of data collected by multiple devices and their sensors. We took advantage of the `requests` package to write a few lines of Python code that could interact with the Intel IoT Analytics REST API.

We used the Intel IoT Analytics web site to set up a device and its components. Then, we made changes to one of our examples to collect data from the sensors and publish observations to Intel IoT Analytics. Then, we learned about the different options that Intel IoT Analytics offers us to analyze huge amounts of data. Finally, we defined rules that triggered alerts. Now that we are able to take advantage of Intel IoT Analytics to analyze huge amounts of data, we are ready to deploy thousands of IoT devices that collect data from multiple sensors.

We learned to use Python and the Intel Galileo Gen 2 board to create low cost devices that collect huge amounts of data, interact with each other and take advantage of cloud-services and cloud-based storage. We can develop IoT prototypes from the hardware selection to all the necessary stacks with Python 2.7.3, its libraries and tools. In case we need a smaller board or a different alternative, we can switch to any of the compatible Intel Edison boards, and therefore, we can switch to this board in case we need to.

We are able to leverage our existing Python knowledge to capture data from the real world, interact with physical objects, develop APIs and use different IoT protocols. We learned to use specific libraries to work with low-level hardware, sensors, actuators, buses, and displays. We are ready to become makers and to be part of the exciting IoT world.

We can start working on fascinating projects that can transform everyday objects into smart devices with sensors and actuators. We are ready to start building ecosystems composed of thousands of IoT devices, with Python as our main programming language.

Exercise Answers

Chapter 1, Understanding and Setting up the Base IoT Hardware

Q1	2
Q2	1
Q3	2
Q4	3
Q5	1

Chapter 2, Working with Python on Intel Galileo Gen 2

Q1	2
Q2	1
Q3	2
Q4	3
Q5	1

Chapter 3, Interacting with Digital Outputs with Python

Q1	3
Q2	1
Q3	1
Q4	2
Q5	2

Chapter 4, Working with a RESTful API and Pulse Width Modulation

Q1	3
Q2	3
Q3	2
Q4	1
Q5	2

Chapter 5, Working with Digital Inputs, Polling and Interrupts

Q1	1
Q2	2
Q3	1
Q4	2
Q5	3

Chapter 6, Working with Analog Inputs and Local Storage

Q1	3
Q2	1
Q3	2
Q4	1
Q5	3

Chapter 7, Retrieving Data from the Real World with Sensors

Q1	2
Q2	1
Q3	2
Q4	3
Q5	1

Chapter 8, Displaying Information and Performing Actions

Q1	1
Q2	1
Q3	3
Q4	3
Q5	2

Chapter 9, Working with the Cloud

Q1	2
Q2	1
Q3	3
Q4	2
Q5	1

Chapter 10, Analyzing Huge Amounts of Data with Cloud-based IoT Analytics

Q1	1
Q2	3
Q3	2
Q4	1
Q5	3

Index

Symbols

7-Zip
URL 29

A

accelerometers
working with 199
actions
firing, when environment
light changes 174-180
**additional expansion and
connectivity capabilities**
recognizing 12-16
additional libraries
installing 50, 51
adxl1345.cxx, C++ source code file
reference 214
ambient temperature
measuring, with analog sensor 224-226
analog accelerometer
used, for measuring three
axis acceleration 203-206
wiring, to analog input pins 200-203
analog inputs
about 161, 162
analog input pin, wiring with
voltage source 163-165
controlling, with wiring-x86 library 180-183
analog temperature sensor
wiring 221-224
analog values
generating, PWM used 107-111
generating, via HTTP requests 114-117

Arduino 1.0 pinout
recognizing 8-12
attributes, IntelIotAnalytics class
account_id 337
account_name 337
component_id_humidity_level_percentage
338
component_id_temperature_celsius 338
component_id_temperature_fahrenheit 337
device_id 337
device_token 337

B

bi-directional communications
working with 289-296
Big Data 319
BoardInteraction class
set_rgb_led_brightness method 178
update_leds_brightness method 178
Bonjour Browser
URL 37
breadboards
prototyping with 62-65
buttons 17-19

C

callback_response_message method 291
components
setting up, in Intel IoT Analytics 328-336
curl utility
URL 93

D

dark_max_voltage attribute 172
darkness level
  determining, with analog inputs and
       mraa library 171-174
data
  publishing, to cloud with dweepy 261-267
  receiving in real-time, through Internet with
       PubNub 275-283
  sending in real-time, through Internet with
       PubNub 275-283
devices
  setting up, in Intel IoT Analytics 324-327
digital accelerometer
  controlling, I²C bus using with
       mraa library 214-220
  used, for measuring three axis
       acceleration 211-214
  wiring, to I²C bus 207-211
digital input pins
  wiring, with pushbuttons 135-137
digital inputs
  reading, with wiring-x86 library 148-150
digital outputs
  controlling, with object-oriented
       code 78-80
  controlling, with wiring-x86 library 87-89
  wiring, with schematics 65-71
digital temperature and humidity sensor
  wiring, to I²C bus 226-229
dweepy
  used, for publishing data to cloud 261-267
dweet.io
  about 262
  URL 262

E

Eclipse Paho
  about 303
  URL 303
Eclipse Paho MQTT Python client library
  reference 303
EEPROM (Electrically Erasable
     Programmable Read-Only
     Memory) 8

error_response_message method 291
extremely_dark_max_voltage attribute 172

F

files
  logging to, in local storage 183-185
firmware
  checking 20-24
  upgrading 20-24
Freeboard
  used, for building web-based
       dashboard 269-275
freeboard.io
  URL 269
Fritzing
  download link 4

G

GPIO (General Purpose Input/Output) 60
GUID (Global Unique Identifier) 262

H

HTTP requests
  analog values, generating via 114-117
  composing 98-103
  sending 98-103

I

I²C bus
  for controlling digital accelerometer,
      with mraa library 214-221
Input/Output
  recognizing 8-12
Intel Galileo Firmware and Drivers
  download link 20
Intel Galileo Gen 2 board
  about 2
  assigned IP address, retrieving 34-38
  components 3-8
  operating system, connecting 39-44
  setting up, for working with Python as
      programming language 27-34

GetRedBrightnessHandler 113
PutBlueBrightnessHandler 112
PutGreenBrightnessHandler 112
PutNumberInLedsHandler 95
PutRedBrightnessHandler 111
VersionHandler 95, 111

U

UART (Universal Asynchronous Receiver/
    Transmitter) port 9
USB attached storage
    working with 186-190

V

very_dark_max_voltage attribute 172
voltage
    measuring, with analog inputs and
        mraa library 166, 167

W

web-based dashboard
    building, with Freeboard 269-275
wiring-x86 library
    PWM, controlling with 124, 125

Made in the USA
San Bernardino, CA
12 May 2018